IN
SEARCH
OF
AFRICAN
THEATRE

IN SEARCH OF AFRICAN THEATRE

Scott Kennedy

CHARLES SCRIBNER'S SONS · NEW YORK

Copyright © 1973 J. Scott Kennedy

Library of Congress Cataloging in Publication Data

Kennedy, Scott.
  In search of African theatre.

  Bibliography: p.
  1. Theater—Africa. I. Title.
PN2969.K4   792'096   72–1193
ISBN0–684–13044–0

1 3 5 7 9 11 13 15 17 19 C/H 20 18 16 14 12 10 8 6 4 2

Printed in the United States of America

For my wife *Janie*—with love

To my son *James Jr.*, and my daughters *Sheila* and *Terri*

To *Mama Kennedy* and my brothers and sisters

To *Daddy Kennedy* who died before this book was
written but who lives in all that is me and mine

And to all of the beautiful people in the world—too
numerous by name—who have helped fill my life with
memorable experiences

in *Love!*   *Peace!*   and *Spiritual Vibrations!*

Acknowledgments

This book owes many debts to many people and places—to Ghana, to Dakar and its Festival in 1966, to Algiers and its Festival in 1969, but especially to the continent of Africa and its many African people around the world.

I express thanks to my understanding and patient editor, Burroughs Mitchell, and especially to my publisher, Charles S. Scribner, for his confidence and his keen perception and understanding.

I wish to thank several people for their critical reading of the manuscript. They include Kwabena Nketia, Tsegaye Gabre-Medhin, my wife Janie, my mother, my brother Joseph, and my sister Mary.

I am thankful also for the critical ears of many people including brothers Don, Doug, and Robert; sisters Maurice, Irene, Lillian, and Adrienne, Walter and Barbara Murray, Perry Knight, Lloyd Hezekiah, Larry Bond, Elenor, D. Parke Gibson, William Marshall, Henry Hall, Okot p'Bitek, Pat Maddy, Femi, Robert Saramagna, Mrs, Zirimu, Efua Sutherland, Bertie OPoku, Dr. Amu, Saka Acquaye, Harry, Vassie, and Maggie Welbeck, Keith Baird, George Matthau, Ed Joel, Errol Hill, Floyd Gaffney, the Davises, the Buchanans, Bobbie and Sarah, and many others too numerous to name.

My thanks also go to my three children, James, Sheila, and Terri for their patience and perception in acquiring their own African experience and adventure which aided me greatly in the writing of this book. Let me also thank Mrs. DeVera Johnson for the typing of the second draft of the manuscript and to Allen Tamakloe for the drawings.

I am especially endebted to Professor Kwabena Nketia, Dr. Kyerematen, and A.A. Opoku for quotes and materials from their books.

Portions of this book have appeared in magazines, journals, and newspapers including *Okyeame*, *East Africa Journal*, *Ghana Research Review*, *The Legon Observer*, and others. I gratefully acknowledge permission to use them here in revised form.

Contents

First Episode

The Night Is Beautiful

So the Faces of My People!

The Stars Are Beautiful

So the Eyes of My People!

Three generations (Janie, Mama Kennedy, Aba, and Scott) (*Frank Silva, New York*)

Beautiful Also Is the Sun
Beautiful Also Are the Souls of My People
"Faces of My People"
Langston Hughes

Ghanaian faces (*Institute of African Studies, Ghana*)

Ethiopian faces (*Orchestra Ethiopia*)

Part One

Chief Bey (*Frank Silva, New York*)

My Own Preface

For many years I have lived both a creative life and an academic life. I have worked within two disciplines, as a creative artist and as an academician. This was especially true during my recent stay in Africa, since I had gone to Ghana hoping to help bridge the gap between the academician and the professional theatre-maker in Ghana's national theatre movement. With all of this in mind, when I began this book I felt compelled to express myself in the manner of the creative artist as well as in the manner of an academician. Therefore, in order to prepare the reader for a shift in style and form, I have divided the book into three parts. Part I focuses on my impressions of Africa and sets forth my ideas about African theatre. Part II concentrates on the theatrical scene in Ghana with respect to materials and techniques for the making of African theatre. It is set forth in an academic, documented manner. It also reflects upon the Dakar and the Algiers festivals. The final section includes poetry and pictures.

Throughout the book I theorize around the unknown as well as around the known, and I am as concerned with the oral literature of African people as history as much as I am with the written literature. No doubt, in time, many of the generalizations suggested in my impressions will be supported or refuted by more empirical evidence and quantitative data than are currently available.

If it had been possible, I would have liked to have had music and sounds accompany this book in order that the reader might

African artist (*Algerian Information Services*)

view the book or the experience as a multimedia or psychedelic experience. This would be similar to my view of African theatre and African people. For you see, I believe that African theatre must be seen, heard, and given witness to. It can't really be treated solely from the word or from a literary point of view. Just as the oral traditions in oral literature come alive through the drama of their presentation, so African theatre must be seen and heard in order to be fully realized. It is music—it is much like jazz music. And, of course, you know that talking about jazz or reading about jazz is a poor substitute for the real thing. It can never be like the experience of making jazz or the experience of giving witness to it. I have, however, concerned myself with the visual aspects of African theatre: The pictures in the book are intended to underscore my impressions and generalizations, while the writing tries to open up an idea or an experience and leave visual space for the reader, much like time space for the listener in music. I am hopeful that this will enable the reader to establish contact, a rapport, and to feel empathy and finally a vibration regarding the African experience and the people-process in African theatre.

I was born AFRICAN PEOPLE and will probably live the rest of my life that way. No doubt I shall also die African people. However, with respect to designation, I have been called many things, including Colored, Afro-American, Black, Negro, Boy, Nigger, and on a rare occasion, American. Of course, it was possible for this to happen to me because what one calls oneself and what one is called may not always be the same. The fact remains, however, that I do not remember having been called American in the land of my birth. At one particular time in my life, though, I was called an American. I distinctly remember it. It was the first time I had traveled out of the USA. It happened in Mexico City. A friendly Mexican greeted me with, "¿Es americano?" I have never forgotten that moment.

I was brought up in a family of "African People," and in a sense, I guess *my search for Africa* has been going on since the early years of my life. I first met Africa through the images and impressions shared by my mother and father with the members of their family.

In addition to having this African experience, my home was

Ghanaian face (*Institute of African Studies, Ghana*)

Ghanaian dancer (*Halifax Photos, Ghana*)

filled with both spiritual and religious vibrations and the richness
of music, poetry, and dramatic experiences. So, at an early age, I
became immersed in dramatic and musical performances; and at the
same time I was made aware of the spiritual forces of life. All of the
children in our family played dramatic roles in church and school
performances. In this sense, then, my search for theatre also started
during my childhood.

As the years passed, I searched the theatre academically, crea-
tively, and professionally. I was in theatre productions at New York
University, and also in off-Broadway and Broadway productions. I
studied theatre in professional schools both in America and abroad.
But it was always in a Western or European frame of reference.
Eventually my own curiosity led me to inspect other forms of
theatre—for example, the Japanese Kabuki and Chinese and Indian
theatre. And needless to say, this inspection enlarged my frame of
reference and led me to make certain discoveries, with respect to
form and concept, about theatre in general.

In 1958 I formed my own professional theatre group, the Scott
Kennedy Players Workshop at 1151 Broadway, New York City. In
an effort to enlarge my own concepts about human beings in
theatre, I sought to form a truly integrated group, including, among
others, AFRICAN PEOPLE (Black Americans, West Indians, Africans),
Koreans, Puerto Ricans, Jews, White Americans, and anyone else
interested in the kind of theatre we sought to create. At that time,
however, I didn't realize that the focus of our theatre group
stemmed from the Black Consciousness of Colored People. It didn't
exclude White people, but the plays that we wrote, acted in, directed, and produced were not typically "American plays." They
were plays springing from an African or Black frame of reference.
And over a ten-year period we performed and produced many
plays, such as, *Improvisatons on the Life and Death Cycle, Yesterday and
Today, Othello Speaks, Commitment to a Dream, Many Moods of the Modern, Behind the Mask, Beyond the Veil, Dramatic Voices of Protest, Negritude: A Speak-Out on Color #1* and *#2, African Moods, The Black
Experience, To Speak of Freedom, The African Experience, Rivers of the
Black Man, The King Is Dead.* We performed in schools and churches
and at colleges, including Columbia University, New York University, and Adelphi College. We also played off-Broadway at Freedom

House, Town Hall, and Carnegie Hall, and on radio and television. The titles of the plays indicate a search for identity and a theatre that reflects or represents Black people or African people.

In 1966 I attended the First World Festival of Negro Arts in Dakar, Senegal, where I was an observer and a participant. There I witnessed the splendor and the spectacle of African theatre. Also at that time I was invited to come to Africa to live and learn and help develop African theatre in the modern sense. I went to Ghana and lived there and worked in many areas of African theatre development. I was a Senior Research Scholar at the Institute of African Studies at the University of Ghana and was also the Head of Theatre Studies and Drama. I immersed myself in the theatre of Ghana and of Africa. Professionally, I acted, directed, wrote, and produced theatrical performances in Ghana as well as in West, East, and North Africa. With me in Ghana was my family. My wife Janie, a professional actress and a scholar in the cultures of African people, helped me in my African quest.

In 1969 an invitation by the Algerian government enabled my wife and me to participate in the First World Pan-African Cultural Festival in Algiers. The following year I returned to my home base at Brooklyn College of the City University of New York (CUNY). (I have been a member of the faculty of the Speech and Theatre Department since 1959.) There, during the years 1970 and 1971, I continued to explore African theatre—Black theatre—through the offering of formal courses, workshops, and a production schedule.

In 1972 I went back to Africa for a short stay to continue research in African theatre on the subject "Contemporary Implications of Drama in Traditional African Societies." Again, my initial thrust was Ghana. In Ghana I delivered graduate seminar lectures on African theatre and gave lectures to undergraduate students on the topic "Relationships Between Black-American theatre and African theatre." I also recorded music and took photographs and made a film strip on the subject "Dramatic Aspects of African Festivals," with a special reference to music and dance. I took part in radio and television discussions of African theatre. From Ghana I journeyed on to Nairobi, Kenya, where I continued my work at the Institute of African Studies at the university and also appeared on radio and television. From Nairobi I went to Cairo, Egypt, to witness African

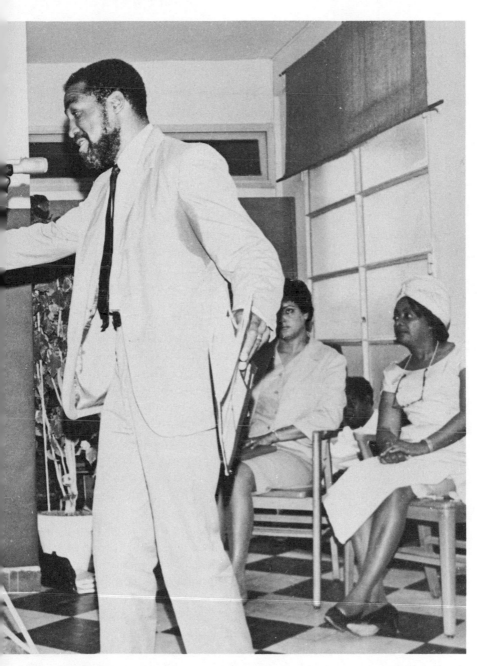

Scott Kennedy, Dakar Festival, 1966 (*U.S.I.A., Dakar*)

theatre from a North African frame of reference. In Cairo I spoke with actors, directors, and producers, and I also "gave witness" and viewed theatre productions in Cairo, just as I had done in Accra and in Nairobi.

As I reflect on these experiences, it would appear as though my *conscious search for African theatre* had come about during these last six years in Africa and in America. During these years in which I have been thinking about African theatre and writing notes for this book, I have also been carrying on a research study of a specific aspect of Black life-styles with regard to expression and communication. The book and the study, however, are quite separate undertakings. The study is limited in scope to specific aspects of the Black man's expression in Africa, in the United States, and in the Caribbean. On the other hand, the book is the result of a search for African theatre that embraced two periods of work. The first, a three-year period of research in Africa, examined materials and techniques for the making of African theatre. The second, a three-year period of research in America, examined attitudes regarding teaching and learning about Black theatre or African theatre and about Black people or African people. The overall study embraced the idea and philosophy of theatre for African people. Underlying it, of course, was the need to inspect theatre in general, that is, as a universal activity and a universal expression of man. The observations, both formal and informal, that I have had to make in the course of the research have been essential to the book, both as data to be reported and as a realistic discipline to my concept of African theatre, including materials and techniques necessary for the re-creation, resurgence, and development of African theatre, and also as a frame of reference regarding African people.

The relationship between the book and the research study is close. The book, however, is not meant to be a full or formal report of my findings. The study was conceived quite independently of this book and had technical and specific purposes that lie, in part, beyond its scope. But the research and study provided an incomparable opportunity, and an obligation, for me to immerse myself in the actual day-to-day activities of theatre-makers in Africa, in a context that kept my mind on the issues discussed in the book. As the research proceeded, I found that what I was learning both

Barbara Ann Teer and Scott Kennedy, New York City, 1970 (*Roosevelt High School, Long Island, New York*)

supported and required me to modify the positions I had been planning to discuss in this book. Despite the fact that my "views" come through the eyes of a research scholar as well as from the eyes of a creative artist, I submit *my search for African theatre* as impressions and hope that other scholars and creative artists will continue to research and create African theatre. By so doing, they will help conceptualize the "idea of African theatre" as a part of a universal mainstream of theatre.

My research was supported by the Institute of African Studies, University of Ghana, and Education and World Affairs (Overseas Educational Services), New York City. A travel grant from the Rockefeller Foundation enabled me to travel to East Africa and make a comparative study of West and East African theatre. An invitation by the Algerian government to attend and participate in the First World Pan-African Cultural Festival in Algiers enabled me to give witness to the festival as well as to view theatre on the North African scene. A research grant from CUNY enabled me to return to Africa for additional research in my continued search for African theatre.

First Movement

Fragments Framed

*T*his book comes out of an African frame of reference. It is orchestrated around the empathy of African people. Orchestrated within the many harmonies and melodies of its people's music. From the beat of Africa to the spirituals, the work songs, the blues, the gospels, the calypso, the jazz, and the soul of African people. Choreographed within the space and time of the dance-movement and a beat—which started in Africa and spread around the world. From the shuffle and the sand to the lindy, the stomp, and the bougaloo, and other dances being created at this very moment.

I hear the sounds of my people throughout the world! Clashing, harmonic, melodious, assonant, dissonant. Never noise or mere sound, but always music. Music created by my people and then imitated, shaped, and distorted by the *man*. Music always borrowed, stolen, or lifted. But music always used and misused.

I vibrate to the movement of my people. Bodies swaying, moving, jumping, running, or at ease—motion and energy at rest. Bodies forever pointed to and connected with the universe.

I commune with the minds and souls and hearts of my people! And my vibrations are at one with them. The definitions of this book are African.

In *your search for African theatre* you, the reader, are the "angles" surrounding the triangle. You are also the "angular existence" of the experience and the search. You complete the circular response regarding the communication. And you soon learn that this book is not an autobiography, or a history, or a text. True, it often embraces autobiography and history, but *the book is meant to be an insight and an experience into a search and a discovery.* Its major bias stems from the fact that the writer is "African people" speaking about Africa.

In *my search for African theatre* I realize that I must try to walk within the culture, the means of communication, and the art forms of Africa. For their theatre, both classical and traditional in nature, is a volcanic eruption of the art forms steeped in the culture of its people. Their theatre is communication. It is culture. Their theatre is *a celebration of life. A communion of vibrations.* However, I learn that I must do more than define their theatre. I must conceptualize it. I must give witness to it. Give witness to both the process and the product. I must try to understand the classical nature of this African theatre. I must see that its people are universal. I must listen to the music of the drum. That instrument which communicates throughout most of Africa. I must try to understand and decode its messages, the language of the drum. I must do more, however, than talk about the language of African theatre. I must learn to use it and interpret it.

I ask myself questions. Shall I consider the music of these people? Consider the sculpture, the dance, and the visuals? Shall I examine the museum pieces and then look at the modern theatre? Shall I examine classical and folk theatre and then look at the definitional difficulties and the frame of reference for the non-African and even for the African? But first I shall look, listen, and learn about *the concept and the idea of African theatre* from an African frame of reference.

Each African art form taken separately has its own language. Imagine the eruption that takes place when these forms merge on the stage to become theatre—when the proverbs, riddles, regalia, tales, dance, music, masks, and ceremonial occasions come together.

African theatre from its very inception could instruct, entertain, please, or provoke action. African theatre today may also do this, that is, if the viewer carries with him few preconceptions about this theatre. Although African theatre in the past, usually nonscripted, played much the same roles as the written theatre literature of the Western world, its functions and purposes must be

Sounds (*Institute of African Studies, Ghana*)

Communion (*Algerian Information Services*)

recognized as something quite different from those of Western theatre. Consequently, the non-African must try to learn to read the language of African theatre. He must try to learn and understand, without preconceptions, the mysteries and magic of the art forms of the African proverb, riddle, tale, music, dance, sculpture, and other visual forms. He must do this in order to understand the values, history, institutions, and sociology of the African people. For African theatre, in its total dimensional form, or even in a diluted dimensional form (that is, when it uses only the word, dance, music, or a single art form by itself), has served as a principal means of communication and a carrier of culture among its people. It has also helped cement its people and connect one generation to the next. For example, theatre—together with the oral tradition through storytelling and dance-drama and the recounting of history, and sculpture—constitutes the principal carrier of the basic knowledge held in common by all members of a culture. This includes the living, the ancestors, and those yet to come. Consequently, African theatre becomes at one and the same time both a "dead language" and a "living language." It becomes both classical and traditional, or folk. It speaks! It speaks of the living and the dead, of yesterday and today. It speaks with great sharpness and clarity to those who try to understand what its symbols are saying. However, its experience is not a representational one, but a symbolic one. *Its purpose is to comment upon nature and life, not merely to reproduce it.*

African theatre conceptualizes. It is concerned with concepts, not definitions. It evokes the wisdom and authority of the ancestors. And in so doing, it speaks of a way of life, or of the way one ought to live. It outlines social responsibilities and speaks of family loyalties. Frequently masks and symbols, which serve literally as teaching aids, are used. Often they are considered principal instruments of social control. They speak clearly and sharply with respect to the role, the relationship, and the responsibility of African people. They deliver the full force of the ancestors.

African theatre is universe-connected. It may be concerned with the wrath of the gods and with the pleasure or displeasure of the ancestors. It speaks of hidden forces of nature that determine success or failure. Frequently it focuses upon what one must do to control the forces of the universe, or at least to check them. From Nigeria, Ola Rotimi's *The Gods Are Not to Blame*, which deals with the Yoruba people, is an excellent example. From Ghana, Sebastian Kwamuar's *The Dagger of Liberation*, about the Ewe people and their history and struggle against the OPPRESSOR. Michael Dei-Anang's *Okomfo Anokye's Golden Stool*, about the Ashanti nation and its coming together. Saka Aquaye's *The Lost Fishermen*, about the Ga people as fishermen and their beliefs and their life-styles. Dr. J. B. Danquah's *The Third Woman*, about the Akan people and their doctrines. From these plays and the characters in them we learn that all African people have unique customs and cultures. We also learn that Africa, a large continent with many countries, has many culture units within the culture of a specific country. And from Ghana, even more conventional dramas, such as Joe DeGraft's *Sons and Daughters* and Efua Sutherland's *Edufa* and *Foriwa*, are revealing to anyone who learns to understand the symbols and meaning of African people.

An understanding of the nature of the African festival and its relationship to the people as a way of life offers many insights about African theatre. For example, when the "festival way of life" reveals itself through *ceremonial drama or theatre*, the audience or the people are often instructed or given practical knowledge about the planting of crops or about the nature of the opening and closing of a lagoon or river.

Our search for African theatre must also be both triangular and circular. At the crux of the search, at the center, is the theatre-maker. The theatre-maker who took his time and energy to commune with me. To share his theatre and his African culture. Standing at the apex of the triangle is the writer. *I, the writer, must give witness to the search and the experience.* In a sense, I am a continuation of the purging of myself for myself. I am to take a walk out of the depths of hell into the limbo and the miasma of that which was my very beginning. My blackness. My Africanesque! Years and years ago. Long before the man tried to dehumanize me. Long before I was NIGGERIZED! Years and years ago. Long before the African-American. The Black. The Afro. The Colored.

Connected with the universe (*Algerian Information Services*)

Celebration of life (mourning) (*Institute of African Studies, Ghana*)

CHAPTER
1
Africa Is a Woman

AFRICA IS A WOMAN! She is both the prediction and the promise. She is always the beginning. But never the end. She is a surrealist. Both the image and the object. She is both art and use. She is truly MOTHER AFRICA. Mother of us all. Yet, to some people, she appears as a phantom in the night. As a spirit haunting their existence. As conscience forever standing over you. But to others, she is their whore. Their pot to piss in. Their scum. Their woman to be raped, ruined, rationalized, exploited. Their exotic delight! And still to others, she is their saint. Their savior. Their survival. Their ritual of life. Their liberty. Their liberation! *But to all, she is forever an* ENIGMA!

Emotionally she surrounds you. And you, as "African people," wish to learn more about her and embrace her. You listen within yourself and recall the words of the anthropologists. "It was out of Africa—East Africa, not Southeast Asia as we once believed—that man first came. *Africa is Mother of us all—black, brown, yellow, red, and white!*"

So whether you like it or not, identificaton with Africa is forced upon you. All of you. But especially this is true of you who are called Black, wherever you are. And to you, twenty-five million Black Americans, Africa is your MOTHER AFRICA in a very special sense. You can run, but you can't hide, for "There's no hiding place down here!" *Africa is your* MOTHER!

Nevertheless, some who are called Black reject an African identification completely. On the other hand, some Blacks joyously and enthusiastically adopt the African identification. Some have always taken this identification-relationship for granted and have called themselves "African people." And yet, as often as not, all American Blacks may have at one time or another felt shame over an identification with Africa. They are ambivalent over "Black Ridicule," and yet at the same time they are proud of people such as Dr. Julius Nyerere, Patrice Lumumba, Jomo Kenyatta, Dr. Kenneth Kuanda, Dr. Kwame Nkrumah, Sékou Touré, Chief Chaka, King Menelik, and Emperor Haile Selassie.

Africa! As a woman she is! Both baffling and agonizing. Exciting. She surrounds you with her mysteries. She teases and tantalizes you with your discoveries about her. At once you think you are beginning to understand her. But suddenly you learn that your lifetime will never be long enough to penetrate her. Physically she is! Emotionally she is! She runs from hot to cold. From the hot humid heat in the Sudan to the cold rains in Ethiopia. From the coastal plains to the rain savannahs and the hot dry north within the nation of Ghana. From the snow atop Mount Kilimanjaro to the torrential rains.

African impressions will forever live within the eye of my brain. Black Beauty is unadorned. It is unfettered. Uncluttered. False eyelashes, paints, and mixtures are not necessary here. Makeup need not masquerade behind her veneer. Humanity, stark and bold, looks at you. Attracts you! Attracts you within the framework of her own unique African beauty ideal. Not within the framework of a Western beauty ideal. Here, the "birthday-suit-human being" confronts you. Africa's reality surrounds you as if from the beginning of man. As if from the beginning of time. Her sights are bright, bold, vivid. Her sounds are clashing, contrasting, dissonant, assonant, overpowering. Africa's smells are sharp, strong, and pungent—the odors of the living. No "double-layer-human being" here, covered with the artificialities of life. Lost in the intricate web of technology. Slave to the machine. No! Africa is different. She is not yet so covered that you can never really see her or touch her. She is naked. Inviting! Her life and her existence beckon you. No frills and idiosyncrasies. No ladylike masquerade. The real lady is thrust upon you, making your sensory perception

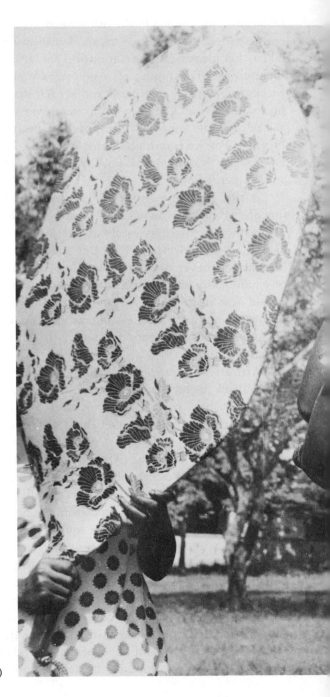

Grace
(*Halifax Photos, Ghana*)

stand at attention. You, the beholder, must give witness. You are provoked, stimulated. Challenged! Challenged to discover your own humanity. Challenged to search for your own unique beginning as a human being. To try to start anew. To be born again. To marvel at the miracle of humanity and the universe. To learn to ask the right questions. To question! To learn to search in the right places. To question? But to begin! *And if man began in Africa, is it not probable that theatre also started there?* At the beginning! Then should I not take my cue from Africa? *Is it here that my search for African theatre must begin?*

Janie (*Frank Silva, New York*)

2
I Dream of Africa

I DREAM OF AFRICA. Land of kings and ancient empires. Land of ancient rituals and unknown mysteries. Land of jungle folk and animals. Or is it? Land of savages inhabited by Tarzan and Cheetah? Dark Continent forbidden to civilized man. A backward jungle? And yet . . . Is this not the land of the beginning of man? The land where Dr. Louis Leakey, British archaeologist, tells us that man has lived longer than in any other place on earth —for more than 1,750,000 years? Have not the anthropologists shown that Africa is where man began? That Africa is MOTHER of us all? That rich civilizations sprang from Africa? That empires existed in Africa when Europeans were still running around in caves? There was GHANA, MALI, and SONGHAI . . . And yet. . . ?

I am a "well-educated Black American"—educated in the best schools of America and Europe. *Is that my problem?* With advanced degrees! I have achieved the highest realm of academia. I am a Doctor of Philosophy. Why I have even done post-doctoral work. And yet . . . *Africa was never a part of my formal education.* Africa was never a part of this *good* education that I have acquired. How then . . . could Africa all of a sudden be important? To me—to anyone? And yet . . . It WAS important to me. Despite my *good education,* I had studied and learned about Africa. *But I had searched for Africa! And now I was searching for African theatre.*

I had searched for everything I learned about Africa, except that which I had learned in my early years from my parents. For most

people, Africa was off the beaten track. And the images of the Black
Man in Western civilization were all bad. Black is bad. Africa is
uncivilized. Black Americans are ex-slaves. Before that, they were
beasts. As slaves they were Black beasts. Chattel! They had no
history. No roots. Everybody knows that. They had no languages.
Just dialects. Oh, they could sing and dance. They could show off
their emotions. They were good for making love and all that stuff.
But they didn't think well. They had no powers of reasoning, and
they never used logic for anything. They never had any real art.
They were born imitators.

My first memories of Africa take me back to my mother's knee.
My mother often read stories to her children. Stories about the
ancient kingdoms and glories of Africa. I was six years old and at
my mother's knee. I remember it well. She covered me and other
members of the family with African tales and told us of the works
of Dr. Carter G. Woodson and Dr. W. E. B. DuBois. And even
at that early age I vowed that one day I would "return in reality" to Africa. I would go home and soak up its mysteries and
wonders!

Years later I realized that I had always carried those first rich
stories of Africa in my head. Of her Black leaders and Black empires, of Ethiopia, the Sudan, Egypt, old Ghana, Mali, and Songhai.
And of that warrior Chief, King Chaka, and also of King Menelik.
So somehow during my school years I was always able to ignore or
refute the many wild Tarzan stories of Africa and the stories of the
exotic, uncivilized Dark Continent. I referred my friends or ene-
mies to the rich sources of Africa's legacy. And certainly whenever
this happened, I was usually carried back to my first contact with
Africa. To those fresh, sharp exciting images of my first childhood
vision of Africa. And yet . . . still I wondered. What was Africa
really like? And when would I actually find out for myself?

In the year 1958 I brushed against Africa through an African,
Dr. Kwame Nkrumah. Ghana had recently become the first "free"
independent African country in modern times. In 1957 she had
entered the select circle of free African countries. Prior to this,
Egypt, Ethiopia, and Liberia had been the only free and Black
independent countries in Africa. The President and Prime Minister

African chief
(*Algerian Infor-
mation Services*)

Osagefo Nkrumah (*Scott Kennedy*)

of Ghana, Dr. Kwame Nkrumah, was visiting New York. A reception was being held in his honor. I was invited. I went. I found myself highly impressed by the wit, intelligence, and perception of Dr. Nkrumah. However, I was particularly struck by the fact that Dr. Nkrumah was an African who spoke of Africa for the Africans. Speaking freely with me and my brother, Dr. Joseph C. Kennedy, and others, he revealed his dream—a dream of Africa for Africa and for African people around the world.

After the reception I went home and reread the speech he had delivered in Ghana on the occasion of Ghana's independence. Several passages stuck with me:

> The achievement of freedom, sovereignty and independence is the product of the matter and spirit of our people. In the last resort we have only been able to become independent because *we were economically, socially and politically able to create the conditions which made independence possible and any other status impossible.* . . .
>
> Independence, is, however, only a milestone on our march to progress. Independence by itself would be useless if it did not lead to great material and cultural advances by our people. In pressing with the advances we shall be doing more than merely benefiting Ghana. If we in Ghana can work out solutions to the problems which beset the tropics, we shall be making a contribution to Africa and to the world as a whole.
>
> In striving to create a modern State dedicated to freedom and justice, *we shall have many enemies to fight against.* Our first task must therefore be to make certain that there is a strong and resolute public opinion which condemns, as anti-social, idleness and neglect; carelessness which destroys valuable crops or machinery; and corruption, which undermines the basis of a sound commercial life. . . . *By our actions the whole future of Africa must be affected.* . . .[1] (Italics added.)

Dr. Nkrumah spoke not only to Ghanaians, and to Africans, but to the entire world. He was especially cognizant of African people. He

[1]Quoted in *Ghana Is Born* (London: Newman Neame Limited, 1958), pp. 54, 56.

spoke of their needs and their relationship to world development. He stressed the fact that Ghanaian people had to create a certain climate for work and development as well as a basis for a sound, commercial life. He was aware of the enemy from within Ghana as well as the enemy from without. He was also cognizant of the importance of image and public opinion with respect to Ghana's direction, and Ghana's direction with respect to its influence upon the entire continent of Africa. I reflected: *Surely within his plan lies a consideration of the cultural resources of African people.*

I decided to reread the speech of the leader of the opposition, Professor Kofi A. Busia. His initial words impressed me.

> We may be permitted to observe that our admission to membership within the Commonwealth drives another nail into the coffin of the crude biological theories of racial superiority by which many have striven to justify the domination of one race by another. We became members of the international fraternity of the British Commonwealth *on the basis of our common humanity.*

As I continued reading, I felt that he was too beholden to Great Britain. He lacked a pro-Ghanaian frame of reference and point of view, especially when he says *"give evidence to our fitness to govern ourselves."*

> *We are aware that we owe this achievement to the people of Britain and other foreign countries,* as well as to our own countrymen. We owe it to many from Britain and other foreign countries who, over the years, as civil servants, service men, missionaries, teachers, traders, and businessmen, *served and taught us;* as well as to many of our own countrymen, political leaders, chiefs, farmers, workers, and citizens in all walks of life who, by what they learned, and what they did, helped to lay our foundations, and *give evidence to our fitness to govern ourselves.*[2] (Italics added.)

[2] *Ibid.*, pp. 4. 56.

I asked myself a question, "What were the Ghanaian people doing before the British came?" I think it is generally accepted as truth now that many of those "outside-insiders"—missionaries, teachers, traders, and businessmen, who *"served and taught us"*—also raped, used, and bought us.

Despite Busia's frame of reference and point of view, I was still impressed with Ghana—with its independence and vision. A few years later, after reading another Nkrumah speech, it became clear to me that I should try to visit Ghana and spend some time at the Institute of African Studies. From the Institute I would examine the cultural scene and the National Theatre Movement in Ghana.

A friend of mine had given me a copy of "The African Genius," a speech delivered by Dr. Nkrumah, at the opening of the Institute of African Studies on October 25, 1963. His words issued a call to African people—a call for them to reclaim their lost heritage and culture. Once again Nkrumah seemed to me to ask some of the right questions and also to point a direction for the answers. He stated that the Institute should be identified with the aspirations of Ghana and Africa. He emphasized a pressing need for "African" studies:

> . . . African music, dancing and sculpture were labelled "primitive art." They were studied in such a way as to reinforce the picture of African society as something grotesque, as a curious, mysterious human backwater, which helped to retard social progress in Africa and to prolong colonial domination over its peoples.
>
> When I speak of a new interpretation and new assessment, I refer particularly to our Professors and Lecturers. The non-Ghanaian non-African Professors and Lecturers are, of course, welcome to work here with us. Intellectually there is no barrier between us and them. We appreciate, however, that their mental make-up has been largely influenced by their system of education and the facts of their society and environment. For this reason, they must *endeavor to adjust and reorientate their attitudes and thought to our African conditions and aspirations.*

> One essential function of this Institute must surely be to study the history, culture and institutions, languages and arts of Ghana and of Africa in new African centered ways . . .

As he continued, I agreed with his conclusion and with his perceptiveness that there is a need to study Africans in Africa as well as Africans outside of Africa.

> Your work must also include a study of the origins and culture of peoples of African descent in the Americas and the Caribbean, and you should seek to maintain close relations with their scholars so that there may be cross-fertilization between Africa and *those who have their roots in the African past.*
>
> An Institute of African Studies that is situated in Africa must pay particular attention to the arts of Africa, for the study of these can enhance our *understanding of African institutions and values,* and *the cultural bonds that unite us.*

When Nkrumah spoke specifically of the "people" and Ghana's National Theatre Movement, I sensed then that he was not only a thinker and a visionary leader, but also a human being interested in the culture and arts of his people. He was driving me closer and closer to Ghana.

> I hope also that this Institute, in association with the School of Music and Drama, *will link the University of Ghana closely with the National Theatre Movement in Ghana.* In this way the *Institute can serve the needs of the people by helping to develop new forms of dance and drama, of music and creative writing,* that are at the same time *closely related to our Ghanaian traditions* and express the ideas and aspirations of our people at this critical stage in our history.[3]

[3]"The African Genius."

CHAPTER
3
Africa Calls

"**C**ome back home to Africa and help us develop our theatre. Come and learn how it all began."

The scene is Dakar, Senegal. The year, 1966. The event, the First World Festival of Negro Arts!

"Come and look at our traditional theatre, and then give us your modern expertise in terms of conventional theatre."

I am listening to a friend, an African leader. We have just witnessed an African play, and we are both excited. Now he wishes to share his "Africanesque" with me through his culture. And I dream of rediscovering, with my own eyes, lost civilizations! Lost civilizations in Africa through theatre!

And so, I went to Africa in search of African theatre. I spent nearly three years there.

"Come on back home to America and help us in our Black theatre movement. We need you!"

The scene has now changed to Algiers, Algeria. The year, 1969. The event, the first World Pan-African Cultural Festival! I am now listening to a friend, a Black American artist. We have just shared an evening of African theatre. We are talking about connections between African theatre and the Black theatre movement in America.

"At home you can help develop the link between Black theatre in America and African theatre. You can tell it like it is."

The scene changes again. This time to New York City. The

year, 1970. I am back home in America. I have just returned from Atlanta, Georgia, where I participated in the First Congress of African People. I am talking to a writer and an activist in the development of Black theatre in America. We are sharing observations on Black theatre and the movement. Our conversation takes me back to Africa and my search for African theatre.

African theatre addresses itself to an African way of life, stemming from its own unique traditions; it is addressed to African man, to African themes, to African moods, to African expression.

In the beginning, there was no need for paid theatre. The theatre went to the people. It was for the people. It was traditional theatre. It took place in the villages and in the centers of African life. It was distinctly people-oriented. *It was a cultural, traditional experience.*

To the non-African, African theatre from Africa is an enigma, as vast, as broad, and as incomprehensible as Africa itself appears to be. Since the theatre may be found in many languages, language alone presents a formidable barrier, not to mention the "special language" of the African ritual, music, mime, regalia, poetry, proverbs, prose, and other art forms, and the numerous aspects of verbal and nonverbal communication. For not only is it possible to find African theatre played in Western languages such as English, French, Portuguese, and Italian, but also in African languages— Ibo, Ga, Twi, Yoruba, Fanti, Ewe, Wolof, Mende, Krio, Luganda, Swahili, Amharic, Arabic, and hundreds of others.

Since anthropologists have clearly established that man began in Africa, probably in Tanzania or Ethiopia—somewhere in East Africa—the dramatic experience must have been seen and felt by Africans earlier than most. Moreover, since African theatre is usually directly related to the traditions, rituals, culture, and art forms of the people, one must conclude that a form of theatre began in Africa as long ago as their community origins. On the other hand, with the current emergence of the "new Africa," one must conclude that African theatre, with respect to theatre viewed in modern terms, is a theatre of evolution, since it is a theatre springing from a continent in transition and from countries in conflict.

Generally speaking, theatre art must derive or draw from the aesthetics or art forms of its locale, and they in turn must draw from the culture. African culture is not like Western culture. In a sense, it draws more directly from tradition. It follows then that anyone training for African theatre must know the culture. He must be steeped in the knowledge of the culture, first as culture, and secondly as it relates to the art forms of the theatre.

Since African theatre is basically a form of communication and expression, it also follows that the makers of African theatre must learn the "language of African theatre." And though the true dramatic experience of all theatre is universal, the receiver—*i.e.* the audience—will usually get more meaningful responses if he knows something about the language of African theatre. Certainly his knowledge of this language helps him complete the circular response in the theatrical chain of communication. This is especially true since the language of the African theatre is much more integrated in terms of total theatre than that of Western theatre.

Take a look at the language of African theatre through some of the art elements and rituals. Then examine their relationship to African theatre. For example, consider the use of ritual, regalia, music, dance, poetry, and the visual arts in African theatre. First you learn that a characteristic feature of African music is its rhythms. There is practically always a clash of rhythms. And you find that for the dancer an understanding of the use of these rhythms is a prerequisite to his art. For the African dancer must learn to control all parts of his body and often set parts of the body to different rhythms within the same dance. His shoulders may be moving to one rhythm, his hands to another, while his feet may play even a third rhythm. Also, the African dancer is usually dancing on his feet rather than on his toes, as is usual in much of Western dance.

Since many African languages are noted for the extensiveness of their vocabulary, the poetry of the theatre may be rich not only in its music, but also in its meaning. Furthermore, since the African image is often a surrealist image (both the suggestion and the creation of the object), it speaks not only in metaphorical language, but also in symbols, colors, rhythms, and stories—all at the same time. Consequently, to the African, the proverb or verse may be more "total" in its being and sensory perception than to the non-African.

It often speaks in powerful symbols and is concerned with concepts. And the art used in African theatre may also be regarded as a language in plastic form.

The richness of African theatre is yet to be explored and developed, both from a traditional point of view as well as from a conventional point of view. Consequently, the maker of African theatre must not only dig back into the roots of African societies to discover existence and meaning for himself and his theatre, he must also stretch and extend what he finds in terms of modern-day communication and theatricality.

He must continue to search for the materials of African theatre, and at the same time develop within himself a technique for the creation of this new African theatre. This holds true for playwright, actor, director, designer, musician, dancer, technician, or anyone else involved in making theatre. This theatre may be either of the traditional or of the conventional mold. Whatever it becomes, however, as theatre, it will form an integral base for tomorrow's student of African theatre and the history of African theatre.

The Elements of Traditional Drama

In African societies, the elements of traditional drama, though similar to the elements of conventional drama, appear more complex, complete, and interdependent or interrelated. For example, in conventional drama, as viewed from a Western mold, the elements emphasized are the word, *i.e.* speech and dramatic communication, and in addition props, costume, makeup, lighting, scenery, and sometimes music and dance. In traditional drama, the ingredients include the elements of conventional drama plus numerous other elements that *spring from traditional drama's direct connection with life.* They include (1) ritual with libation and prayers; (2) verse with spoken forms and sung forms, including speech surrogates such as drums, bells, and flutes; (3) music and dramatic communication, including instrumental symbolism, instrumental sounds such as signals, speech surrogates, music, song forms, and chorus, including the use of proverbs, tales, and riddles; (4) regalia, including the use of masks, stools, skins, and weapons; and (5) dance and movement expression.

Since ceremonial drama and traditional drama are usually staged outside, lighting and sets per se are not usually needed. *The staging is natural, based on man's relation to the universe.* That is to say that the choreography of the audience-performer relationship is natural, based on the African's normal way of seating himself, whether outside or inside. Special dress and costumes are also dictated by tradition.

With regard to dance, it may be necessary for the theatre-maker to have knowledge of the historical, social, and cultural background of the dances as well as knowledge of the organization of performers and their relationships and roles. He should also know something about the dance types and the categories of dances: religious dances, ceremonial dances, festival dances, and recreational dances. Certainly he should be aware of the use of costumes, makeup, props, and regalia and of the correlation between music and dance movements. He should also have insights regarding communication through the dance with respect to folk opera, concert party shows, and dance in the drama of contemporary African plays.

With regard to music, the theatre-maker should possess knowledge of the use of music in ceremonies and rituals. He should know song types and categories of songs, including religious songs and work songs. He should have basic knowledge of the use of musical instruments, the music of royal courts, the use of drum music, the music or musical roles of households, the musical interaction among ethnic groups, and the music or musical roles of individuals. Certainly it is advisable that he have knowledge of the use of music in contemporary drama. He should also have a knowledge of African tales, proverbs, and riddles.

In the BEGINNING theatre was a communion of vibrations, a sharing of ideas and emotions—a communicative force. Theatre came out of man's way of life, out of his life-styles. Theatre came out of the incantations, the rituals, the festivals, and celebrations of life—in the communal society. THEATRE WAS A CELEBRATION OF LIFE. Theatre was communicated and articulated through man's modes of expression. Man danced. Man sang. Man spoke. He expressed himself through movement, mime, word, and music. As man's imagination and perception developed and he became more of a social animal, he expressed himself more and more by oral means: through his proverbs, riddles, poetry, and prose. MAN BEGAN IN AFRICA.

All of these means of expression were a part of the African's traditional life-style. Rarely, if ever, was any of this viewed as art for art's sake. Consequently, this form which today we call "theatre" was then an integral part of man's communal existence. For example, storytelling drama, dance-drama, and ceremonial drama were and still are an integral part of communal existence. So today we speak of African theatre as being closely connected to the "culture concept" and the "integrated arts concept." Another way of viewing this is to say that African theatre is closely connected to the traditions in African culture and daily living, and that the theatre utilizes any and all of the art forms for a unified whole called "theatre." *African theatre may be viewed as a total creation, a volcanic eruption of the art forms caught in the middle of the culture of a particular African society.*

Often when one sees African theatre in this light, the theatre, though classical in nature, appears as simple and unstructured. Thus non-Africans and even Africans call it "primitive" theatre. They do this usually because of their hidden biases about Africa and its people, and because to them this theatre is simple. Perhaps this theatre is easy and simple to the artists and innovators who know their medium and their art, those artists who have discovered the discipline of their craft. And we must remember that it is the true artist who often has the ability to make his art appear very simple. This perhaps is the true essence of its beauty and the profound nature of its being. It is true that the African who has lived connected and in the midst of his own culture, not removed from his people, knows his own culture. Also he may know the meanings and nuances of African proverbs, riddles, poetry, and prose. He may know his own drumming and music, his dance and his gestures. That is to say, he knows his culture without trying to be a profound, erudite, scholarly dispenser of the arts. *He is* the embodiment of his arts, caught in his culture and communication. He does not profess to be; he is. And often he is this way without even knowing he is this way. That is, until he is "discovered." And before being discovered, he knows and understands his rituals, festivals, and celebrations. He experiences the depth and breadth of his culture. In other words, he has an idea of his culture, *but he also has the experience beneath the idea.* He thinks it. Feels it. Gives witness to it. *He is comfortable in being himself through his art.* Expressing himself through his art, celebrating his life-cycles through his art.

The moment he becomes removed from his African culture, however, or the moment he removes himself, he faces a dilemma. He becomes an African caught in a great culture conflict, an African caught in mixed worlds of transition. His problem then becomes one of retaining his own culture and its values. And at the same time, because of technological advances in the world, he finds that he must also learn about the modern contemporary technological age and its highly competitive nature among societies of the world.

The non-African asks the question, "What are some of the basic differences between African theatre and European, or Western, theatre?" There are some very basic differences as we have already seen with respect to the traditions and the culture concept and the integrated arts concept.

Also, African theatre is more directly concerned with the poetry of life and its rhythms and life-cycles, whereas the essence of the current concept of Western theatre is clash or conflict. Another basic difference is this: in Africa, people generally GO to see and PARTICIPATE in the theatre, to share and to COME TOGETHER, especially in the traditional theatre. For them, theatre is an occasion of a COMMUNION of VIBRATIONS and a CELEBRATION of LIFE.

Often Western theatre thrives on the idea of ESCAPE for its audience. An audience goes to the theatre to escape. African theatre is participatory theatre. Western theatre is player-oriented and often passive from the audience's point of view. *In African theatre a unique relationship exists between the audience and the performer.*

African theatre utilizes all elements of the art forms and non-verbal and verbal communication. It is a total fusion. *At any given time any of the art forms may tell the story or enhance the dramatic or theatrical experience.*

Classical African theatre is loose, like jazz; it is free to be opened up and fully realized on the spot. It is improvisatory, though highly structured. It is an *on the spot-giving witness to-celebration of life-process.*

The dramatic consciousness of African people expects these modes of expression and communication.

Traditional African drama is indigenous or ethnic drama of a high classical mold and has specific elements, including the following: (1) *Ceremonial Drama,* which is dramatic expression associated with social, ritual, or ceremonial occasions; (2) *Storytelling Drama,* which is a composite of narrative and dialogue, music, poetry, mime, and the movements of the dance; and (3) *Dance-Drama,* which is drama expressed through music, poetry, mime, and the movements of the dance. In dance-drama usually the master drummer dictates the tempo, holds the rhythm section together, and sometimes choreographs the pattern. At any given time these three elements may come together to form a unique dramatic experience in theatre. And rarely, if ever, does this theatre exist as something separate from social life; rather it is a necessary contribution to its fulfillment.

On the other hand, *conventional African drama or theatre* is often very similar to Western theatre and includes plays written in English, French, or other European languages by the playwrights and theatre-makers of the new Africa. *Popular African theatre* may also be included in this category, although it is often viewed as a separate category. Its themes are the conflicts between modern society and its values and traditional society and its values.

The Western mind tends to categorize African theatre as FOLK, PRIMITIVE, POPULAR, and LITERARY. Of course these categories may be used as long as the user understands the high classical nature of the traditional theatre, as well as the negative connotation of the words "folk" and "primitive." *Image-doors must be open-doors in order to understand African theatre and African people.*

In a real sense African traditional theatre may be viewed as classical and folk theatre at the same time. It is theatre of a high order, which is understood and accepted by the people—African people—which thereby conveys universality to those people who crawl inside the "African people experience." It goes back into antiquity and is with us today. It is of the people, by the people, and through the people. Consequently, it is also *folk* and theatre of the people. When viewed this way, as a theatre of high dimension, being both classical and folk, it is often possible to understand the many facets and dimensions of African theatre. When something erupts in front of your eyes, when something penetrates your entire perceptive being, through not one art form but through many, and at the same time speaks of years, of yesterday and today, this "something" has to be of a high order and not primitive or basic. *African theatre communicates to you in this fashion.* However, the viewer's perception cannot be and must not be ANTI-AFRICAN or ANTI-MAN. His perceptions and values must be humanistically oriented in order to *step inside the African theatre experience.*

In a world in which four-fifths of its population is *colored* (nonwhite), that portion of the world, by virtue of its commonality of experience and circumstance, is, in a sense, already close to the "African people experience." In most instances they have begun to understand the nature of the African theatre experience. Also, although there are many differences between Asian theatre and African theatre, there are some basic similarities. Chinese theatre, the Japanese Kabuki theatre, and Indian theatre all have elements of ritual and spectacle and also use music and dance. As we have already learned, African theatre is filled with ritual, spectacle, music, dance, and other art forms, and is usually connected with the traditions and the history of its people. In discussing Kabuki theatre, A. C. Scott tells us that

> a general understanding of the social and psychological background of Japanese society in the past is a valuable aid towards a richer appreciation of the dramatic construction of the Kabuki. . . . The Kabuki, like the Chinese theatre, lays great stress upon the virtuosity of the actor. He supplies the motive for the whole drama. He must play to an audience which knows the rules of the game and which is primarily interested in the way he recreates a stage character in a traditionally accepted mold. At the same time his performance must contain an individuality beneath the unchanging conventions, his symbolism must be something more than imitative repetition.

These same words could be used in speaking of the African actor, inasmuch as he is also the embodiment of his culture and the exemplifier of his art forms. Scott goes on to tell us that in Chinese theatre, one of the primary requisites of a good actor is a fine singing voice in addition to his other accomplishments; on the Kabuki stage he is not required to sing, but he must with few exceptions be a first-class dancer. Dancing plays an exceedingly important part in the Kabuki drama. There are a large number of plays in the repertoire which are dance pieces pure and simple, others in which dancing is an underlying feature of construction, even in the dialogue plays a dance passage is often introduced.[1]

In African theatre there are celebrations in dance-drama. And even in the conventional form of African theatre, dance and music often play an integral part. It is true, however, that most Asian theatre is highly stylized, while African theatre is not. We must also remember that African theatre, when played in a borrowed language, is often bound by a Western form. In other words, when African theatre is played in English or French, by necessity the form usually gravitates toward a Western conventional form. By virtue of this fact it is safe to say that the one-fifth noncolored population of the world can also easily understand a great deal of the new developing African theatre, especially when it is in the conventional form. As we have already said, image-doors must be open-doors in order to understand African theatre and African people.

A brief consideration of examples of African Traditional Festivals usually offers the "outsider" additional insights with respect to an understanding of traditional African theatre. For example, in West Africa, and especially in Ghana, at least four specific types of festivals may be found. They are (1) *A Festival of the Gods*, a festival in which the public collective rites center around the gods of a given locality; (2) *A Festival of Nature*, a festival in which reverence for nature as something to be drawn upon for the benefit of man is stressed, such as the opening and closing of rivers or lagoons; (3) *A Festival of a Specific Area*, a festival usually emphasizing the solidarity of a local area; and (4) *A Festival Devoted to Ancestors*, a festival commemorating historical events relating to the ancestors.

[1]A. C. Scott, *The Kabuki Theatre of Japan* (New York: Collier Books, 1966), pp. 5, 15, 16.

In addition to a study of African festivals coupled with the study of the traditions and the cultures of Africa, a historical thrust should permeate the total framework of African theatre or Black theatre. Also, in order to understand Black theatre and its development, one must seek at least an overview of the "Black Experience," the culture, the life-styles, and art forms of Black people, beginning with the Motherland—Africa.

Some basic considerations with respect to the performer-audience relationship should now be mentioned. Drama permeates all of living throughout the world. Man is forever playing a role and engaging in dramatic conflict. When one speaks of theatre, one must be careful to distinguish between this kind of life-drama, or role playing, and the drama of the theatre. Though drama and theatre have long been a part of the cultural activities, the rituals, the festivals, and everyday living in Africa, rarely has there been drama or theatre as art for art's sake. Today, however, this situation is slowly changing and bringing with it specific problems of communication and production.

For example, traditional theatre or ethnic theatre is an integral part of the society and its living. The audience is usually familiar with its form, its motivation, and its artistic elements. This is so, because the basic forms and patterns have become established over a period of time. Consequently, the audience knows the story and the form. It knows just what is going to happen, and moreover it expects it to happen that way. It expects the drama to express and reflect a traditional way of life or to reiterate life-forms in certain rhythms and patterns as they are reflected in daily life. Repetition is both expected and desired. Moreover, the dramatic experience is more directly shared by performer and spectator as a community activity. And by now we certainly understand that ceremonial drama, storytelling, and dance-drama fall into this category. These dramatic expressions associated with social rituals or ceremonial occasions and narrative drama, including dialogue, music, dance, and mime with more spontaneity than formality, and dance-drama movements may all be well known and expected by the audience. And this audience-ritual-identification may keep the spectators involved for days or weeks without their becoming bored.

Conventional theatre, on the other hand, presents a special

problem with respect to communication, attention span, and audi-ence-performer relationship. In this new theatrical situation the drama is consciously organized, staged, and designed by a director for a general, impersonal audience, and for a specific length of time, usually two or three hours. Although the theatrical process is still one of sharing, involving a circular response, the responsibility for the quality of the performance and presentation rests more with the performer, for his audience is more of an impersonal receiver.

Usually the dramatic experience is not directly shared by per-former and spectator in conventional theatre. Here the attitudes are more "show me" or "make me laugh or cry," but above all, "enter-tain me." Consequently, the technique of the performer and the way in which he communicates play a different role in the circular response of the dramatic experience. The performer must at all times capture and hold the attention of his audience. He must hook his audience, and then he must make his audience understand him and believe him. True, he must share the dramatic experience, but the burden is more upon him as the theatrical medium, or the link between the playwright and the audience. This particular audience demands variety, contrast, and communication of a specific dra-matic experience or idea. So we see that the functions of traditional and conventional theatre are quite different and place different de-mands upon the actors or performers. For both, however, the per-former must be cognizant of the culture and the art of his society, and he must be steeped in the technique of the theatre. He must develop theatrical awareness, involvement and concentration, and then he must adjust technique to the situation of traditional theatre or conventional theatre. And even for the purely imitative theatre of the Western mold, the African performer must be skilled in theatrical techniques and discipline.

It is correct to say that "to understand African theatre in the contemporary Black World is to get closer to a better understanding of culture and communication in Africa." However, Africa is . . . ? . . . ? . . . ? That is to say, when one speaks of Africa, one speaks of a vast continent of many complexities. For within the continent of Africa there are many countries. And within the countries of Africa there are many nations, tribes, and cultures. Therefore, Afri-can drama and theatre may be as various as its tribes or nations, and

African ethnic groups or tribes may range in size from two hundred thousand to twelve million people. Each tribe has its own social organization, political organization, religion, language, music, dance, and drama. Some ethnic groups or collections of tribes have become nations. For example, the nation of Ghana is comprised of numerous groups, including the Ewe, the Ga, the Ashanti, the Fanti, the Nzema, and the Dagbani. In many parts of Africa the general pattern is to emphasize the relationship of the drama and the music to the other activities of the people, especially those activities that are recreational, ceremonial, and ritualistic. Ritual music and drama are performed for worship, and there are particular songs to be sung by women, children, and mixed groups at the royal court and the market place and when sowing, harvesting, and cutting bush.

For some individuals, learning music is an inherited obligation. The players of the "talking drum," by which messages are sent long distances, must know all the tribal traditions as well as the music. In some tribes there is a custom of imitating musical instruments vocally. Music societies are very common in Africa. It is considered to be the duty of a person's musical group to come when he needs the members to perform for a celebration or to provide appropriate music for a sorrowful occasion. People make their own music much more in African countries than in those of the West. There is drama, ritual, and ceremony in nearly every phase of life.

Part Two

I went to Ghana in search of African theatre. And since I was on Ghanaian soil, I felt a need to renew my acquaintance with the African kingdoms of the past, so I decided to work my way from the old Empire of Ghana to the Gold Coast, before finally immersing myself in the traditions of the Ghana of today.

Along the way, searching for seeds of African theatre, I would sharpen my sights by paying particular attention to African man's traditional way of life, including his mode of expression. After traveling an abbreviated historical journey, I would examine the drama springing from the traditions of the people, and then reflect upon the modern scene by taking a look at Ghana's current national theatre movement.

With my journey before me, I began to reread the story of OLD GHANA.

Old Ghana was an ancient kingdom and was mentioned by historians in the eighth century. There is little doubt, however, that it was a powerful nation long before that time. As an empire it had a central government, a regular army, and a civil service. Its people were steeped in Africa's traditional way of life. Its leader, a "divine king," was also its religious leader. He emerged from Africa's special forms of tribal organizations, customs, and culture.

The empire of Ghana flourished during the Iron Age in West Africa. Its rulers, understanding the nature of an effective trading system, emphasized a sound export-import policy. From the fringes of the Sahara, where salt was plentiful, the Ghanaian leaders imported large quantities of salt. They also exported enough gold to pay for their imports of salt. Their abundant supply of gold helped them to maintain their royal power and also made it possible for them to bestow regular gifts upon the chiefs and governors through whom they reigned. With control over the import of salt and the purchase of gold, they were able to make all merchants pay large duties on the buying and selling of salt and other commodities. In turn, these duties or monies were used for the upkeep of their courts, their armies, and their administration.

Thus the kingdom of Ghana was important commercially. With Spain and Portugal and other countries, they traded in gold, ivory, animal skins, kola nuts, and cotton. At the height of Ghana's power, Egyptian, Asiatic, and European students flocked to Ghanaian universities, where they learned philosophy, medicine, mathematics, and law. There was even an exchange of professors between the University of Sankore in Timbuktu and the University of Cordova in Spain. There is little doubt that during this time Old Ghana's traditional theatre flourished with all of its ritual, regalia, and dramatic elements, and that the splendor and pride of the empire was evidenced through its music, drama, and ceremonial spectacles.

Eventually, however, constant attacks from nomadic peoples further north and internal dissension shook the foundations of the empire. Many of its inhabitants migrated. Those who remained behind were attacked and defeated by Mali in 1240. Sumanguru, the king of Old Ghana, was defeated by Mari Djata, or Prince Lion. The town of Ghana was destroyed, and the country of Old Ghana became part of MALI.

Mali's territory and influence spread from the Atlantic to the borders of modern Nigeria, and from the fringe of the forest lands far northward into the Sahara. Mali became one of the world's largest empires. Like Ghana, it too was noted for its gold. It was also noted for its ceremonial splendor and spectacle, ritualistic drama, and traditional culture.

In the Madingo language, *mansa* means "king." And Mansa Kankan Musa was perhaps the greatest of Mali's kings. He reigned for twenty-five years and was noted for his justice, piety, love of learning, and wealth. During his reign, Mali reached the height of its power and development. And, generally speaking, there was peace and happiness in the kingdom. The fame of the Mali Empire was known all over the world and several distinguished travelers, like the geographer Ibn Batuta, visited it. The university at Timbuktu was remarkable for the opportunities it afforded students.

In time Mali also met its downfall. Internal confusion set in, tribes revolted, and Mali then became an easy prey for neighboring countries like Mosi and Songhai. The people of Songhai, formerly subjects of Mali, were to become independent. Timbuktu was to be captured by the Tuaregs. And finally, Songhai was to take the empire away from Mali piece by piece.

The first home of the Songhai people included the area around Dendi, which lies northwest of the place where the Gulbin Kebbi joins the Niger, just inside the modern boundaries of Nigeria. From this point they spread northward along the banks of the Niger.

Thus in the middle of the fifteenth century, Mali became part of the Songhai empire. Starting as a small kingdom south of the Niger, Songhai took advantage of the weakness of Mali and moved its capital to Gao, further upstream, in order to facilitate trade with the north. It was from that point that Songhai was soon able to conquer Mali.

Askia Muhammed, or Askia the Great, as he was often called, was one of the great leaders of the Songhai people. Under his rule, the University of Sankore in Timbuktu became the center of Muslim learning in Africa. Nor was learning merely confined to the University of Sankore alone. Other universities at Mali, Aiwalatin, Jenne, and Katsina flourished. New schools and mosques were built and old schools were improved and enlarged. In general, "culture" spread throughout Timbuktu. And there is little doubt that Timbuktu was the center of rich music, dance, and drama experiences. Askia the Great reigned for thirty-six years. During his reign, his empire stretched from Cape Bogador on the Atlantic Coast along the northern desert to Marzula and Augila, which is a hundred miles from the border of modern Egypt.

In 1591, however, on the battlefield of Tondibi, the last of the great kingdoms of the Niger Bend fell a victim to the Moorish

troops of the Moroccan Prince, El Mansur. Such was Old Ghana
and succeeding empires. But what of New Ghana, the Ghana of
today?

On the basis of archaeological, sociological, and linguistic evidence, it is generally believed that *the Akans of modern Ghana were
closely associated with the ancient kingdom of Ghana,* if they did not form
part of it.

After the fall of the kingdoms, trade, religion, culture, and
other influences reaching the inhabitants of the forest belt from the
north were slight. On the other hand, there was extensive contact
between the forest people and the Europeans who came to West
Africa by sea. This contact was to have its effect upon the culture
and the traditions of the people. For in time, the culture conflict
would affect the direction of drama in Ghana.

Europe "discovered" the Gold Coast in 1471. The Portuguese
came first. They discovered the gold-producing districts between
the Ankobre and Volta rivers. And subsequently they named the
area *Mina,* meaning "mine." The French called the area Côte d'Or,
or the "Gold Coast," a name that was later adopted by the English
and applied to the country as a whole. In 1482 the Portuguese built
the Castle of Saõ Jorge de Mina. This gave them exclusive rights
over the area and enabled them to obtain an impregnable trading
center.

At first the Portuguese concentrated on the natural resources
of the west coast, such as gold, pepper, and ivory. Later came the
trade in human beings. And from its inception in about 1515, the
slave trade became very lucrative, and soon largely eclipsed the
trade in gold and other commodities. Slaves soon became the "gold"
of the Gold Coast. The discovery and colonization of the Americas
in the fifteenth and sixteenth centuries, along with the establishment of sugar and cotton plantations in the New World, created the
need for a regular supply of slave labor. And so profitable did this
trade in slaves and gold increasingly become that other European
traders "invaded the market" and gave the Portuguese competition.
Thus from 1598 onwards, it was first the Dutch, who captured the
Elmina Castle from the Portuguese in 1642, then the English, the
French, the Danes, the Swedes, and the Germans who steadily
entered the field. Consequently, by the middle of the eighteenth

Regions in modern Ghana (*Allen Tamakloe*)

Languages in modern Ghana (*Allen Tamakloe*)

Precolonial empires and states (*Allen Tamakloe*)

century, cut-throat competition for the trade was raging all along
the west coast. However, by the beginning of the nineteenth century, only the British, the Danes, and the Dutch were actively
operating on the Gold Coast, with the British controlling about half
of the trade. The numerous forts and castles that still dot the coast-
line of Ghana are monuments to the exploitation of the Gold Coast
by the European people. One can only speculate regarding the
effect this slave mongering had upon the traditions of the Ghanaian
people and their traditional drama. It did, however, set the stage for
the "missionary movement" which was to follow, bringing with it
the early missionary dramas and another approach to African
drama and theatre.

It is important to note that, until this time, Europeans had
concentrated their activities entirely along the coast and had remained largely ignorant of the peoples of the hinterlands. Primarily
they concentrated on gold and then on the slave trade, and certainly
showed no concern for the welfare or the education of the Africans.

Then came the missionary societies. They aimed at "converting" and "educating" the Africans instead of enslaving and selling
them. Again one can only speculate regarding the results of this
policy of attempting to press the African into a new mold, into new
traditions, and into a new culture. This period was no doubt the
precursor of the era of the African caught in culture conflict and the
African caught between two worlds. For along with the missionary
societies came the missionary dramas, European concerts, and theatrical presentations. Certainly the words *concert* and *theatre* were
alien to the ears of most Africans. And of course the missionary
dramas were quite different from the traditional dramas that most
Africans were truly at home with. Efua Sutherland speaks of the
word *concert* in telling us about the evolution of "concert parties"
in Ghana.

> The story of the new evolution towards theatre in European
> images has similar characteristics in most African countries.
> For, once upon a time, Africans did not stand on a platform
> to sing songs and say things, and dance to entertain static
> audiences ranged on chairs before them. Then came Euro-
> peans who started new institutions called schools. The chil-

dren of these schools learned among other things to stand on platforms and give what they called a CONCERT. This concert was a performance of songs, mostly in English.... The crowds flocked to the Concerts and were thrilled by the jolly chorals in English rendered from the platforms before which they sat in chairs arranged in rows. Although the scope of the performance expanded, it made no difference what the bill of fare, it was all CONCERT to performers and audiences alike. ... To date, the average Ghanaian goes to a Concert, meaning by that, any performance by actors on a stage, that is, an acrobatic display by a Chinese troupe; straight Shakespearean drama by a British troupe; a performance of modern dance by an American dance troupe. . . . The words Drama and Theatre are foreign words and imcomprehensible to everybody else except a mere sprinkling of people. But CONCERT has become a Ghanaian word which is comprehensible, and for the people who use it, it serves instead of drama and theatre. ... It is not surprising, therefore, that the first locally evolved form of theatre has become popularly known as the CONCERT PARTY.[1]

By the 1870s, instead of slaves, palm oil, peanuts, and cotton had become the main exports. In the missionary field, the Basel Evangelical Society had, for instance, firmly established Christianity in the Akwapim and Akim districts, and had opened the Akropong Training College, the Aburi Girls' School, and ninety other shcools. The Bremen Mission had become firmly entrenched in Eweland. The Wesleyan Missionary Society had won hundreds of converts in Fanteland, and was running the Mfantsipim Secondary School as well as over forty elementary schools, including the first elementary boarding school in Cape Coast, which Dr. Kwegyir Aggrey, one of Ghana's famous educators, attended. Consequently, after the abolition of the slave trade and the acceleration of missionary activities in the nineteenth century, a revolutionary change occurred in the nature and scope of European interests and activities in West Africa in general and on the Gold Coast in particular. *By the middle of the nineteenth century, the Europeans had pushed inland*

---

[1]Efua Sutherland, "Theatre in Ghana," in Janice Nesbitt, editor, *Ghana Welcomes You* (Accra: Orientation to Ghana Committee, 1969), pp. 84–85.

and were "educating" and "converting" the Africans. They were now trading in legitimate articles such as gold, palm oil, rubber, and cocoa. *The Africans became "educated," Christians, and even professional ministers of "religion," school teachers, lawyers, journalists, and politicians.*

Almost all Ghanaians are Sudanese Africans, although Hamitic strains are common in northern Ghana. The country has been peopled during the past seven hundred to one thousand years. Most of the ethnic groups moved into the country from the north, and a few probably came from the east.

Those coming from the north included the Guan groups, who first moved in along the Volta gorge and spread along the coast between Winneba and Cape Coast. They were followed by the Fantis, who were the vanguard of the largest group and occupy roughly the present Cape Coast district. Later, the Twis followed the Fantis and spread over most of Ashanti and the forest country further south between the Volta and the Tano and north of the Fanti and Guan areas.

Of those coming from the east, the Ewes claim to have come from farther north in Togo and the Ga-Adangmes from along the coast from Nigeria. Beliefs and customs prevailing in the northern regions indicate that aboriginal agricultural populations were subjugated by conquering warrior bands. The main groupings of the population are: Gonja in the center and northeast; Kassena, Nankanni, and Builsa in the central frontier; and Wala, Dgarti, and Sissala in the northwest.

Between the eleventh and sixteenth centuries, Ghana was populated by the Ga-Adangme peoples moving from the west along Ghana's eastern coastal areas. They were followed in the eastern inland areas by the Ewe people. From the north at about the same time, Akan peoples, known as Ashanti, Akwapim, and Fanti, moved southward into the forested areas of Ghana. Numerous savannah peoples moved southward from the Upper Volta. Among the differences in tradition were the languages, so that although English is the official language of Ghana, you will hear Ga, Twi, Fanti, Ewe, Hausa, and many other languages.

Ghana consists of three geographical zones: northern savannahs, forest lands, and a flat coastal belt. In the north, the country

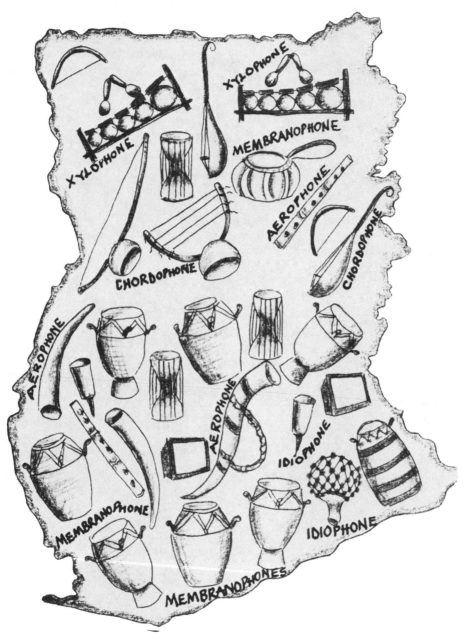

Musical map of Ghana (*Allen Tamakloe*)

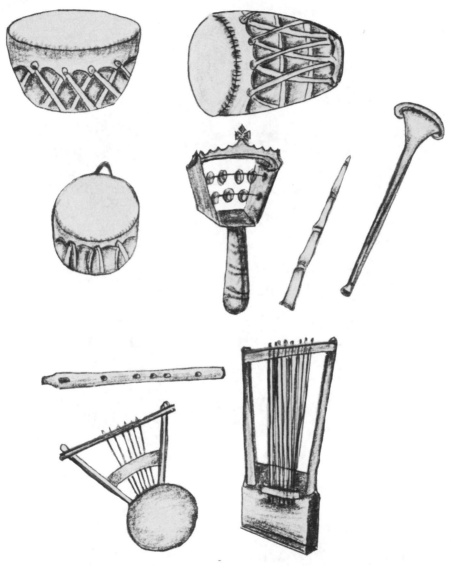

Ghanaian musical instruments (*Allen Tamakloe*)

is open, the climate is hot and dry, and the farmers grow corn and millet, or raise cattle. In the forest areas of the central and western parts of the country, rolling hills and dramatic ridges are covered by tall timber trees or numerous cocoa farms. The climate there is often hot and humid. In the eastern coastal plains, the land is flat and the climate is warm and dry. Ghana's seasons are the wet season, from May to September, and the dry season, from October to March or April. In general, the weather is summerlike all year round.

Ghana has a population of approximately eight million with a variety of historical traditions. Densities are highest (sometimes over four hundred per square mile) in the northeastern and northwestern frontier districts, around Kumasi, and then in the south toward Obuasi and east into Kwahu, the southeastern, Cape Coast, and Ahanta districts. Densities are lowest in the southwestern frontier areas south of 7°N and in the middle of the country in a belt extending from the western frontier between 8° and 10°N across the Afram Plains right up to the Togo border between 7° and 8° 45′ N. Ghana has an area of approximately 92,000 square miles, and is about the size of Oregon. About 350 miles wide and 400 miles in length, it is a few degrees north of the Equator, on the Greenwich (0°) Meridian. It is bordered by the French-speaking countries of Togo, Upper Volta, and the Ivory Coast, and it is trisected by the Volta River and its two tributaries, the Black and White Voltas.

New Ghana was born on March 6, 1957, when the country became the first British colony in Africa to gain independence. The former Gold Coast was declared an independent state and was re-named Ghana after the ancient Sudanic Empire.

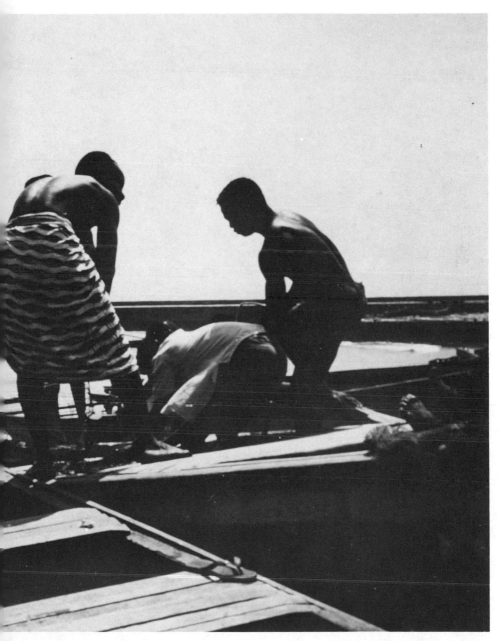

Fishing (*Scott Kennedy*)

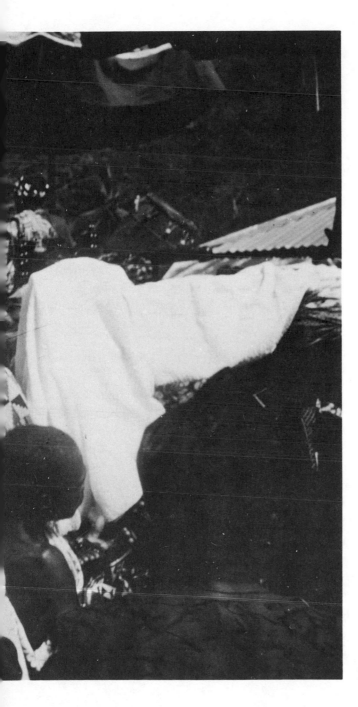

Festival (*Scott Kennedy*)

CHAPTER
5
Drama in
Traditional African Societies

The African festival is the lifeblood of African people. To look at the festival is to learn about the culture of Africa—to learn the African's mode of expression and communication and his religion, and to understand the WHY of his politics and his economics.

Most Africans have evolved traditional rituals for all the important events of life: for child naming, for puberty and initiation, and for marriage and death. More important than the rituals, however, is the festival. In fact, according to A. A. Opoku, "The annual and seasonal festivals, which bring together the whole people of a town, and indeed, the whole tribe, are far more important than the rituals, which are performed only by the little family or clan circle."[1]

Festivals and rituals share a common dramatic experience in a communal setting through group participation. They celebrate life and examine the survival scene. And in the midst of this communion of vibrations is the use of regalia, dramatic expression, and music and dance.

According to John Mbiti, "African man lives in a religious universe. He sees and experiences life through his religious understanding and meaning. Religion is the strongest element in traditional backgrounds and exerts probably the greatest influence upon

[1] A. A. Opoku, *Festivals of Ghana* (Accra: Ghana Publishing Corporation, 1970), p. 4.

70

Ghanaian man mending a net (*Scott Kennedy*)

Festival dancers (*Scott Kennedy*)

the thinking and living of the people concerned, for wherever the African is, there is his religion."

Traditional African theatre is couched in action-centered ceremonies, rituals, and incantations told through storytelling or dance-drama. Religion is the African's celebration of life and his source of survival. The traditional theatre is his way of giving witness to his celebration of life and his means of survival.

In one sense, "African philosophy" may be found in the religion, proverbs, oral traditions, and ethics of the society concerned. And in another sense, African philosophy may also be found in African theatre as it celebrates life, as it erupts within the art forms and the culture of its people. Certainly, as Mbiti informs us, "Religion itself can be discerned in terms of beliefs, ceremonies, rituals, and religious officiants."

The African's traditional drama is an extremely religious act, just as his music, his dance, and his celebrations are often religious acts. But the reader must be reminded that traditional religions are not primarily for the individual, but for the community of which he is a part, for "in traditional society there are no irreligious people. To be human is to belong to the whole community, and to do so involves participating in the beliefs, ceremonies, rituals, and festivals of that community. Everybody is a religious carrier."[2] Everybody is a participant. From the time he is born to the time he dies or enters upon another journey called death, he is forever a social being participating within a communal setting. Rarely if ever is he functioning or acting for or by himself. Others are involved. And from this, too, he can run, but he can't hide.

In a nontraditional setting, however, life often takes another course—the course of the individualist, for self-aggrandizement and self-perpetuation. This, all too often, is the course offered by the forces of modern life and the highly technological age, which are in the race for supreme power and control of tomorrow's world.

Ghanaians usually express themselves traditionally through their art forms, rituals, and regalia, which are necessary elements in their mode of communication and expression. This drama of life

[2]John Mbiti, *African Religions and Philosophies* (Garden City, New York: Doubleday Anchor, 1970), pp. 1–3.

and a traditional way of expression and communication form the legacy and the food for the emergency and reemergence of Ghanaian theatre both in the traditional sense and in the conventional sense. This Ghanaian way of life erupts upon the stage as the art forms appear caught in the middle of their unique culture. And always the PEOPLE are the focus of this special relationship between the performer and the audience, as together they share an experience. To them, theatre is an experience, a people-oriented experience, not yet technologically oriented or controlled by gadgets or things.

Dramatic aspects of African culture and African art forms permeate the continent. They spring from the music and poetry of the universe. They lurk within the heart of nature. They speak of the Africa of yesterday and today and cry out for use by the makers of modern African theatre. They are at rest within the funeral dirges, in the songs of praise, or in the songs of criticism. And at the same time, they breathe life and spring alive in the recreational and incidental music of Africa. They flow in the streams of folk music, popular music, and "fine art music."

Professor J. K. Nketia tells us that "the traditional music of Ghana is essentially folk music developed and maintained by oral tradition by each group, and organized and practised as an integral part of everyday life . . . and . . . that music making is socially controlled."[3] For example, he informs us that "Akan custom requires that the singing of funeral dirges shall normally be an integral part of the funeral celebration, providing it with its atmosphere and underlining its activities, while giving the participants opportunities for displaying their thoughts and emotions and for paying tribute to the deceased."[4]

Stressing a strong relationship between the dramatic and musical expressions of the Ghanaian people and their traditions, he says, "as a creative verbal-musical expression, the dirge takes its place alongside the poetry of songs, drums, horns, and pipes." "In studying the dirge, we . . . [study] not just individual utterances but social

[3]J. H. Kwabena Nketia, *Folk Songs of Ghana* (London: Oxford University Press, 1963), p. 1.
[4]Nketia, *Funeral Dirges* (Achimoto: University College of the Gold Coast, 1955), pp. 3, 5, 6.

expressions and aspects of the culture of the Akan people." In Ghana the folk songs are still a part of the life of the people today, "for while the songs are sung by 'simple' agricultural communities sharing common ideals and beliefs, common customs and institutions, common folk tales and oral traditions, they are by no means songs of a forgotten past. They are still widely practised and perpetuated by oral tradition among those who have kept to traditional ways of life."[5]

The word *regalia*, to the non-African, carries many connotations, including the insignia of royalty used at coronations and at similar occasions. For the Ghanaian, however, the word covers a wider range of objects: the Golden Stool of the Ashanti and the Stool of Precious Beads of the Denkyiras, and things like an imported siphon, which quenches the chief's thirst with its aerated water and also delights his subjects with the hissing sound it makes. The regalia also includes the various forms of Ghanaian traditional crafts: weaving, embroidery, carving, pottery, and works in leather, brass, bronze, silver, and gold. According to A. A. Y. Kyerematen, "a study of the regalia of Ghana's traditional rulers reveals much about her cultural heritage, and therefore these regalia are important to the Ghanaian in many ways." They are important for their historical connections, their social and ritual functions, their symbolic meaning, and also for showing the imagination and ingenuity of the Ghanaian craftsman. Kyerematen informs us that "the regalia of Ghanaian chiefs have been of special significance in that they have not been merely symbols of the kingly office but have served as the chronicles of early history and the evidence of traditional religion, cosmology and social organizations. It is customary for the regalia to be paraded whenever the chief appears in state at a national festival or durbar, so that all who see them may read, mark and inwardly digest what they stand for."[6]

The chief emblem of royalty for British and Norwegian monarchs is the crown and for other Scandinavian rulers the bracelet. "In Ghana, the stool and the skins of certain animals are the most

[5]Nketia, *Folk Songs of Ghana*, p. 2.
[6]A. A. Y. Kyerematen, *Panoply of Ghana* (New York: Praeger, 1964), p. 1.

important of the chief's regalia and the sine qua non of his high
office. Stools are found among the Akans, the Ewes, the Ga-
Adangmes and other tribes of Southern Ghana, i.e. among the
Ashanti and in states on the littoral, while skins are used in Northern Ghana."

Included in the regalia of Ghanaians are many objects, including stools, skins, and chairs; weapons, including spears, arrows,
clubs, swords, and guns; figurative weights; musical instruments,
including drums, flutes, horns, gongs, and rattles; and personal
ornaments. The Asantehene's categories of swords include those
used for different purposes and made of iron, brass, gold dust, and
silver. Personal ornaments include the main body garment and
ornaments for other parts of the body—head, feet, neck, and fingers.
You will find robes, headdress, sandals, jewelry, and other regalia
including umbrellas, palanquins, and staffs of Office, like the stick
of the *okyeame* or official linguist. We learn from Kyerematen that
the legacy of the Ghanaian craftsman include: (1) regalia as the
people's spiritual fortification; (2) regalia as symbols of authority; (3)
regalia as a guide to the study of Ghanaian society (cosmology,
religion, nature of man, social values); and (4) regalia as works of
art.[7]

Ritual Celebrations

A chief, one of the most important figures in Ghanaian society,
has had his role clearly defined by traditions, as Kofi Busia points
out in his book *The Position of the Chief in . . . Ashanti.*[8] Felix Yamoah,
in his study *The Installation of an Ashanti Chief,* stresses the importance of the dramatic experience, and drumming and dancing in the
installation ceremony. The three stages of the installation ceremony
include: the nomination, the swearing of the oath, and the formal
installation act—all three embrace formal dramatic elements.
"When a stool becomes vacant in any Ashanti state a new chief is
made within the first fortieth day to occupy the stool. Arrange-

---

[7] *Ibid.,* pp. 101–16.
[8] Kofi Busia, *The Position of the Chief in . . . Ashanti* (London: Frank Cass and Co.,
Ltd., 1968).

ments are made to install him on a day fixed by the elders." The reader is asked to notice the importance of the music, drama, and dance during the occasion. For example:

> He [the chief] is carried shoulder high amidst singing and dancing and then taken to Apatam where he is taught the history of his people and all about the ceremonies. . . . After the ceremony the new chief dances to the Asantehene's frontomfrom music. The chief has four different types of drums at his court, and during festivals his drums play for him while he rides in the palanquin. On the fortieth day following the death of the late chief, the new chief wears the batakarikesee to celebrate the funeral rites. In this celebration he dances. . . . Drum sounds signify the end of the enstoolment. People come to sing for the chief.

Yamoah specifically refers to the drama when he tells us, "there are ritual and ceremonial performances which are celebrated with pomp. There are many dramatic elements in these activities. Drumming and dancing form a major aspect in the making of enstooling a chief."[9] At the conclusion of his study Yamoah says that it would be virtually impossible to consider the ritual of installing a chief without the use of specific art forms and modes of communication, including the use of regalia, drama, music, and dance.

A close study of Ghanaian festivals and rituals shows us that the dramatic experience and the use of the art forms, such as music, dance, and visual elements, appear to be necessary to the fulfillment and execution of most Ghanaian festivals and rituals.

Francis Yartey in her study of the puberty rite of the Ga-Mashie underscores the importance of dramatic elements and the use of music and dance. The Otu puberty rite, a custom of the Ga-Mashie people of Ghana, is used to strengthen the moral and spiritual outlook of youths in order that they may face the future courageously. Among other things, "it includes formal presentation of the girls to the custodians for training in the ceremonial fetching

---

[9]Felix Yamoah, *The Installation of an Ashanti Chief: A Study of Movement and Customary Behavior,* unpublished thesis, University of Ghana, 1971.

of water, formal presentation of gifts to the candidates at a ceremony called 'Mandzranobaa,' storytelling, ceremonial washing of hair, and also drumming and dancing, which are the keynotes of the ceremony." We learn much about the importance of music and dance in this rite. For example, the candidates must go through a course of instruction to learn how to master the movements of the dance, how to sing the special Otufo songs dedicated to all aspects of the ceremony, and how to respect and be loyal to everybody with whom they come in contact. We also learn about the *forms of the dance, the performance, the use of music,* and the *manner of dress.* Regarding the forms of the dance, Yartey says:

> The dance takes three forms, they are: Otufo, Saayole, and Sidaa; each form has a function in the ceremony. The Otufo form is identified with Oko, the Saayole is a revelation of worship and the Sidaa of thanksgiving. To ensure that nothing goes amiss, special roles are assigned to specific people. The chief custodian known as Otufowulomo is the "master of ceremonies" throughout. He is assisted by a woman refered to as Otufoanye. She is in charge of the welfare of the candidates. Next in rank is the linguist to the Otufowulomo and finally the master drummer and his subordinates.

The staging of the performance and the use of music are also considered:

> The men form the actual ensemble at one side. They face the women at the other end while the spectators, who in some cases play active part in singing, flank the other sides to form a rectangle. The singing takes the form of "solo and chorus" while the melody is basically built on the indigenous pentatonic scales with some modifications. The membranophones and an idiophone are the types of musical instruments used. Each one has its own tonal values, which contribute to the overall pattern for the dance.

With respect to the manner of dress, Miss Yartey states:

The participants do not have special outfits for the occasion, except the Otufo girls themselves who have their own special costumes which identify them wherever they go. The latter are adorned with very rich and beautiful beads and ornaments around their waists and are smeared with Kloboo. At the end of the ceremony the "graduates" wear white cloths to say "thank you" to all who in various ways have contributed to the success of their initiation. There are particular kinds of costumes for particular phases of the ceremony. At one point they wear the beads with an ordinary "boi" and at another point they replace the boi with another one called "titriku," the most valuable possession which qualifies them to enter the spirit world when they die.[10]

Ghanaians celebrate the inevitability of death with funeral ceremonies and with other kinds of rituals. In the Lobi and Dagari districts the people have a special way of announcing a death and a special ritual for the funeral. The messenger carrying the news of a death is identified by his manner of dress. He has a hoe hanging around his neck and a goatskin bag slung over his shoulder. His wrists are tied with fiber. Upon delivering his message, he is presented with some cowries. On his way back home he spends part of these cowries, and he uses the remaining part to buy pito for the person to whom he sent the message, when he arrives at the funeral. Although the Lobi and the Dagari have no special cloth for mourning, there are ways of identifying the people directly connected with the deceased. For example, close relatives of the deceased have their wrists tied with fiber and attendants control the relatives' movements. This is done to prevent the relatives from running away to commit suicide. The widows have their waists tied instead of their wrists. The dead person, dressed in his or her best attire, is placed on a chair on a raised platform in the open yard. Men are placed in such a way that they face east, and women face west. The explanation for this is that men look to the east for the sunrise so that they can go to the farms to work, and women look to the west

[10]Francis Yartey, *Otufu: A Study of Music and Dance of the Ga-Mashie,* unpublished thesis, University of Ghana, 1971.

for the sun to set before they start to cook for the family. Children may face any direction.

The deceased, enthroned on the raised platform, remains there for three days or more in order that friends from far and near may come to see him. The occupation of the deceased is displayed on the platform. If he or she was a good farmer, grains and other farm products are heaped on the left side of the platform. A smock with talismans is hung at the back of the platform if the deceased is a jujuman.

Musicians comprising xylophonists, guard-drummers, and singers take their place close to the raised platform. The songs of the musicians reveal the deeds and achievements of the deceased. In appreciation of the music, some sympathizers dip their hands into their goatskin bags for cowries, which are thrown to the musicians. If the deceased was a great man, the weeping often becomes uncontrolled. The mourning and crying from the relatives and other sympathizers continues until the corpse is buried. A close associate of the deceased presents him with a cock, which signifies the end of their friendship.

The Lobis and the Dagaris dig their graves in such a manner that it is possible for them to open the grave three years later and bury another corpse. Sometimes one grave can accommodate about seven or eight people. First a calabash is turned down and a line drawn around it. The circle is then the entrance of the grave. The depth of the grave is about six feet. The small circle, about one and a half feet in diameter, leads to the first chamber and from the first chamber to the grave proper.

For the burial procedure, one man gets into the chamber and receives the body through the small hole and places it in the grave proper. Then a big stone is placed at the entrance. The morticians collect the millet and the cock and dismantle the platform. They then cook and eat the millet and the cock. Three days after the burial, the deceased's widow is smeared with white clay for a period of two to three months, after which time she can remarry.

A careful study of the festivals also reveals some common features and Ghanaian beliefs. Opoku tells us:

There is, first and foremost, the belief in life after death and in the nearness of dead ancestors to their living descendants. Secondly, through these festivals, the people remember their past leaders and ask for their help and protection. Thirdly, the festivals are used to purify the whole state so that the people can enter the new year with confidence and hope. . . . It is also noted however that the people today tend to emphasize the social aspects of the festivals with the drama, song and dance and the pageantry and feasting.[11]

Outstanding Ghanaians in many different fields of endeavor, including Kofi Antubam, Dr. J. B. Danquah, and Dr. Kyerematen, have all spoken of the beliefs of Ghanaians and the importance of their religious traditions and culture. It is essential that the non-Ghanaian recognize the importance of these deep-seated beliefs and their relationship to the Ghanaian's way of life. With this thought in mind, let us pay particular attention to the use of stools and skins and learn how and why they came to be used by the Ghanaian people. This knowledge will certainly help us to understand the significance of the feeding of the black stools and the use of skins. Dr. Kyerematen gives the following information:

The reason given for the choice of a *stool* or a *skin* as the principal object to betoken the office of a chief is the one-time existence of a special relationship between the people and these articles. For the peoples of the north, who in the past were mostly nomadic and pastoral, a skin was a ready and indispensable possession. The owner would sit or sleep on it during his travels, and, if he was a Moslem, would have daily need of it for his prayers. It was sometimes used as clothing and sometimes to gird a corpse as a loincloth. Certain animals were thought of as ancestors and a particular animal might be regarded as the alter ego of a given person, particularly if his birth or some other event in his life happened to coincide with the appearance of that animal in the village or with some incident connected with it. The skin of that animal would in such an event have a special meaning for that person, and his

[11]Opoku, *Festivals of Ghana*, p. 4.

contact with it was believed to bestow on him the qualities of
that animal, the valour and strength of a lion, for example.

Explaining the significance of the *stool,* he says:

> Among the settled people of the south, the acquisition of a
> stool was regarded as a prime necessity. The first gift to be
> made by a father to his child when the latter began to crawl
> was a stool. Crawling signified that the child had come to stay.
> A young girl undergoing the rite to mark her attainment of
> puberty was placed on a stool, and it was customary for a
> husband to present his newly married wife with a stool to
> make sure of keeping her. It was on a stool that a deceased
> person was bathed before being laid in state.[12]

Because of this close association between a person and his stool
—there is a saying, there can be no secrets between a man and his
stool—it was believed that his spirit inhabited the stool he regularly
used and this was true even after his death. When vacating one's
stool, one was supposed to tilt it on its side to prevent someone else's
spirit or an evil spirit from occupying it.

The skin or the stool thus became stamped with one's personality and it is understandable that it should also be used to mark the
position of a chief vis-à-vis his subjects. The personality or soul of
the personified state or chiefdom was similarly denoted by the skin
or stool of the founder of the state or chiefdom, or of the most
distinguished of its rulers, or by a special skin or stool believed to
have been received miraculously from the Supreme God as a gift.

In northern Ghana the skin serves as the throne of the chief,
the equivalent of the stool in the south. It may be the skin of a goat,
sheep, cow, hyena, buffalo, leopard, lion, elephant, or other mam-
mal. He can sit on any number of these skins at any given time. The
number of skins used is no indication of his place in the hierarchy
of chiefs, but the type of skin used is an indication of his status in
the state. The fiercer the animal whose skin is used, the more powerful the chief who sits on it is considered to be. Five cushions are
usually placed on the skins: one for the seat, one for a backrest, two

[12]Kyerematen, *Panoply of Ghana,* p. 11.

for armrests, and the fifth as a footstool. Tie cushions are cased in soft leather with beautifully embroidered appliqué and incised ornaments. The backrest is placed against a tree or a wall.

In southern Ghana the ancestral stools, otherwise called the "black stools, " were usually taken to the battlefield; if the army was in danger of defeat, the captain would stand on an ancestral stool to give orders to his men to press on. Standing on the stool was regarded as an abomination, an insult to the ancestors. To avoid doing this, and to prevent the enemy from seizing the stool, the men would brace themselves and fight to the last man. The chief target of an army was the seizure of the captain of the enemy and his ancestral stool.

Among the stools of chiefs in the south, apart from those used for domestic purposes such as dining *(dididwa)* and bathing *(adware dwa)*, there are the black stools and the ceremonial stools.

Black stools were originally the special personal stools used by rulers while alive, and after they died the stools were smoked or blackened by being smeared all over with soot mixed with the yolk of an egg. These are preserved in their memory in the stool-house. As already mentioned, it is believed that the spirit of the ruler enters into or saturates his stool while he is alive and this "habitation" persists after his death.

Black stools, being the abode or shrine of the spirits of the ancestors, became the chief sacramental object and the pivot of the rites connected with the ancestor cult. Ancestors are regarded as lesser gods, and although they are believed to live with and form part of the Being of the Supreme God, it is assumed that they retain in the supernatural world the mode of living to which they were accustomed while on earth. Thus they require food and drink and these are offered to them by being placed on their stools on appointed days. In the Dome Division of the Anlo State in the Volta region the stool-house at Anloga has an annex with bath and kitchen facilities, which is believed to be used by the ancestors when they visit the stool-house.

The feeding of the ancestors is the underlying principle of various national festivals held throughout southern Ghana, such as the Adae, Odwira, Homowo, and Unntum festivals, which are invariably connected with the first harvest or the first catch and also with the custom of pouring libations. Through this feeding and pouring of libations the ancestors are kept in constant touch with their descendants. They punish those who neglect them and do wrong to their neighbors, but they also bestow their blessings of peace and prosperity on those who have shown them due respect and lived by the accepted canons of proper behavior.

Opoku tells us that there are two types of annual festivals in Ghana. They are the harvest festivals, like the yam festival of the Ewe and the Homowo of the Ga, and also those which mark the period of remembering the dead. The most typical among these is the Adae of the Akan (Twi).

The Akan calendar year is divided into nine cycles of forty days, called Adae. The adae, however, does not merely mark a period in time, but it is also observed as a special day of worship. It is the day on which the chief and his elders go to the place where the sacred stools are kept.

The spirits of the departed chiefs, it is believed, rest in the stools kept for them after their death. These stools are blackened with soot and the yolk of eggs to make them last long. They are sometimes wrapped in camel-hair blankets and laid on their sides in the dark room called nkonguafieso, or stool-house. Only chiefs who do well in office are honored in this way because, the Akan say, "It is the good spirit that deserves the feast of sheep."

The sacred stool has two uses. It is the shrine into which the spirit, or soul, of good chiefs may again be called upon to enter on special occasions such as the Adae. It is also a means by which we can tell the number of chiefs that have ruled over the tribe. *Adae* means "a" resting-place. It is the name of the special day on which we are allowed to go into the room where the spirit of our forefathers rest.

The Akan live with the spirits of their dead. They believe that the souls of their dead relatives are still near to them and they call upon them in times of trouble. They ask for their guidance and make them offers of drinks and eggs, chicken and sheep.

On adae days, water, food, meat, and rum are taken to the

shrines. The dead are then invited to continue to help those over whom they ruled when they were alive. Not all people are allowed to go into the stool-house. Only those who perform the rites and a few who are related to the chief go there. Of those who go in, only the chief and the royal princes wear their sandals.

The day immediately before the adae is called Dapaa. There is the Saturday that comes before the Sunday adae, called Memeneda Dapaa. The Tuesday preceding the Wednesday adae is also called Benada Dapaa. Children born on the dapaa days are called Dapaa just as those born on adae days are called Adae. The Dapaa is the day of preparation for the Adae.

Foodstuffs, firewood, water, drinks, chicken, sheep, eggs, and all the articles required for the celebration of the Adae are brought home on the Dapaa. On Adae days, no work or travel may be done except duties connected with the celebration.

The Dapaa is also the time for tidying up the house and its surroundings. Villages and towns and well as footpaths leading to them are also cleaned.[13]

Festival Celebrations

We have seen that the festivals and rituals attest to the Ghanaian's constant use of ritual, dance, music, and dramatic situations. We have learned that they are also a rich source of material for the modern theatre-maker. We will continue to look closely at a few more Ghanaian festivals, especially with regard to their use of drama, music, and dance. By looking at these celebrations of life we will know more about the contemporary implications of drama in traditional African societies. For example, let us consider the Akwamu Odwira Festival, a yam festival, filled with story, spectacle, music, dance, and ritual—witnessed by a people with a continuous connection to a traditional timeless past.

The Akwamu were among the original settlers who migrated from the Kong mountains of West Africa to the forest region of Ghana, thus breaking away from the mainstream of emigrants. They settled successively at Hemang, Abakrampa, Asamankese,

[13]Opoku, *Festivals of Ghana*, pp. 7–8.

Nyanawase, and finally crossed to the eastern bank of the Volta after their defeat by the united forces of the coastal tribes whom they had dominated for the best part of a century.

In 1553, the Akwamu defied the rule of the king of Denkyira and moved to Asamankese. It was during the flight from Denkyira that a section of the tribe broke away and settled in the Ivory Coast, where they later assumed the name of Agni or Anwi or Sanwi.

The valiant deeds of these warlike people, who are said to have fought as many as sixteen battles between 1553 and 1872, are known beyond the boundaries of Ghana. In fact the large bunch of keys now held as part of the regalia of the Paramount Chief of Akwamu is a tangible proof of their prowess, for it is the prize they carried away after the occupation of Christiansborg Castle for fourteen days by one of their captains, Asamani.

Throughout their travels and settlements the people of Akwamu never forgot their ancestral leaders and national gods who led them and brought them safely to their present home.

The Akans and many other tribes in Ghana regard yams as the most important crop. This makes the crop not only sacred but also venerable, especially when it is first harvested. The ritualization of the crop or festivals associated with yams are celebrated throughout a wide area of Ghana.

In Akwamu the yam is associated with the Odwira festival. The people celebrate this festival on the fall of the ninth Adae. The festival has a threefold significance. First, it is a period of remembrance: a time when the people are reminded of the warrior kings who helped to found their state. It is also a time when the chiefs and their people bring sacrifices to their gods to thank them for the mercies of the past and to ask for protection in the future. Above all, it is a time when people come together to renew their family and social ties. In other words, it is a political, religious, and social festival.

It is during this festival that the black stools are "fed" with the firstfruits of yam. When the new yams are harvested, they are first served to the black stools to give the ancestors an opportunity to partake of the firstfruits and to bless the crop before their descendants eat it. It is therefore considered ominous to eat or to bring fresh yams to the town before the Odwira festival.

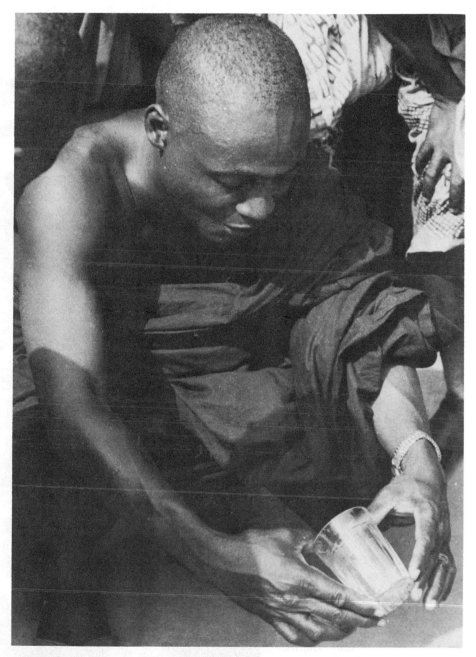

ODWIRA FESTIVAL Pouring libation (*Institute of African Studies, Ghana*)

ODWIRA
FESTIVAL
Procession
and prepara-
tion (*Institute
of African Stud-
ies, Ghana*)

ODWIRA FESTIVAL   Tuber of yam and firewood (*Institute of African Studies, Ghana*)

The main activities of the Odwira ceremony are as follows:

1. Weeding the path leading to the royal mausoleum. (This is to inform the ancestors that the year has ended and that they are about to be called upon to test fresh yams.)
2. Mourning the dead.
3. Feeding the black stool.
4. Holding a durbar to end the ceremony.

The celebrations last a whole week, beginning on a Friday evening. The Saturday following is called Odwirahuruda or "the day that brings in the Odwira." It is a day of national mourning and fasting. The omanhene, or paramount chief, goes first to his father's

house and then to his mother's to pour a libation to his departed
relatives. All the clan heads do likewise. After this the omanhene,
his subchiefs, captains, and state executioners form a funeral procession and parade through the streets to a sacred place called
Akyeremade, where the omanhene pours libation upon the relics of
generals or chiefs or important people killed in ancient battles.

On the day of the feeding of the black stool, the head of the
family in which there is a black stool has to present the stool with
a sheep, a tuber of yam, and three pieces of firewood. These are
brought before the stool three times. On each occasion the spokesman for the stool says that the year has come to an end and that the
occupant of the stool presents this sheep, a tuber of yam, and three
pieces of firewood for the sacrificial rites. Another attendant dips
leaves in a bowl of water and sprinkles the stool, sanctifying it.
Some of the hairs of the sheep are forcefully pulled out and placed
on the stool. The sheep is then slaughtered on the black stool. The
front left leg of the sheep is removed and placed in front of the stool;
afterwards, half of it is roasted and shared by the elders. The remaining half is cut into bits and dotted on the stool, which is lying
on its side. Two plates of mashed yam, one mixed with palm oil, are
placed near the stool. An attendant makes balls from each plate and
places them on the stool. This act of placing these items on the stool
is the actual feeding of the stool.

Libation is poured and the door is opened for anyone with a gift
to offer. Some people enter and make a vow that if the stool helps
him or her to achieve his or her aim, or if there is progress in the
coming year, he or she will offer a sheep or something equally
important as a gift to the stool. Others also donate small amounts
from ten pesewas onwards and ask for protection.

The food on the stool is left over for the night and the following
day it is believed that the ancestors have manifested it with an-
tidotes for all kinds of diseases.

Of all the days, Sunday appears to be the most important day.
On Sunday the warriors of Akwamu meet in battle array to present
arms to their captain. This martial parade, which starts in the early
morning, is followed in the early afternoon by a rally of state executioners, who are to play quite an important role in the ceremonies
that follow.

At one o'clock the Akrahene, or the chief of the soul washers who are responsible for the cleansing of the soul of the chief, leads a band to the Volta and fills a covered brass pan with water from the river. He brings it home under the shelter of a state umbrella, preceded by state sword bearers, and takes it to the house of the Kyidomhene, chief of the rearguard. This is the water with which the omanhene is to cleanse his subjects.

The crowd of celebrants and spectators swarm up to the open courtyard in front on the palace to await the omanhene, who is now busy putting on his battle dress. Meanwhile the talking drums are sounding the praises of the chief.

As soon as the final notes die away, the omanhene appears at the top of the flight of steps wearing "the cap of the devastator." It is made of leopard skin surmounted by the feather of an eagle, two horns, and a crown of solid gold. He wears a battle dress studded with talismans. His shoulders are smeared with red clay and a bullet wallet is strapped across his left shoulder. Six double-edged knives also hang down the same shoulder. His eyes are as red as blood. (An important part of this festival is the carrying of the paramount stools to the royal mausoleum. There the spirits are invoked to look after the omanhene and his people.)

The chief of the rearguard steps forward with the basin of water from the Volta and the paramount chief takes three handfuls into his mouth and spouts them out. He then sprinkles some of the liquid upon himself and upon the crowds who bow down in obeisance and shout AKOSEE, meaning "blessing!" Next, the priest of Mfodwo presents him with water from the god, which he uses in a similar manner. Then follows a calabashful of water from the god Mpen Kwadwo. This contains three knots of green grass. He picks one up and places it between his teeth. Then follow the waters from Obohene and Totoabo, Mfodwo, and Mpen Kwadwo—Obohene and Totoabo are gods of war. Finally, there is water from Odassikyi, the god of cataracts and falls that capsize the canoes. When he has done with this last one, the omanhene upsets the calabash container and places his right foot upon it three times.

The chief now mounts his palanquin and rides to one end of the town amidst the deafening noise of drums, horns, musket firing,

ODWIRA FESTIVAL   Tasting yam (*Institute of African Studies, Ghana*)

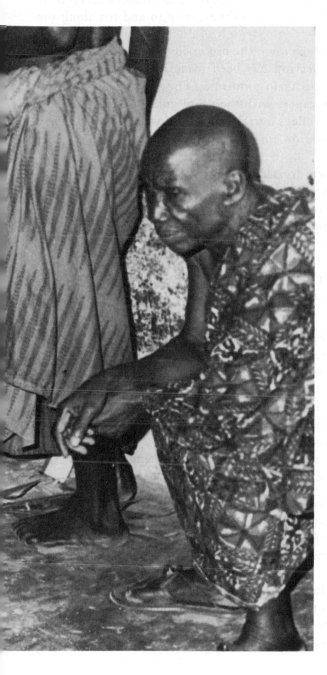

ODWIRA
FESTIVAL
Feeding the
black stool (*In-
stitute of
African Studies,
Ghana*)

singing, and shouting. At this stage the executioners carry their fetishes and become possessed as they sway to and fro along the course.

From the end of the town the procession returns to the durbar grounds, where a clearing has been made in the center for the military display by the Asafo companies. The gunners march, saunter, crouch, and cut capers with their flint guns in their hands. At a signal they all fire volleys into the air and reload as quickly as they have fired. This goes on for a while and then they march and countermarch.

Bands of women dressed in white move from one end of the grounds to the other, singing and dancing, and once in a while running to the omanhene to fan him with their stoles and sheepskins to demonstrate their affection and loyalty.

The omanhene now rises up, and holding his war sword, advances majestically before the Adontenhene. He renews his oath of office and pledges his service and protection to the state and to all those who hold him as their ruler. Dramatically, he swears, in effect, the following:

> I am the great-grandson of Akoto;
> I am the great-grandson of Ansa Sas raku;
> I am the great-grandson of Akono.
> You have made me your chief.
> If the Akwamu State calls upon me
> By day or night and I do not respond,
> Or if in time of any national crisis
> I malinger and turn my back to the enemy,
> I violate the great oath.

The drums then peal forth the omanhene's praises and he walks back to his seat to the rhythm of Mpintin drums. He presents rum to his chiefs and subjects, and then the crowd disperses.

The final ceremony of the day follows at about seven in the evening. An hour before that time, a gong-gong is sounded to warn the people to stay indoors. A great hush descends upon the town. Why? Because soon the muffled notes of the small drum that herald the approach of the "messengers of death," the executioners, become audible. They die away in the distance and the phantom figures of the executioners recede into the dismal gloom of the night. They are on their way to the foot of the hills to the south of the town, those sacred hills that enshrine the mortal remains of past rulers of the state. Every soul is cowed with fear and doubt. In fact the very air is charged with anxiety over the result of this ritual that will determine the welfare of the state in the ensuing year. At the stroke of eight, a shrill voice pierces the stillness. It is the voice of the chief executioner calling upon the Odwira spirits. As soon as his voice dies away, a distant voice shouts in response. Shouts of joy come spontaneously from the people, as if they had all been set off by machine. But soon they are hushed again. The mystical voice that has just been heard was that of the male Odwira spirit. There is yet the response of the female to pray for. Again the executioner's voice goes up and once again comes the audible response. A gunshot is heard in the distance and soon there is a stampede past the palace where a vigil is being kept. It is the executioners running home after consulting the oracle of the Odwira festival. Everyone is now assured of a happy year, for the spirits have, by their clear responses, accepted the invitation of the living to join with them in celebrating the past and calling in the new year.[14]

The Aboakyer is another Ghanaian festival filled with spectacle, splendor, conflict, music, dance, ritual, and rich theatrical material. Winneba, a district along the coast, about thirty miles from the city of Accra, is the scene of the Deer-Catching Festival of the Effutu people. This festival, more than three hundred years old, dating from the time that the Effutu first settled in Winneba, draws record crowds from all over Ghana. Years ago the Effutu, in search of a safe place for the installation of their tribal god, Penkye Otu, had settled in Winneba. Penkye Otu demanded an annual sacrifice from his people. The victim was to be a member of the royal family. To prevent the possible extinction of the royal family, the god was made to agree to a substitute of a live leopard to be caught with bare hands. The leopard hunt was carried on for a number of years but later abandoned, because many people died or were seriously injured during the hunt. Later, the god agreed to accept a live deer as a substitute, also to be caught with bare hands.

[14] *Ibid.*, p. 27.

The Deer-Catching Festival takes place in April or May, though it is prescribed or calculated long before then. The chief matron of the shrine, an old woman, calculates the exact time of the festival by performing her own special ritual, at a time that usually coincides with Easter. The chief priest in turn informs the paramount chief of the Effutu state. The priest then enters into confinement and remains there until he has sanctified himself and the sacred stools.

While the priest is going through the lustral rituals, the paramount chief assembles the two principal asafo companies and breaks the news of the coming celebrations to them, ordering them to hold themselves in readiness for the day of the hunt. The captain of each company presents a demijohn (a large potlike bottle) of wine to the tufohene who, in turn, shares it with the members of the company. This is a sign that he has given them due notice of the time for the festival. Then every member of the asafo, including every citizen of Winneba, busies himself with preparations for the hunt that is to follow in two weeks' time.

On the Thursday following the Monday of drinking the asafosa, or "company wine," the captains of the two companies put on traditional battle dress and present themselves to the paramount chief. The captains of the Tuafo ("number 1 company") wear short smocks and carry cutlasses. Their men wear a variety of clothes made from blue and white materials. The captains of the Dentsifo ("number 2 company") wear chain mail and iron helmets and carry traditional war swords. One captain, called Enyinda, from the Dentsifo is also allowed to carry a cutlass. The members of the company dress in red and gold and wear all sorts of ingenious fashions that are calculated to excel and impress.

On the eve of the day of the Deer Hunt, an all-night vigil is kept. Old and new charms are offered sacrifices so that they may aid their wearers in the next day's hunt.

At cockcrow next morning all the members of the two companies assemble, armed with sticks and cudgels. Each company has three subcompanies. The subcompanies of the Tuafo group are the Apayofo ("fire strikers"), the Akomfoadzefo ("priestly band"), and the Kyiramimfo ("fraud deterers"). Each subcompany is further divided into three categories—adults, youths, and children or fledglings—these being called Mpanyimfo, Mfinimfinifo, and Asam. The three principal subcompanies of the Dentsifo company are Patufo, Etsiawafo, and Asomfo. These are the adult, youth, and children's groups respectively.

The Tuafo company is the first to set off, since their field of operation is farther away than that of the other company. They start at five o'clock. However, before setting out, they go to the chief. The captains now make sure that every section of their company is fully marshaled. Leading the march are the adults of the first subcompany, then come the youths, followed by the children in the rear.

After the departure of the companies, the stage is taken up by the Adenkum and Adzewa dance ensembles, the traditional minstrels and the priests and priestesses. This situation is much as it was when in time of war the women were left behind to organize dances and processions to keep up their own morale during the tense moments of doubt and waiting.

An hour or so after the departure of the last companies, the omanhene and his subchiefs, courtiers and spokesmen form a procession to the open space on the outskirts of the town, facing the hills beyond which the dentsifo company operates.

The first company to catch a deer rushes back home with shouts of victory and places the deer in the center of the grounds. Their captain then walks up proudly to the front of the dais and with a great deal of martial ceremony informs the spokesman that he should tell his lord that his company has won the chase and are inviting him to come forward to receive their prize. Meanwhile the members of the company stampede about with war songs and drumming, in a display of health, strength, and agility that fills the people of Winneba and all spectators with pride and confidence.

When the chief comes to the spot where the panting deer lies securely tied up, he slips his right foot out of its sandal and places it three times upon the animal. Turning around and bidding the company "well done," he then retires to his seat to await the other company.

Members of the winning company are now free to go home, to rest and put on their finery for the gala display and dancing that follow the morning's hard work.

The chief waits patiently until the second company brings its

Aboakyer
(deer hunt) (*In-stitute of
African Studies,
Ghana*)

Aboakyer (deer hunt) (*Institute of African Studies, Ghana*)

quarry. He is enjoined by custom to remain seated till the last man has returned safely from the chase. If it should happen that the other company fails to catch a deer, their captain and field marshal should come before the chief and inform him that they have done all they can but have not succeeded. They therefore respectfully request him to accept their dismissal drink in order that they may retire home.

Now the captive deer is borne upon the shoulders of its captors to the shrine of the Penkye Otu god at the center of the town. The omanhene joins them in procession along with the asafo companies and the spectators. Leaving the deer at the shrine, they all retire to their homes.

On occasions when both companies succeed in catching a deer the merriment and jubilation defy description. All and sundry parade the streets in their groups, wearing the diversified uniforms of white and blue, red and gold. The companies sing songs of challenge and hurl taunts at each other. These are all taken in good humor as a necessary part of the celebration.

> The manhene emerges from his palace dressed in shades of purple. He is neither blue nor red. His unique position as the hub, unifying the different elements that consitute the Effutu State, requires him to avoid party rivalry. He is borne in a palanquin and paraded through the principal streets of the town amidst drumming, flourish of horns and shouts of adoration from his loyal subjects. The captains of the various companies lead their bands and supporters, who now number thousands, in this gay procession that usually continues till dusk. Very few pageants could excel this one in color and gaiety.[15]

The companies assemble before the Penkye Otu god again at two o'clock on the following day—Sunday—to ask the oracle what the gods have in store for the state in the new year they have just entered. The chief priest draws four parallel lines on the ground, one in white clay, one in red clay, another in charcoal, and the fourth in salt. He places a pot upside down at the head of the lines.

[15] *Ibid.*, pp. 37–38.

The cloth covering the fetish is then removed and rolled into a carrying pad, which the priest places on the bottom of the pot. He picks up the little round stone that lies before the fetish, puts it upon the pad, and invokes the spirits of the seventy-seven gods of the Effutu state to descend. He invokes Penkye Otu, calling him by his several names. As soon as the priest stops speaking, the stone rolls down and rests upon one of the lines drawn on the ground. This is repeated a third time. He then announces the results to the people.

If the stone falls upon the white clay line, it signifies that there will be a great drought during the new year. On the other hand, if it rests upon the charcoal line, it portends heavy rains. If the stone stops on the salt, it indicates that there will be plenty of fish and food for all. If it settles upon the red line, it argues war and strife.

After this mystical consultation, the prize deer is slaughtered and sacrificed to the god. The festival is then over, but not for the Penkye Otu priests. They have to sleep in the open until such time as the first rains fall. To them, as to those waiting to sow their new crops, this is a happy occasion. The priests can now wash pots and utensils used in connection with the celebrations and return to their homes.

Dance Celebrations

We have looked at drama in traditional African societies as evidenced through the rituals and the festivals, but what of the modern forms? Perhaps a look at some of the dances will further underscore the connection between the traditions and modern dramatic forms; in this instance modern dance forms that are currently being used in dance-drama and dance performance in the theatre. According to Bertie Opoku, many of the modern dance forms are directly connected to the traditions.[16] His insights regarding the current trends in dance in Ghana have greatly aided Ghana's national theatre movement. We learn from Opoku that the "Atsiagbekor" is made up of modern inventions based on the older "Agbekor." *Atsia*, like the Twi *akyea*, means "to show off," and it is the

---

[16]A. M. (Bertie) Opoku, "Thoughts from the School of Music and Dance," *Okyeame*, Vol. 2, No. 1, 1964, pp. 51–56.

Female trio in Slow Agbekor
II (*Halifax Photos, Ghana*)

modern Anlo's version of what must have been a serious expression of prowess, suffering, and hardship by people who had been in battle. In effect they are stylizations of Western arms drills blended with the traditional war movements. The dancers tend to show off with movements that display agility and strength.

The Lobi dances exemplify a festival of work and happiness. The dances are adapted from the working songs and movements of the Lobi to express their love for communal labor. A house is built by this means and this provides an opportunity for the "Babina Dance," which is performed by two girls with a chorus; then follows the "Sebire," characterized by the infectious abandonment, energy, manliness, and dignity of the male dancers, and the fascinating rhythms. This tremolo of fast contraction with release is the special technique of Lobi dances. Dynamism, dignity, and controlled inner strength are the characteristics of the Sebire dance. The so-called convulsive movement shows restrained power and strength to frighten an enemy.

The "Agbekor," upon which the Atsiagbekor is based, is essentially a soldier's dance. The Agbekor dances are fairly widely distributed and variants are found in Dahomey, which is where the Anlo-Ewe-speaking people migrated. To watch the Agbekor is to watch scenes that may have their origins in the battles that were fought as the Anlos trekked through hostile country in search of peace. The two slow Agbekor are processional in the original form to illustrate the trekking and are marked at intervals with halts, during which short episodes are danced. Some episodes show the periods of relaxation when the warriors play games, and the fast Agbekor shows the times of retreats and counterattacks.

The "Sikyi" is a gay dance of the twenties. It is flirtatious in character. Its characteristic form is strutting and bobbing up and down and a display of theatrical elegance (sikyi). In his arrangements, Opoku seeks to clarify the mild but innocent playful flirtation of the boys and girls as expressed during the period of the popularity of this dance.

The "Adowa" is a dance that was originally a funeral dance and this character is preserved in the graceful, dignified walking movement. It is usually preceded by a chorus of voices and two gongs— two drums joining later. When the mood has been suggested in song, the Atumpan drums pick up specific rhythms from particular drums for motivation while the body turns; spins and bows are suggested by the melody of the gong. As a dance it is popular among the Twis, the Fantes (who call it "Adzewa"), and also among the Gas. The Ashanti "Adowa" now has about eight forms derived from other dances. Thus the "Ahunum" is a modified "Akapoma," a dance form that the "Adowa" superseded.

The "Kundum" is a dance that expresses the spirit and sentiments of the Nzema and Ahanta people during the Kundum Festival. In spirit, the Kundum is a warriors' dance. While the men dance to express bravery, prowess, endurance, and determination, the womenfolk inspire and hail them as conquerors. As a Harvest Festival Dance it also expresses thankfulness for the fruits of the earth —symbolic of rebirth—and departed friends and relations are remembered.

As one begins to understand the dramatic forms and their connection to traditions in one African society, it becomes easier to realize and to recognize reasons for similarities in another. For example, I recall my response to African dramatic forms and African theatre at the Dakar Festival in 1966. There I witnessed African theatre, side by side so to speak, from all over Africa. And I believe I detected similarities. Certainly I sensed similarities between the dances of Nigeria, Ghana, Sierra Leone, and other West African countries; I even saw similarities in dances from West to East Africa, as far as Ethiopia. But I wasn't sure, since I felt that I had little basis upon which to rest my judgment.

Then I went to Africa to live, seeking from the continent some basis for my judgment. And soon I realized that the basis was at rest within the African traditions. In essence the African approach to life is similar from country to country, and consequently the African's approach to drama is also similar. How it is presented depends largely upon a mode of traditional expression.

When once again I saw the theatre of Africa at the Algiers Festival in 1969, I understood why I sensed these similarities between the dances and the theatre from country to country. By then, I was viewing them with a more critical and perceptive eye.

Finally when I was able to help bring together Ghanaian and

Ethiopian culture on the same stage in a "shared theatrical performance" in Algiers, I was able to view the forms on a one-to-one
basis. And though dissimilar in some ways, I witnessed many
similarities between Ghanaian and Ethiopian dances and music.

For example, Tsegaye Debachen's Ethiopian troupe does the
"Gambella War Ballad," which in a sense reminds me of the spirit
of Bertie Opoku's Ghanaian Atsiagbekor and Agbekor dances. The
Gambella War Ballad has some of the same ceremonial splendor to
it as the Atsiagbekor. Here a warrior returns from battle and is
received with a great pomp and ceremony: "You are the most brave
of them all."

From another point of view, both the "Menjar Folk Song" and
the "Harrar Kotu Dance" of Ethiopia are similar to the Lobi dances
of Ghana. Throughout the years the Manjares have been dancing
and singing while at the same time thrashing their harvest. The
Manjares are a sect of the Shoa Amharas, whose farm life is charmed
by this harvest song. The Harrar Kotu Dance is a folk dance inti-
mately related to the agricultural life of the people. In this dance,
a young farmer is seen chasing birds away from his farm when his
work is interrupted by the appearance of a young girl.

The "Cotton Plantation Song" is another folkloric example
that shows the relationship between music and dance to work activities of the Ethiopian. This dance is an instance of how Ethiopians
enliven their work by singing and dancing while planting, picking,
and spinning cotton. An Ethiopian, whether busy plowing and
cultivating his farm, hunting in the forest, or marching to war,
always accompanies his activities with a song or a dance.

The "Medinnana Zlzegna" is a song of praise, the rhythm of
which depends solely upon the expression conveyed by the words
themselves. It gives impetus to a style of Ethiopian music removed
as far as possible from the rhythmic folk music.

To give witness that her people have always had the better of
Mother Ethiopia's nature, the songs and dances are often matched
with the flowers and plants that happen to grow during the seasons
when the various national holidays take place. For the New Year's
celebration, young maidens sing the popular "flower-picking" folk
song.

The "Isa" and "Ougaden Folk Dance" are also revealing. The Somalis who inhabit the Ogaden area in the southern part of Ethiopia have developed a culture that is in harmony with their environment. Two of their most charming dances are the "Dagger Dance" and the "Umbrella Dance."

CHAPTER
6
Making Theatre
in Ghana

I really wanted to know about this African theatre in Ghana, therefore I decided to immerse myself in the life of Africa as much as was humanly possible. Reading about Africa is one thing, but being a part of the life of Africa—intellectually, physically, emotionally, and spiritually—is something else. I wanted to become connected with the expression and the communication of the people. I wanted to be right in the middle of their arts and their culture.

Fortunately for me, my assignments at the University of Ghana and at the Ghana Drama Studio placed me directly in the middle of Ghana's national theatre movement where I would become associated with the visionaries of the movement and the theatre-makers of Ghana. I would have the opportunity to become an integral part of the process involving research scholars, producer-directors, and other creative persons. Not only would I be able to see modern theatre trends evolve but also I would be able to connect myself with Africa through a study of the rituals and the traditional festivals.

I found myself working very closely with many Ghanaians, among them Kwabena Nketia, a scholar, a composer, and an ethnomusicologist. He was also the director of the Institute of African Studies. One day, in his usual soft-spoken, sincere, and understated manner, Kwabena said to me, "Africans speak languages." I listened, and I thought, "So what! Big deal, now isn't that a profound statement."

I was with him in the Institute office preparing to look at some of the dissertations on music, dance, and theatre. The phone rang. Kwabena's secretary was out of the office, so Nketia answered the phone himself. "Agoo! Yo! Yoo! . . ." He was conversing in Twi. Now they were speaking in Ga . . . and now English. "Yes, yes! . . . All right! . . . Yo! . . . Yoo! . . ." and the conversation continued as he switched from one language to another without missing a musical beat. I was impressed, greatly impressed. I realized that Nketia hadn't expressed himself in that manner in order to impress me—he was expressing himself naturally. His versatility in languages was a natural aspect of his everyday mode of communication and expression. He was Ashanti, and therefore his first language was Twi. English is the language of instruction in Ghana, so naturally he spoke English. However, he also understood Ewe, Fanti, and Ga, and often found it convenient to use these languages from time to time. By necessity he was multilingual. I reflected. *So Africans do speak languages!* And I was soon to learn that even the untutored African is usually multilingual. Consequently, in addition to speaking his own language, he is usually conversant in other languages and dialects. For him, this is a necessary—he has to do this in order to communicate with members of different tribes. I reflected again. *The African language situation is certainly different from that in the Western world, especially in the United States where people usually master only one language.*

We had traveled to the village about thirty miles from Kumasi. The Ghana Dance Ensemble was there to perform for the people of the village. Bertie Opoku, visual artist, choreographer, and Artistic Director of the Ensemble had been telling me what to look for in the dances that were to be performed. He had also informed me that some of the people would join the Ensemble and dance with them. The drums beat, and the dancers began to perform. Soon several of the village people joined them. I patted my feet as my body began to sway to the music. Bertie whispered to me, "Let the dance consume you." I nodded my head and continued to enjoy the music and the dancing. An African lady came to me, extended her hands, placed some beads around my neck, and proceeded to draw me in the circle of the dancers. And before I knew it I was in the circle enjoying myself. I was part of the group, and the dance had truly consumed me.

Later on that evening, as Bertie and I talked about the experience of the afternoon, Bertie said to me. "You are Ashanti people." I smiled. He looked at my feet and repeated himself. "I tell you, you are Ashanti people." Quite pleased, but a bit puzzled, I responded, "But Bertie, why would you say that? Are you serious?" "Sure, I'm serious! Look at your feet, man! And pay particular attention to your toes. You have Ashanti feet. You are one of us."

In Ghana, much of life centers around movement and dance. Dance is an integral part of the rhythms and cycles of life. Dance may be ceremonial, recreational, or religious, for it is a language, a mode of expression or a form of communication that permeates everyday life. To the Ghanaian, dance is drama based on specific movements couched in the music and the poetry of the people. It is drama depicting the experience beneath the idea, a specific moment of sadness or happiness within the rhythms of life. Consequently, it is not surprising to see the Ghana Dance Ensemble emerge as a leading force in the national theatre movement. Their successful concert tours through Nigeria and the United States and to Mexico City and London, have prompted them to look back on the dream of yesterday as an impetus for tomorrow's successes.

Born in 1962 as a collaborative effort between the Institute of Art and Culture and the Institute of African Studies, the Ghana Dance Ensemble was officially inaugurated on Saturday, November 11, 1967 at the Arts Centre in Accra by A. K. Deku, National Liberation Council member responsible for sports, arts, and culture. Thus in this relatively short span of time the experiment has proved successful enough to make the Ghana Dance Ensemble known throughout Ghana and in some of the major cities of the world as well. But what was the experiment, and how great was the challenge? Let us look at the birth of this dance ensemble and follow its growth.

The project-model was sound enough. Select a group of dancers and musicians from a variety of tribal backgrounds to be the instruments of a new dance ensemble. Place them in the hands of research scholars and theatrical artists to be trained and developed. Watch them become immersed in the arts and cultures of Ghana. Help them learn about the history and the institutions of Ghanaian societies. Try to instill within them a theatrical attitude and the discipline of the craft. Mold them as living instruments of dance-theatre —as instruments equipped to perform not only the dances of their own tribal areas but also dances from other parts of Ghana and West Africa. See them grow and become the nucleus of dance traditions and drama. And then? If the experiment works? Begin to extend the dance company into a theatrical company. In any event, you have already started a flame in the national theatre movement. You will have created not only a professional dance company but also a training center, a citadel for dance, theatre, and music history— tomorrow's insurance for continuity in Ghanaian and African dance traditions. Tomorrow's school of dance, music, and theatre studies specializing in African theatre!

And now, today, let each Ghanaian dream of his successes of tomorrow. Let him be proud of Ghana's artists who are steeped in the dance traditions of the country. Let him acknowledge the growth and development of the School of Dance, Music, and Theatre, which is housed in the Institute of African Studies at the University of Ghana. Let him talk about this school that is equipped to teach the dances as they are performed in the villages or to present them in the new theatrical forms of contemporary life. Let him be aware of the miracle of the small bridge between the academic and the professional in the theatre. And moreover, let him be assured that this dance troupe, by its very nature, has helped to encourage creative cooperation and integration of the arts.

The visionaries of the dance ensemble and the school were committed to African theatre and its development. Their rationale was sound. Their dedication encompassing. Kwabena Nketia, Executive Director of the Ghana Dance Ensemble, was using his musical skills and knowledge in the molding of these dance performers. And Bertie Opoku, Artistic Director, was devoting his perception and energies to the shaping of the dance skills and talents of the troupe. These were the two men most directly responsible for the dance ensemble.

Certainly dance is at the center of life in Ghana, but without music one could hardly have dance, for the beat and the melodic frame are ever present in most walks of life. Since music is also a most vital aspect of Ghanaian life, it is not surprising to note the force of music in the national theatre movement. Choral singing has long been one of the outstanding forms of entertainment in Ghana, and one of the first Ghanaians to recreate traditional music for publication was Dr. Ephraim Amu.

Dr. Amu was showing me the basics of the Anteteban flute. He said, "Our students must learn something about their own culture. We must guide them in that direction." I asked him if he would let me have some copies of his music. As he reached in his files to get the music he continued, "Certainly we want our students to learn something about music from other parts of the world, but they must begin with their own roots."

Years ago, Dr. Ephraim Amu, composer, musical director, and maker of African instruments, recognized the great need for studying Ghanaian music and re-creating it in written form in order to preserve it. The publication of his *Twenty-Five African Songs* in 1933 by Sheldon Press paved the way for a new idiom of African music. It also prepared the way for new and undiscovered African composers.

In recent years Dr. Amu has served as head of the School of Music and Drama at Legon where he emphasized the importance of Ghanaian music and culture. His work and creativity often focused attention upon the singer and the musician in Ghanaian society. Another of Dr. Amu's outstanding accomplishments was the creation and formation of the Legon Choral Ensemble, an all-male group of singers who play the flute and drums and specialize in traditional Ghanaian music. Dr. Amu was also the director-conductor of this group.

Before his recent retirement, Dr. Amu accompanied the Legon Choral Ensemble on a tour of the United States where they performed for enthusiastic audiences. He and the ensemble hold fond memories of this tour and especially of their performances at Lincoln Center in New York, at the Washington Cathedral in Washington, D.C., and at the Hampton Institute in Hampton, Virginia.

My wife and I also have fond memories of our creative associations with Dr. Amu and the Legon Choral Ensemble with its forty-piece orchestra. Janie and I performed with them on several occasions. And this is how it came about.

Shortly after the family and I arrived in Ghana, Efua Sutherland thought that a special performance would be a creative way to formally introduce the Kennedys to the Ghanaian family. We discussed the idea and thought about an appropriate presentation. After viewing a few Ghanaian performances in Twi and in English we reached a decision. We would celebrate Langston Hughes in Ghanaian style. But since English would be our vehicular language, we would need something African in the celebration, something like African music or dance. The answer to our needs was the Legon Choral Ensemble; we would ask them to collaborate with us in the creation. And since Janie and I had previously celebrated Langston Hughes in New York City and also in Freetown, Sierra Leone, fortunately we already had working materials at our disposal.

Next came the creative process of sharing ideas with the Legon (Anteteban) Choir. In a relatively short time we arrived at the format and prepared the script. Then came the rehearsals. And finally on Thursday, November 9, 1967, at the Ghana Drama Studio in Accra, we made our debut before a Ghanaian audience.

Due to the success of the performance,[1] it was evident that repeat performances would be necessary not only in Ghana but elsewhere on the continent of Africa. And during the next few years the most memorable of those performances, including the Ghana Drama Studio performance, would include the performances at Ambassador Franklin Williams' outdoor garden in Accra, in Freetown, Sierra Leone, in 1968, at the University of Ghana in 1969, and in Algiers in 1969.

In Ghana the performances entitled "The Poetic Life of Langston Hughes," "The Black Experience," and "The African Experience" had come about as a result of experimentation, innovation, and creativity in the area of the African celebration. Some of the traditional music used included "Akatin," "Drum Kete," "Drums and Flute Sokpote," "Puberty Song," "Ndubli-Kaayona," and "Kyen-Kyen-Bi."

Enthusiastic responses from Ambassador Williams, Gordon Winkler, head of USIS, and his Cultural Affairs Director, Stella

[1]"Delightful Poetic Night at Drama Studio," *Accra Daily Graphic* (November 10, 1967).

Davis, initiated another presentation in which I used the works of Langston Hughes.

Gordon wondered whether I could celebrate other American poets in a similar manner. I got the picture. Certainly I could do this after some hard work on the writing of a script and the rehearsing of the performance. After all, I already knew many American poets from my previous years of research in the area of American literature and especially Black literature. But since this was not meant to be a Black celebration but an American celebration, we decided to use Langston Hughes, Carl Sandburg, and Robert Frost. I said that I would need an African collaborator in order to make the project a more meaningful experience to me and to the people of Ghana.

I went to see William Amoako, Ghanaian musician-performer and the Associate Director of the Legon Choral Ensemble. We discussed the idea and he agreed to provide the music for the celebration. Discussions followed by trial-and-error rehearsals finally brought us to a final script to be used in a series of performances designed for teacher-training colleges and secondary schools throughout the whole of Ghana. In the series I wanted to celebrate Langston Hughes and the other poets and at the same time examine certain aspects of life in America through drama and poetry. The means of expression and communication would be a mixture of Ghanaian and Afro-soul. And our music and movement were certainly designed to help us in this respect.

The result of our collaboration was a theatrical piece entitled "They Sang of a Nation," also sometimes called "The Poetic Life of America." By combining traditional African music played on flutes and drums, dramatic scenes, and dance, we created a celebration. Some of the traditional music included "Drum Kete," "Flute Sokpote," "Ghu Drum Solo," and "Ewe Kete."

Because of these performances I was able to conduct valuable research on audience behavior and also to initiate an important dialogue with many of the youth of Ghana.[2] One of the extra rewards came when the University of Ghana decided to offer a Lang-

[2]Scott Kennedy, "The Ghanaian Audience Response and Behavior to a Theatrical Experience of Poetry and Music," Institute of African Studies, *Research Review*, Vol. 4, No. 3, 1968, p. 81.

ston Hughes creative writing award to the most promising
Ghanaian student. I have often reflected upon that award and remarked, "Now Langston Hughes has gone back to Ghana to visit
the family."

Another direct premium from the performances resulted when
I was asked to write a book entitled *Three Poets*, which was published
in Ghana. And although William and I enjoyed the "experience" of
the celebration as well as the enthusiastic responses from our audiences, we both agreed that the highlight of each celebration was a
segment entitled "A Portrait of a Black American."[3]

Another choral ensemble, the Damas Choir, one of the oldest,
most talented, and versatile choirs in Ghana, is extending its hori-
zons through a new theatre company idea in its theatrical productions of *The Lost Fishermen*, a Ghanaian folk opera and a celebration
of the life of fishermen.

Begun more than three decades ago as a theatrical club called
the Dama's Club (the initials of Dodoo, Attoh, Mallet, and Amar-
tey), the group originally performed primarily on the stage. In a
sense they were the popular theatre of the day, playing to audiences
of all ages and tastes and maintaining a box-office appeal. During
their early period they popularized minstrel shows and tap-dancing
acts like those featured in the movies of the time. Perhaps their
greatest early success was in 1945 when they appeared at the King
George V Memorial Hall in a presentation of *Christopher Columbus*,
a Gilbert and Sullivan-type operetta written and arranged in a
classic dialogue with colorful music, to which they added their own
interludes, dances, and touches of humor.

When the membership of the club grew, the club became a
choir and began to concentrate on singing. Recently, under the
direction of Ishmael Adams, talented singer and choirmaster, the
Dama's Choir has merged with Saka Acquaye, one of Ghana's leading sculptors, dramatists, and composers, to produce his production
of *The Lost Fishermen*. Already they have had success in staging the
play throughout most of Ghana and hope to embark upon an American tour.

---

[3]After the "portrait" segment which ended the performance, the dialogue started.
The youth wanted to rap with me about Black Americans, Black Power, and brotherhood. Generally their response was, "Why don't you come home? We're brothers!"

Concert Party Theatre

It would be very hard to discuss the national theatre movement in Ghana without paying attention to the importance of Ghana's popular theatre, the concert party. This particular style of theatre provides one of the most popular and common means of entertainment in Ghana today. It is essentially the Ghanaian equivalent of vaudeville.

Bob Johnson (Ishmael Johnson), the "father" of the concert party, is the oldest comedian currently engaged in this comic art. Influenced by the minstrel and vaudeville shows from America and England, Bob Johnson introduced vaudeville, via the concert party, to Ghana. In 1920 he founded and led "The Versatile Eight." In 1930 he followed his first success with "Two Bobs and Their Caroline Girl." Bob Johnson tells us, "I was greatly influenced by Al Jolson in *The Jazz Singer*, which gave me many ideas regarding the direction of my concert shows."

The early concert shows were staged around itinerant guitar bands and employed the use of an all-male cast. Today, the performers, essentially comedians, concentrate mainly on entertaining their audiences and making them laugh. Nearly all of the shows are in Akan, but since they are usually unscripted and rely mainly upon improvisations on a general theme, other languages are often interspersed. Rarely if ever are the concert parties presented in English.

The theatrical style, similar to the commedia dell'arte, relies heavily on adaptation and improvisation. The shows are staged either inside on a modern stage in a city theatre or outside on an open stage in the courtyard of a village compound with an improvised setting of a raised stage on boards and cement blocks. No curtains are used, since the use of music and dance helps to suggest scene changes and keeps the plot moving.

Although these comic plays are presented essentially for entertainment and recreation, they also serve a social function by affording the audience the opportunity of releasing emotions and tensions. Each play has a theme that carries with it a moral and "mirrors life" with respect to specific relationships between the male and the female in the home and, in general, shows Ghanaian life in the village and in the city. Today approximately forty companies of concert parties are in operation in Ghana.

Efua Sutherland considers the concert party theatre Ghana's indigenous theatre: "Concert Party Theatre is the only fully evolved indigenous form of theatre at present. It is also the only professional theatre. It enjoys a countrywide appeal and it is completely supported by the large, enthusiastic audiences it can draw in city, town and village."[4] Knowing Efua's involvement in traditional Ghanaian theatre, I presume she speaks in terms of modern conventional theatre. I also suspect that she uses the term "professional theatre" here because many of the concert party groups support themselves solely by way of their theatre productions.

The Ghana Brigade Drama Group, a concert party company, was attached to the Ghana Drama Studio for a period of time. Their involvement with the Studio included an intensive training and development program. It was through this connection with the Studio that I came to know Mr. G. Kitson-Mills, company theatre manager and producer of the group. Mr. Mills is also a talented magician who studied the art of magic in China. I have vivid memories of the first time I saw him work his magic and later watched a spirited production of concert party theatre presented by the Brigade Drama Group. My family and I were at the Arts Center in Accra to witness a special celebration for the National Liberation Council. The Center was crowded. There was standing room only. We were fortunate enough to have special seats along with the invited guests. My son James was seated next to General Lieutenant Joseph A. Ankrah, chairman of the NLC. He sensed the importance of General Ankrah's position because of the attention paid to him by members of the audience. James wanted to meet him. General Ankrah was cordial and engaged James in a conversation about Kitson-Mills' magic act. The magic act was followed by a hilarious presentation of "Crazy Gang," a concert party show. Sometime

[4] Efua Sutherland, "Theatre in Ghana," in Janice Nesbitt, editor, *Ghana Welcomes You* (Accra: Orientation to Ghana Committee, 1969), p. 85.

later my wife and I were to perform in Algiers on the same stage with this talented company and I would learn to know more about the talents and techniques of both Kitson-Mills and his group.

Celebrations—Traditional African Theatre

Today I was to give witness to a form of traditional African theatre. Efua Sutherland had invited me to a festival. As we sped along the open highway on the road to Mompong, Efua and I talked about the significance of the festival.

"This is the Nmayem Festival, celebrated by some of the Adangme tribes to mark the end of the old year and to herald the new year."

The festival, to be held in Adumasi, was an eight-day festival, beginning on Monday, October 16 and lasting through Monday, October 23. *Nmayem* means "eating the millet," and the festival is celebrated during the millet harvesting season. *Nma*, which has now become the common name for all kinds of food, originally meant "millet," for a long time the staple food of the Adangmes.

"The celebration of the festival starts with the reaping of *Nma*, which is not eaten until after the priests have offered some of it as a token of gratitude for the year's harvest, at all crossroads and shrines. The various tribes, clans, and families who trace their ancestry to a common ancestor celebrate the occasion at a tribal gathering with the tribal chief, on a tribal day."

Manya Krobo has six major tribes whose tribal days are: Djebiam—Mondays; Peigwah and Manyayo—Tuesdays; and Akwenor, Suisi, and Dorm—Thursdays. These six major tribes are again divided into twenty-four clans.

"The ceremony is observed by all members of the family squatting around a big bowl of a meal prepared with powdered roasted corn cooked in palm soup, and each member eating with his fingers from the common bowl."

Meat or chicken is eaten with this. As a second course, mashed yam with eggs, without soup or stew, is eaten. There is drinking of palm wine and other liquor and general merrymaking. The festival culminates on the Friday of the celebration week with a grand durbar at which all the tribes and their chiefs meet the paramount chief.

"At this durbar the high priest pours a libation for prosperity (pouring libation is similar to saying a prayer) for the ensuing year, after which the priestly families assist the high priest in scattering nma to the crowd. Everybody (including the visitors) is expected to eat the grains which fall on him, as it is symbolic of the whole tribe eating from the common bowl."

Like most festivals, Nmayem has its significance in the history of the tribe. The year is reckoned by the priests of Kloweki, namely the high priest Nimo Okumo Madjamor Atreku and the priest Nimo Asikpe. The last day of the year is the full moon day of the thirteenth month, which falls either in October or November. There are a number of minor activities during the week-long celebration, for example, Akleme ("silent day").

"Akleme is fixed for Wednesday when men visit the burial ground early, before dawn, and pour libation. They return at sunrise amid drummimg and firing of musketry and are met at the outskirts of the town by women carrying green leaves and singing. No food is eaten until sunset."

Akleme is the name given to the ancestral home that is now conceived to be in the spirit world, but it is most probably the name of an ancient capital or city. The name is now given to the mausoleum where chiefs and dignitaries are buried.

"The celebration is for all the tribesmen, of whatever religion or creed. One significant feature is the large number of marriages and the amicable settlements of family, clan, and tribal disputes during the period."

My eyes drink in the beautiful African terrain, decorated by the majesty and splendor of its tear trees and cottonwood trees. Today is Friday, October 20, 1967—the day of the Nmayem durbar at Laasi. I soon learn that I can expect to see everyone descending upon the town in celebration.

Stretched ahead of me, high on a hill is a retreat, Puadasi Lodge, built by former Premier Kwame Nkrumah. Now we are reaching Mompong. Children, old men and women, youths and middle-aged alike, throng the streets. We soon become a part of the crowd.

Different melodies and rhythms fuse into one harmonious orchestral sound as dancers sway back and forth, bringing on the chiefs, the queen mothers, and other important members of the village tribes and communities.

After passing through the streets we find ourselves at a village square where people of all ages have arranged themselves as an audience. The young children and babies are attentive, not restless, seemingly unaware of such a thing as a short attention span for children. They are involved in the action. They are participants in the celebration of the festival. Their focus of attention is clear. The storyteller holds the center of the stage. Each character plays his role—the executioner, the dancers, the chief, the audience. They all form a network of stimulus-responses. This is the CELEBRATION—the festival. Here I am giving witness to a sharing process—real honest communication in the arts—where the play IS the thing, with all the actors playing their part and with an audience that knows the story of the play, just as well as the players. Here is a fusion of dramatic dialogue, dance, and music—into one spectacular dramatic experience.

At 9:20 A.M. the chiefs and people begin to assemble on the durbar ground for drumming. There is a great assortment of musical sounds. I hear and see drums, sticks, gongs, gourds, and horns of many kinds. I am reminded of the biblical saying, "Make a joyful noise unto the Lord." For here I see and I hear a real CELEBRATION OF LIFE, within the heart of a religious experience. It is a multimedia happening. I hear and see many modern instruments—saxophones, trumpets, and electric guitars—the modern blending in with the past. I see clothing all colors of the rainbow. The music engulfs me and the dance consumes me. The drumming is all around me. The many rhythms—counterpoint, assonance, dissonance—create a symphony of the universe.

At 9:45 A.M. the guests begin to arrive. We are in the courtyard. A few minutes later the special guests arrive. At 9:58 Konor arrives. And all throughout this event of the coming and going of people, drumming is continuous.

At 10:00 A.M. the members of the N.L.C. arrive. The drumming reaches a climax, and then at 10:04 it ceases. The Konor delivers his address. There is much singing and dancing in the background. I am carried away to another time—to another land—to another place. I hear a bass drum and a trumpet. And within the limbo line of my listening, perhaps within my subconscious mind, I also hear jazz resting on top of carnival music. I am now truly within the celebration.

The principal address is delivered in Ada, one of the many African languages. The audience's response to the speech has much emotion, movement, communicative drive, fire, and feeling. The background music is much like a chant with many open tones, such as *oo, ah,* and *ay.* Man, I really dig that open instrument, somewhat like a bugle, also the reed instruments, but especially the drums. Yes, especially the drums. But now I have passed the stage of empathy and have moved right into the middle of the vibration.

Now the Ewes do their dance.

It is 10:25 A.M. The Nmayem ceremony begins. This involves the scattering of the nma. It is much like a sprinkling of rice or corn. At 10:30 we hear an address by a special guest, the chief of police. At 10:45 we see the guests' courtesy greeting of Konor. There is more drumming and excitement. At 11:00 A.M. the Procession of Konor and chiefs go to Konorwem.

Well this is it! For me, this has been festival theatre. A Celebration. A Total Creation. Is this the ACT or the PRESENTATION of the act? Or both? Or does it matter? Does it really make any difference? The ingredients of theatre as theatre is known today are prevalent here. The food for the creation and re-creation of that thing placed on the stage before an audience, another kind of re-creation.

I muse. But is this celebration cloaked in a theatrical form for a specific audience at a specific time? Sure it is. And it involves freedom, imagination, and an on-the-spot involvement, concentration, and discipline. So this is the drama or the theatre of the festival! And it serves the people. So I ask, must it be compressed and placed on a proscenium stage to serve a few people, to serve commerce and our modern times—to serve our "modern idea of theatre"?

Ghana Drama Studio

During the late 1950s and the early 1960s the Ghana Drama Studio in Accra emerged as one of Ghana's leading theatre centers.

In a sense the Studio evolved around the efforts, insights, and talents of Efua Sutherland, Ghanaian playwright and producer. Today the Studio still houses one of Ghana's best outdoor theatres. It was here, from this Studio, that much of my work would be done.

Since the Studio was a structural arm of the Institute of African Studies at the University of Ghana, Professor Nketia envisioned a cooperative plan and relationship between the Legon drama students and the professional theatre groups attached to the Studio. With this idea in mind, from the Ghana Drama Studio, Efua and I would initiate a graduate program in Experimental Theatre Productions and Professional Theatre Training.

One phase of the plan would include a graduate seminar program with Sandy Arkhurst and Allen Tamakloe, both recent graduates of the School of Music and Drama at Legon, as the initial graduate interns. Our program was to concentrate on professional training and experimental productions. The experimental productions would include productions in Akan, for example. The Workers' Brigade Drama Group, attached to the Studio, would provide the required human materials of the Akan productions. Allen Tamakloe was assigned to direct children's plays. Adult plays would be directed by Sandy Arkhurst; he was also to direct the Atwia Project, an experimental village theatre project conceived by Efua, which included both teen-age and adult groups. She would supervise the Atwia Project. I would provide the professional training and direction for Allen and Sandy and the various projects. Efua and I would work very closely together in all other activities.

We began our experimental project by reorganizing the former Studio Players Company. The major focus of the New Studio Players Company was the development of a basic philosophy and rationale with regard to theatre company development in Ghana. It was to focus on the development of a professional company utilizing both children and adults in a bilingual situation. The first thrust of the work was to include the creation of an acting company trained to do plays in English and in Akan. Our work was to include all phases of theatre training for the actor, with major concentration on the use of language. It was necessary, however, first to instill within each player the idea of theatre African theatre and the need for discipline of the craft. The "tune-in" and "unlocking process"[5] were also necessary before any intensive work on acting technique could be undertaken. The company soon realized that it was not designed merely to put on another play but to learn how to best put on plays—in the manner of a repertory company—and to learn the discipline and work of the craft. As the company developed, the nature of the multilingual African society and its relation to theatre productions would be explored and exploited.[6]

As time went by and the training and development phases continued, the number of people in the company diminished. Some members balked at the idea of emphasizing discipline, training, and the development of technique for the theatre; they were content to continue the process of trial and error in theatre-making. Other members strongly resented the bilingual nature of the company and the "work method" approach to theatre and productions, which was exacting, taxing, and new to most members. Also they preferred to have the plays presented only in English and not in the vernacular, Akan.

A second phase of the company development program began when Efua decided to form the Kusum Agoromba from a nucleus of the New Studio Players Company. Since the experimental work in Akan that she and I had been doing with the Brigade Drama Group had come to a formal end, she felt the need for an "Akan experience" in the theatre and so formed another company that would perform plays in Akan. Consequently our emphasis shifted temporarily to this new company. Sandy Arkhurst would direct the company and Allen Tamakloe would be company production manager. Funds became available for the new company and a production schedule became a reality when the company launched its production of *Odasani*, an Akan version of *Everyman*, the medieval morality play.

The initial concern of the Kusum Agoromba Company and its production of *Odasani* was to develop audiences, especially church and school audiences. Moreover, a professional company perform-

---

[5]Scott Kennedy, "The Use of Language and the Ghanaian Actor's Technique," Institute of African Studies *Research Review*, Vol. 4, No. 2, 1968, p. 61.
[6]Scott Kennedy, "A Bilingual Approach to Theatre Development in Ghana," in Gilbert Ansare, *Ghanaian Languages* (Ghana: Ghana Publishing Corporation, 1969).

ing in the vernacular was felt to be desirable and a necessary step forward in the development of the theatre movement in Ghana.

Following the completion of their *Odasani* productions the Kusum Agoromba Company presented an Akan version of *Foriwa*, a play written by Efua Sutherland. They have recently completed a successful tour of Ghana with their Anansegora repertoire based on Ananse stories under the watchful eye of their writer-producer, Efua Sutherland.

When funds eventually became available for the New Studio Players Company it too launched its production program. The initial productions of *Ananse and the Dwarf Brigade* and *Tweedledum and Tweedledee* assured the company that both the rationale and the method were sound.[7]

Our work in theatre development at the Ghana Drama Studio was concerned with many things, including the following:

1. The training and formation of acting troupes (artistic and technical).
2. The training of business and administrative officers to handle company matters.
3. Theatre research in training programs for African theatre, company management, audience behavior, and audience development.

School of Music and Drama

In Ghana's current theatre movement, one cannot underestimate the importance of the role of the Drama and Theatre Studies Division at the University of Ghana, Legon. In the first place, the School of Music and Drama, by its very existence, has focused attention on the theatre. The student, forced to look at theatre from an academic point of view as well as from a professional point of view, soon realizes that theatre must be taught and that it also must be made. Some of the students who will eventually become teachers, administrators, and community leaders will have an awareness of the rich potential of theatre with respect to cultural development and communication. Others, who will become "makers of theatre,"

[7]"Unique Performance at Ghana Drama Studio," *Ghanaian Times* theatre critic, Saturday, June 1, 1968, p. 7.

will form theatre companies and establish professional standards. And from this professional company framework, playwrights, actors, technicians, designers, and "models of excellence" may emerge.

In the early stages of the development of drama studies at the university, the teaching of drama was the major interest. The division head, Mr. J. C. DeGraft, playwright and teacher, concentrated mainly on preparing teachers of drama and producers in a college setting. At the same time, however, he also worked out of the Ghana Drama Studio as an actor and a producer in the Studio's experimental production program. At present DeGraft is not in Ghana but is working with UNESCO as a teacher of English as a second language in Nairobi, Kenya.

In the current stage of development at the university, new directions in the Drama and Theatre Studies Division have begun to emphasize the company idea and professional standards of excellence with regard to technique and performance. Within this new direction the school is searching for a "character" and a "concept" of African theatre for the university and for Ghana. The company idea of African theatre has already moved past the idea stage and the university is eagerly anticipating the emergence of the University Players' Workshop Company. Of course the development and direction of this company depend largely upon the philosophy and energy of the teaching staff and production personnel within the school. The structure does, however, envision staff and student cooperation with respect to major productions throughout the year. The first-year students will begin as apprentices in the company and gradually advance until they become resident members within the next two years. Each player will have the opportunity of learning theatre both from an academic point of view as well as from a professional point of view. Despite the fact that professional standards of company development are being stressed, the academic studies within the university structure still remain in the program. The visionaries of the plan are hopeful that the students will profit from the advantage of working closely together over a period of three or four years. This togetherness will enrich the company and the school and advance the idea of a concept and a character for African theatre. It will also enable the company to examine techniques for African theatre within the framework of a training program.

Scott Kennedy with University Players (*U.S.I.A.*, *Ghana*)

Forest Orchestra of New Studio Players (*U.S.I.A., Ghana*)

Professor Nketia and I however soon realized that these new directions in the Drama and Theatre Studies Division would of course necessitate a strong and a close relationship with the music and dance divisions. Therefore we sought to build this positive relationship between the drama, music, and dance divisions. We also understood the necessity of considering and stressing priorities within the national theatre movement. We both felt that the concept and idea of African theatre was perhaps the most important aspect to be stressed. Next was the need for trained specialists. And for this phase, money was needed to bring these people in to work within the movement. On the other hand, in a developing country like Ghana, a country with great economic needs for its internal development, the problem of securing financial aid for a national theatre was most pressing. Foundations and philanthropic organizations are more prone to support agricultural and educational reforms and developmental programs before supporting theatre. The question

Anteteban Choir (*Dr. Amu*)

was, considering the limited budget for theatre development, where could Ghana find trained theatre specialists willing to devote several years of their life to the movement? And where could Ghana find "seed" money to overcome some of the basic financial problems inherent in the theatre movement? For example, the problem of transportation in Ghana, especially around Accra, pointed to the need for transportation and hardship budgets for persons involved in the theatre—persons who must rehearse long after public transportation has ceased to operate. Or just transporting the students from Legon to the Ghana Drama Studio would cost money that really wasn't available. Seed money, however, would pay for a company bus and gasoline, which would then make it possible for interested performers and technicians to become a part of the current movement. Perhaps it would then be possible to create and support traveling companies.

Even though our staff at the university was limited, we still envisioned a program of experimental productions along with the regular university academic program. Sophia Locco and John

Kedyanyi, production assistants Allen Tamakloe and Sandy Ark-hurst, and I were the nucleus of this staff. We selected the following plays for our initial experimental project: Wole Soyinka's *Trials of Brother Jero*, James Henshaw's *Jewels of the Shrine*, Efua Sutherland's *Foriwa*, my own *Gospel Suite for Dr. Martin Luther King*, and my *Mourning Memorial* (based on a poem by Darwin Turner and with African music by Kwabena Nketia).

An opportunity to enlarge our theatre staff with trained specialists did present itself, and we had to consider whether we wished to avail ourselves of the opportunity. The American Peace Corps had selected Accra as the site for a conference of Peace Corps directors in Africa. The Peace Corps was already supplying Ghana with teachers, agricultural specialists, and other needed educators. I speculated. Why not begin a training program for theatre specialists from the Peace Corps? No such program existed within the international framework of the Peace Corps. Nketia and I talked about the idea. He liked it. Why shouldn't we work with the idea. The Peace Corps Directors descended upon Ghana. My brother, Dr. Joseph C. Kennedy, was the Peace Corps Director for Sierra Leone. I spoke with him about the idea. He thought we could realize it only if Ghana wanted such a program and requested it. Of course the head of the Peace Corps and the US Government would have to agree to the plan. Inasmuch as the Conference of Peace Corps Directors in Africa was underway, several meetings were arranged between the principals involved to discuss the theatre project. Finally it was agreed by the group that such a project should be tried. Jack Vaughn, Director of the Peace Corps for the USA, C. Payne Lucas, Director of the Peace Corps in Africa, Dr. Jim Kirk, Director of the Peace Corps in Ghana, Carrol Buchanan, Associate Director of the Peace Corps in Ghana, Joe Kennedy (at the request of Jack Vaughn), Kwabena Nketia, and I, with a representative from the Ministry of Education, in a meeting at the Ambassador Hotel in Accra, finalized the plan.

We would begin with a very select group of Peace Corps volunteers. Carrol Buchanan would search for this group of volunteers in America. After completing orientation in the United States they would then have to engage in an in-service training program in

Ghana.[8] I was asked to help set up, shape, and coordinate the program. The principals involved felt that these volunteers, though trained in theatre and specific technical aspects of the arts, should still be required to engage in a specific training program for African theatre and the related arts before being assigned to work within the theatre movement in Ghana. Five persons were selected, each with special training in the following areas: theatre per se, production, cinematography, music, and dance. This was the starting point for a program that is still in existence, a program designed to aid Ghana's theatre movement via a Peace Corps involvement. Ghana welcomed this means of getting trained personnel and theatre expertise, fully aware that such an arrangement would benefit both parties concerned. While aiding Ghana in its theatre movement the Peace Corps would provide rich opportunities for the PC volunteers, trained in Western theatre techniques, desirous of learning something about the arts and culture of Africa through an African theatre program.[9]

Playwrights in Ghana

Any theatre movement needs active playwrights and published plays, and in Ghana's case, plays in English and in the vernacular are required. From the point of view of published plays in English, Ghana has been involved in the process for about thirty years. *The Fifth Landing Stage* by Dr. F. K. Fiawoo, a play in five acts, was published in 1942. In 1943 *The Third Woman*, a play in five acts by Dr. J. B. Danquah, was published. Twenty years later in 1963, *Akomfo Anoche's Golden Stool*, by Michael Dei Anang, was published. It was followed in 1964 by *Sons and Daughters*, written by J. C. DeGraft, and in 1965 by Ama Atta Aidoo's *Dilemma of a Ghost*. In 1969 Miss Aido published another play, *Anua*. Efua Sutherland published *Edufa* and *Foriwa* in 1967 and 1968 respectively. Both Joe DeGraft and Efua have written other plays, which have not yet been published. However, plays continue to be written in the vernacular, and several young playwrights are creating plays in English, although they have not yet been published.

---

[8]Scott Kennedy, "An Approach to African Theatre," Institute of African Studies *Research Review*, Vol. 5, No. 2, 1969, p. 80.
[9]Scott Kennedy, "Communicating Culture Through Theatre and the Arts, Institute of African Studies *Research Review*, Vol. 5, No. 1, 1968, pp. 81–83.

Most of the new playwrights are graduates of the School of Drama at Legon, and they have all written at least one or more plays. The playwrights include Martin Owusu, who wrote *The Mightier Sword* and a short play, *The Story Ananse Told*, which was published recently; Allen Tamakloe, who wrote *Kokoroko*; Sebastian Kwuamuar, who wrote *The Dagger of Liberation*; and Emmanuel Yirenchi, who wrote *The Shadow of Living*. And of course there are other writers outside of the School of Drama, for example, Kwah Ansah and Ivan Annan. Upon completion of a theatre study program in America, these two young men returned to Ghana to write *Mother's Tears* and *An Ancestral Dialogue: The Linguist*, respectively. As writers continue to graduate from the School of Drama and new theatre companies continue to be formed, the prospects in Ghana become brighter for the emergence of more new young playwrights.[10]

African Plays

At the School of Drama, in attempting to develop an African concept and idea of theatre, we stressed the inclusion of plays from all of Africa. And of course we studied these plays from an African frame of reference. Since Nigerian plays usually headed our list of plays for inspection, perhaps we should now consider some of Nigeria's dramatists and theatre-makers.

Wole Soyinka, one of Africa's leading playwrights, creates plays that utilize the infinite possibilities of the theatre and the stage. He creates plays that stretch the imagination of the director and the player—plays that usually integrate dramatic conflict with dance, music, spectacle, mime, and poetic diction. Soyinka creates African plays—plays that make us remember that theatre sprang from ritual, song, dance, and a *celebration of life*. His plays never let us forget that the roots of African drama and theatre—the roots of the African CELEBRATION or TOTAL CREATION—rest within tradition and ritual observance.

Soyinka's world of theatre links modern themes with tradi-

---

[10]Scott Kennedy, "University of Ghana Graduates in Drama and Theatre Studies —Direction and Careers," Institute of African Studies *Research Review*, Vol. 5, No. 2, 1969.

tional African life and the Africa of yesterday. And within this world he examines the life-death-scene within the limbo line of the African's dilemma: the conflict between his new values of progress and his old values of tradition.

Soyinka is a playwright who has great talent, skills, and technique and who seeks to examine the dramatic experience through the use of total expression in the anticipation of the creation of a total theatrical experience. In 1960 he founded the Masks and the Orisun Theatre, and since then he has been actively connected and committed to drama and theatre development in Nigeria. After attending Government College, Ibadan, he went on to the University of Leeds. In London, he joined the Royal Court Theatre, where he had his first play, *The Inventor*, produced. For some time he made his living as a full-time playwright, poet, and producer. He has also been a research fellow at the University of Ibadan and a lecturer at the University of Ife. Since his release from prison, for his alleged political activities in the recent Nigerian war, he has been busily engaged in movie-making, writing plays, and serving as director of the School of Drama at the University of Ibadan.

It is as a playwright that Soyinka is perhaps best known. Therefore we shall examine several of his plays, and as we shall soon see, his plays do exemplify a basic concept of African theatre as a celebration of life and as a total creation. In order to become African theatre, such dramas demand the use of inventive, well-trained actors and directors, sensitive to the structure, style, and concept of African theatre.

The Swampdwellers, a one-act play, was written when Soyinka was still a student at Leeds University. The story is one of disappointment and frustration, revealing the evils of too great an emotional attachment to superstitious beliefs. We see a young man who is alienated from both the soil and the city and who witnesses the dehumanizing aspects of city life as well as the destruction of his farm by flood. "It was never in my mind . . . the thought that the farm could betray me so totally, that it could drive the final wedge into this growing loss of touch."

The theme suggests that superstition is the enemy of progress and economic development. Symbolic characters—such as the Blind Beggar, Kadiye, the Priest of the Serpent, and Igwezu, who loses his belief in the religion of his home place because of his hard times in the city—help spark the dramatic interest in the play. The Beggar, set against Kadiye within the focus of the dramatic situation, helps provide the play with a dramatic experience of compression and immediacy. Kadiye represents hereditary corruption, a spoiler of the earth, while the Beggar must redeem the land from him.

The Lion and the Jewel, one of Soyinka's most popular plays, is also one of his most theatrical. Here he provides us with both verbal and visual interest by using free verse and a mixture of song, speech, dance, and mime. Once again he testifies and gives witness to African theatre as means of expression and communication and as a total creation by utilizing several art forms within the framework of both verbal and nonverbal communication. In this play Soyinka achieves harmony by the masterful blending of form and content. This fusion of an African mode of expression with content produces a powerful dramatic experience that orchestrates verbal, emotional, and physical rhythms around a score that is both humorous and serious.

The Lion and the Jewel deals with African tradition in conflict with Western ideas. It is an examination of the conflict of the new order with the old order about social customs, in this case, marriage customs. It also focuses on a struggle between progress and tradition. The lion in the play is Baroka, Bale of Ilujinle, a reputedly important and aging tribal ruler, who is set against a progressive young school teacher in a contest for the belle of the village, Sidi, the jewel of the play. Lakunle, the village schoolmaster, represents the new order in society. However, he is no match for the Bale, who is neither impotent nor senile, but is steeped in traditional wisdom and strength and instinct still determines his actions. The Bale tells us, "I do not hate progress, only its nature, which makes all roofs and faces look the same." He merely fears the "reckless broom that will be wielded in these years to come," to sweep away all traces of his culture.

Soyinka integrates structure, form, and style by using to great advantage song, dance, ritual, and mime, and to dramatize episodes from the past, he uses flashbacks. This approach is especially effective in the scenes dealing with the Bale's supposed impotency and the visit of the photographer and his glorification of Sidi.

The Trials of Brother Jero satirizes religious sects in Nigeria.

Brother Jero, a religious leader, makes a living by duping others in the name of religion. In this play African chants, music, drumming, mime, speech, and song are utilized. The way Soyinka mixes conventional speech with the popular vernacular is truly a "page from African communication and expression." During moments of stress and excitement, or for relief, the characters move freely from one language or level of language to another. Chume, when pleading with Jero for permission to beat his wife, switches from one level to another: "Just once. Just one sound beating and I swear not to ask again" to "In' go beat 'am too hard. Jus' once small small." This switching brings to mind the approach of the "old Negro preacher" or the Black preacher in America today, pleading with his congregation through rich storytelling. He moves from one level of language to another and from voice level to chant; he lifts the language and expression from one dramatic line to another to involve his congregation and at the same time to relieve himself within his storyteller's role.

Soyinka manipulates Jero as both narrator and character, thus making it possible for Jero to comment upon his own actions and thereby provide an element of sophisticated objectivity. His use of Jero as both narrator and character also establishes contact and a relationship between Jero and the audience. The play thereby places itself within the African theatre concept of participatory theatre.

A Dance of the Forests was first performed as a part of the Nigerian independence celebration—an occasion marked by great festivities and gatherings. And the play is indeed a celebration, rooted in African values and beliefs, in this instance, the African belief in the continuity of the human community. Though *A Dance of the Forests* celebrates and satirizes African chauvinism, Soyinka speaks of the gathering of the tribes, reincarnation, and ancestral worship. Structurally he utilizes African dramatic and theatrical elements by employing mythology and by having the climax of the play in dance rather than in words. The conflict within the play arises from the desire of the living to glorify and ennoble the past while seeking to overlook and evade its judgments and accusations. The play, divided into two parts connected by a dance, introduces many characters, some as individuals, some as social types or representives of groups.

Soyinka's sharp vision and poetic gift attack those who romanticize the glories of Africa's past but who continue to perpetuate the evils of the present. The characters in the play refuse to "leave the dead some room to dance." However, Forest Father intervenes and four human beings are forced to confront the two who have returned from the dead to accuse them. Around this confrontation the play moves to a climactic struggle for the possession of unborn generations.

This is a highly theatrical African play and once again we witness Soyinka integrating the nuances of word, song, dance, mime, music (drums, bells) and audio and visual aspects of theatre to provide a stage spectacle within an African dramatic experience —to make spectacle and drama explode before your very eyes.

As the play opens, two of the dead push their heads through the soil. In the second act the dances of the Half-Child and of the Unwilling Spirit provide beautiful stage spectacles. These episodes together with the climax of the play in dance point to a particular direction in African theatrical presentations. Such a direction seems to make use of many modes of expression and communication and in a sense deemphasizes the use of the word standing by itself as it were, as it often does in the European literary approach to drama. It is merely a matter of emphasis: European drama focuses upon dialogue and African drama focuses upon modes of expression and a theatrical celebration.

In *The Strong Breed*, Soyinka calls attention to a system that he feels needs immediate reform. In this play he again attempts to integrate both form and content. The Carrier dies for the sins of the community, but his death does not result in any noticeable improvement in public morality. The setting is a New Year's celebration in a village during a significant ritual in which the Carrier is selected to carry away the sins of the previous year in order to prepare for a new year of purity and peace. The play takes its title from the hero's family: in the village of his birth, one member of the family is chosen to be the carrier of the canoe, made each year at the flood's regress, to symbolically carry away the sins the villagers committed in twelve months. The play is firmly rooted in dramatic ritual and reveals itself on several levels, including individual psychology, mass psychology, and the religious experience.

In *The Road*, as in *Brother Jero*, Soyinka uses the various levels of English that the Nigerian uses, and he also gives us an idea of how important the lorry, or truck, is to the life of the average Nigerian.

One of the major characters, the Professor, searches for the Word that will unite two worlds, the world of the spirit symbolized by the rainbow and the world of the flesh symbolized by the palm tree and the wind. The Word, however, is never found, except in death. The theatrical power of the "Dance of the Mask" and finally the reenactment of the lorry's destruction serve to remind us of the talent, technique, and power of Soyinka as an exemplifier of African theatre as a celebration of life and a realization of a total creation —one that is to be seen, heard, and felt on a multimedia level as opposed to that kind of drama which is merely to be read or witnessed from a distance.

John Pepper Clark, another outstanding Nigerian playwright, attended Government College, Warri, and the University of Ibadan. Clark has been a journalist in Ibadan, a features editor of the *Daily Express* in Lagos, and a lecturer at the University of Lagos, where he is currently a research fellow.

Clark's plays, all tragedies—*The Song of a Goat, The Masquerade, The Raft,* and *Ozidi*—examine the conflict between Nature's law (God's) and society's law (man's). Through his plays he examines the life of his people, their social practices and beliefs, their shortcomings and their difficulties.

The Song of a Goat, based on a pre-dramatic ritual—a cleansing sacrifice—raises a moral issue. The story is about an Ijaw fisherman and pilot whose wife, made restless and resentful by his impotence, turns to his brother. The fisherman performs a sacrifice—a real sacrifice of a live goat—in which he reveals his knowledge of the adultery. The fisherman, Zifa, impotent and unable to have any more children by his wife Ebiere, goes to a masseur. The masseur advises him to let his brother "take" his wife. Though Zifa rejects this advice, Ebiere and Tonje, the brother, do become intimate. Zifa learns of the this. Tonye, trying to escape his brother's wrath, hangs himself, while Zifa wades into the sea and disappears. All of the characters are caught up in a dilemma and caught within the web of the tragic flaw because of a curse that has been put on them.

The Masquerade is a family tragedy in which Dabiri brings death to his daughter and her suitor.

The Raft tells of the ordeal of four men who are hired to take a raft of logs down a river. The raft goes adrift and it seems that Nature herself had a hand in their fate.

The concert party and the traveling theatre companies of Nigeria are very important to Nigeria's theatre movement. Hubert Ogunde, a pioneer in concert party theatre, began performing and adapting school plays from Bible stories in 1943. In 1944 he founded his concert party group, and the following year his play *The Strike* was acclaimed throughout Nigeria. In 1947 a tour of Ghana convinced Ogunde that he should include more music in his plays. With this thought in mind he reworked his concert party concept, and when he returned to Ghana in 1948 he was more successful than ever. Ogunde's ability to retain salaried actors and stage managers makes it possible for him to have few staff changes in his company. Also the fact that he has married most of the female members of his concert party group and includes his children in his cast enables him to keep his company together. He has gained considerable knowledge of the theatre through his extensive travels in Africa and overseas. Hubert Ogunde is no doubt the most widely acclaimed and most popular dramatist in the concert party field.

Two of his political satires—*Yoruba Ronu* ("Let the Yoruba Think") and *Otito Koro* ("Truth Is Better")—deal with the political events in western Nigeria that led to the declaration of emergency in 1963. As a result of his production of these two plays the government banned Ogunde and his concert party from performing in western Nigeria. Ogunde's plays, in concert party manner, are not scripted or written.

Duro Ladipo, actor, composer, director, and playwright, has the Duro Ladipo Theatre Company. Ladipo started his career by adapting church stories for the stage and by accompanying church songs with traditional instruments. In 1962 he founded the Mbari Mbayo Club at Oshogbo. His most important plays are *Oba Moro*, *Oba Koso*, and *Oba Waja*, which premiered respectively in 1962, 1963, and 1964.

Oba Moro ("The King Overcomes the Devil") examines Yoruba history at a time when the king of Oyo wielded both temporal and spiritual power. The king displays his superior power over his councilors, who are at odds with him because of his decision to move his kingdom. They are forced to acknowledge his supremacy when he checks them in their attempt to use household evil-spirit carriers to prevent him from moving his kingdom.

Oba Koso ("The King Never Hangs") won the Nigerian Federal Government award for the most significant contribution to culture in 1963. It was also well received at the Berlin Festival in West Germany in September 1964 and is perhaps Ladipo's most popular play. It re-creates the uneasiness that preceded the decline and the fall of the ancient Oyo Empire. The king and his councilors are tired of the warlike activities of two warrior chiefs, Gbonka and Timi, and arrange for the assassination of at least one of them. Gbonka emerges victorious and soon challenges the authority of the king. Deserted by his councilors and later by Oya, his wife, the king hangs himself. Finally, amidst lightning and thunder, the frightened subjects sing a mournful dirge that their king is not dead but has ascended to heaven.

Oba Waja ("The King Is Dead"), based on a true experience that took place in the late 1940s, also examines an aspect of the history and culture of Oyo. The clash between British and Nigerian people with respect to culture and values explodes in a confrontation expressed in music, dance, and words.

In Act 1 we witness a celebration of the death of the king. The people are mourning the death of their king. It is evening. We overhear a conversation between the District Officer and his Wife. We sense the clash and the tragedy that is to follow.

In Act 2 we experience life in the king's market. We learn more about the culture of the Oyo people. We learn that the Commander of the King's Horse (Olori Elesin) must accompany his king in death. For this, there is a celebration in the market. The District Officer and his men interfere with this celebration and the customs of the people. They arrest Olori Elesin and take him away.

In Act 3 we see Olori Elesin being confronted and criticized by the Oyo people, who are ashamed of him. We then see him being criticized by the Spirit of the Alafin, the dead king.

In Act 4 we give witness to life in a Ghanaian Bar-Nightclub. We meet Dawudu, the son of the Commander of the King's Horse. Dawudu learns of the death of the king, the Alafin. Now he knows that his father must also die and that he must go home to bury his father. He responds to his duty and obligation. He and his wife prepare to go home to Nigeria.

In Act 5 we are in Nigeria in the home of Olori Elesin, where Dawudu confronts his father when he finds that he is still alive. We then witness the result of the prophecy of the Spirit of the Alafin who has said, "I will not cross the river alone."

The play ends with another confrontation between the Oyo people and the District Officer who now recognizes the tragedy that has occurred.

Duro Ladipo's plays are written in Yoruba and are often described as "Yoruba operas." They are a fine blending of cultural content and an African mode of expression which utilizes music, dance, mime, song, and dialogue. Ladipo is a gifted African theatre-maker skilled in the various art forms of Africa and capable of examining all aspects of Yoruba cultural conflict in the form and style of a celebration of life and a total creation. Such dramatic examinations and experience provide theatrical presentations which appear to explode in front of our eyes. They are truly volcanic eruptions of the art forms caught in the middle of the culture of the people.

CHAPTER
7
Observations and Impressions
Dateline—Ghana, 1967, 1968, 1969

Giving witness to African theatre at the Dakar Festival had opened my eyes and had given me certain insights and impressions that would aid me during my stay in Africa. Immediately I had seen that African theatre was similar and yet dissimilar to Western theatre. African theatre was explosive, rich in culture and art forms, rituals and regalia. I saw African people examining African themes in an African way. *Kongi's Harvest* and *Danda* from Nigeria, *LeRoi Christophe* from Senegal, and *Hannibal* had all impressed me, but in different ways. *Kongi's Harvest*, though in English, was rich in African things. *Hannibal* was in Amharic and was historical; and *LeRoi Christophe* was in French an was historical. The plays were African, yet they were similar and dissimilar in style, language, and presentation. I saw an abundance of "materials for the creation of African theatre." And I was struck with the fact that both talent and technique lurked somewhere within these creations. I was overcome with one basic question, "What kind of special technique is necessary for the creation and the execution of this kind of celebration, total creation theatre?" "What were the language and communication problems for the playwright, the director, and the performers?" Perhaps a special technique was needed. But how did you get it? Where did it come from, and who taught it? How would it be learned? The technique for this special kind of creation, but not a technique that would rob it of its African character! In Dakar I began to accelerate my search for this special kind of technique. And now six years later I am still connected with the search.

When I traveled to East Africa in 1969 looking at the theatre scene before the Pan African Cultural Festival in Algiers, I saw essentially theatre in Africa. For example, I saw *Lock up Your Daughters* in Uganda (Kampala), and *Pink String and Sealing Wax* in Nairobi, Kenya. I had previously seen *The Crucible* in Ghana. But these plays were theatre in Africa and not African theatre, for they were not essentially connected with the lives of African people. At the same time I did see plays in East Africa that I would call African theatre, but of course technique is needed for both kinds of theatre, whether it be African theatre or theatre in Africa.

Upon my return to Africa in 1972 I witnessed *Anansegora* in Ghana. This was African theatre. In Nairobi, Kenya I saw *Othello*. This production was theatre in Africa. In Cairo, Egypt I saw mainly African theatre along with some theatre in Africa. In reflecting upon my impressions regarding the nature and development of theatre in Africa I sensed a basic problem in respect to both the concept and the technique for anyone involved in the creation of theatre in Africa or the "creation" and African theatre.

Before schools and missionary institutions came to Africa, technique for the culture and the art forms had been learned from the carriers of culture. For example, the master drummer had selected children at an early age to begin to instill within these children the skills and the techniques of the craft of master drumming. However, after learning the skills and developing the art of drumming these youngsters still had to jump the hurdle of "becoming" a master drummer approved and acclaimed by the members of his society. Consequently, the process of becoming a master drummer was usually a long hard process. The same could be said about the process of becoming a storyteller. The storyteller had to be a master performer. He was a "carrier of culture," consequently he had to know the folklore of his society. He also had to be able to create, re-create, interpret, dance, sing, mime, and do anything else that was necessary to fill his slot as a performer and to execute his role as a storyteller. And finally he had to be approved and acclaimed by the members of his society. In other words, TECHNIQUE for the celebration and total creation of theatre in traditional African societies

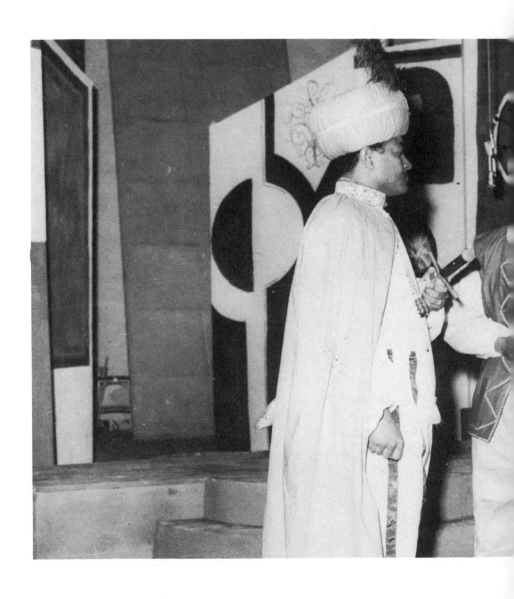

El Sultan El-Haier, Khartoum
(*National Theatre, Khartoum*)

was a learned process, involving hard work, beginning almost from birth. So at that particular time in history, the African child had a predisposition for his skills, his culture, and the TECHNIQUE leading to his art as a master performer, master drummer, master dancer or musician, or what have you. He was almost "born into the technique of performing."

Then came the schools. And the children were "removed" from their immediate society. And in a very short time they were taught to aspire to become Westernized or "modern." In a real sense they were taught to hate and despise most things African. And this naturally included their traditions, their art forms, and their culture. They found themselves abandoning an African way of doing things and striving for another way, usually a Western way, or the way of the imposed culture of the imperialistic conqueror. Their language usually was the first thing to suffer. They strove to learn English or French or German or Italian or some other Western language. And perhaps even more debilitating than this was the fact that they were "removed" from the carriers of their own culture— removed from their roots and their models of excellence. And gradually they began to lose their predisposition to African culture and their natural spirit as performers. The schools were "run" by the outsiders. And the outsiders certainly taught from outside to inside and never the other way around. For example, in teaching the English language, little or no concern was paid to how the Africans had learned their own vernacular languages. Little or no concern was paid to the African's physical habit patterns, his melody patterns, rhythmic patterns and intonations, or other aspects regarding their original languages. So by necessity the Africans approached their language learning from outside in rather than from inside out. And such was the case in most of their learning that did not stem from an African way of doing things.

Now that the schools, in a sense, have become a part of an African way of life, a new approach must be found to dispense and teach technique, especially as it relates to African culture, an African way of doing things, and the African's mode of expression and communication. But before this can be done, generally speaking, the African must learn to lose some of his self-hate. He must begin again to appreciate and love his own culture and his own way of doing things. He must find a way to break some of the old imposed bad habits learned during the period of the coming of the schools. And of course he will forever be aware of the fact that it is often harder to break old habits and instill new ones than it is merely to begin to learn the new habits. And naturally since he is in the middle of a culture conflict and a continent in transition he will have to search for his original roots upon which to build his world of today and tomorrow. A way of working and a new technique then becomes very important.

If the African goes to the schools to learn and no longer gets his learning from traditional societies, then the technique must come from the schools and the institutions of learning in Africa. It follows then that these institutions must first, however, conceptualize a philosophy and a way of working (a technique) for those Africans coming to the schools to learn.

Certainly then a concept of African theatre must first be realized by anyone wishing to learn how to make African theatre. And along with this concept must come technique, a way of working. But of course the institutions themselves must first become "African." And the technique must stem from African-centered approaches to life, creation, and celebrations, and African traditions.

A brief sampling of my impressions in diarylike form should illustrate the direction of my search in respect to technique in African theatre. As you will see my major concern in the observations addressed itself to technique, mainly for the actor and the director. I tried to answer some basic questions, using the celebration or the total theatrical experience in conventional theatre as a point of departure. Usually I asked myself, What is he doing? How well is he doing it? And is it worth doing? Is he believable, and do I understand him in light of the experience and the theatrical celebration? Is he involved in such a manner that he also involves me in the experience? I decided to save the "raw material of the play script" for some future date. At this particular point I was more interested in the process of theatre making and the product of the actor, especially since theatre had to be made and the player was one of the major links in the theatre-making process of the celebration and the total creation.

Trinidad in Ghana

On October 5, 1967, Janie and I went to see *Moon on a Rainbow Shawl* at the Ghana Drama Studio in Accra. I have called this experience Trinidad in Ghana simply because the play was written by Errol John, a Trinidadian actor. It was directed by Roy Watts, a West Indian. And the play itself focuses upon the "wasted dream" of the Trinidadian. Errol John, the actor, has performed in London with a number of repertory theatre companies, including the Old Vic, and has also appeared in a television series. Errol John, the playwright, won first prize in the *London Observer* 1967 play competition with *Moon on a Rainbow Shawl*. Roy Watts, the Producer-Director, is from Jamaica, West Indies. He came to Ghana several years ago and became involved in making movies for Ghana television and working in the theatre. Currently he is employed by GBC and is also working at the Institute of African Studies at Legon.

The play takes place in Trinidad in a crowded poverty-stricken backyard. It depicts the multitudinous problems and the difficult existence of the people living there. The rainbow of racial colors represents the many people who come from the variety of national origins found in the West Indies. The characters include Ephraim, a trolley bus driver who wants to go to England to better himself. In doing so however he will leave behind sweet innocent Rosa who loves him and will bear his child. Mrs. Adams, the backbone of her family, is the "ear" for nearly everyone in the neighborhood. Her husband, Charlie, who was once a famous cricketer, now lives in his dream. He has no job, and appears to have lost his ambition and hope. Ephraim and the Adams' clever young daughter Esther offer alternatives to this difficult rut in which the Adams seem to live. Esther is a good student in school and may well win a scholarship to further her education. Mavis, blunt, sarcastic and a realist, sells herself in order to pay the rent on time. In spite of her particular life-style she manages to get engaged to Prince, a flashy character who likes her the way she is. Old Mack, a lecherous, old rascal who owns all the houses in the neighborhood and also runs the local café, is the villain in the play.

This play was presented by The International Drama Group

which includes Ghanaians as well as expatriates. Among the expatriates are found West Indian, Afro-American, British, and White-American players in the troupe. Gwendolyn Benyard, as Mavis, was one of the most consistent, believable, and imaginative players of the cast. Gwen, an Afro-American, is a most talented and perceptive player. During the day she worked as a school teacher in the Accra Girls School but diligently pursued her acting career after school hours. Joe Akonor, Ghanaian, and a graduate of the School of Music and Drama of the University of Ghana, played Charlie Adams. Although physically he looked the part and also possesses a beautiful voice, I think he missed the essence of Charlie's dream. Better acting technique would have enabled him to have a stronger characterization of the "wasted Black" as seen through the eyes of this "trapped Trinidadian." Theresa Dadzie, also a graduate of the School of Music and Drama, played Esther Adams. Although she appeared to have the physical and visual aspects of young Esther as well as the right voice for her character, Miss Dadzie seemed to be "playing the character" and not "creating the role." As a result of this kind of acting she was often in and out of character and unable to sustain the essence or energy of Esther. Pearl Jones-Quartey, wife of the writer and educator Professor Jones-Quartey, played Rosa and evidenced a good feeling for her role. Evans Hunter of the Arts Center gave a good characterization of the Taxi Driver. Thomas Gunning and Claudia Slemp, both White Americans from USIS, played the soldier and the fisherwoman respectively. The sound effects were produced by Beattie Casely Hayford, a maker of movies for GBC. Prompting was by Helen Odamtten, and makeup was by Francis Sey, another graduate of the School of Music and Drama.

All in all the play provided the audience with an interesting evening. I do think however that both the director and the players as an ensemble missed the quality of the dream and the essence of struggle as depicted by the writer, Errol John. Essentially I think that they missed the mark here mainly because of the lack of significant technique both by the director and the players. I learned from the cast and the producer that much time had been spent on sets, costumes, lighting, and various other matters. I do wish that more time had been spent on the *people-element* of the play.

Why Do Africans Laugh at Tragedy?

On November 15, 1967, Janie and I went to the Accra Community Center to see two plays by The International Drama Group. The first play presented, *Three Women*, was a premiere performance. It was written by Ayi K. Armah, author of the novel *The Beautiful Ones Are Not Yet Born*. A Ghanaian, educated at Achimota School and Harvard University, Armah is presently living and working in New York City. He is a former staff member of Jeune Afrique in Paris. And although he has written several plays this is his first to be produced. The Director was Patricia Calder and the music was by Allen Tamakloe. The cast included Albertha Watts, Betty Bossman, Mary Yirenkyi, and William Okae. Bossman and Yirenkyi are graduates of the School of Music and Drama; William Okae is connected with the Accra Arts Center; and Albertha Watts is an Afro-American school teacher in Accra. On the whole the acting was adequate if not spectacular. All of the actors appeared to have grasped the essence of their characters in this short opening play.

A Yorkshire Tragedie is a revival of a previous experiment of touring theatre. With this same cast the play toured from January to March as a part of a Workers Brigade Show around the café-bars of Accra and its environs. At that time, for the tours, the rest of the evening's entertainment then consisted of band, cabaret interludes and a full-length musical drama—all in local languages. This was the first play in English, and the first one using a mixed cast to be taken to the café-bars. The play proved a great success even where audiences had almost no knowledge of English. The only change made in this performance tonight was that the first comic-exposition scene, which was then done in a Ga version, is now performed in the original English.

Both plays concern themselves with the problem of the abuse of power and examine the legal and personal obligations of the individual in his society.

The Three Women was an interesting play and merits publication. Although the performance was enjoyable the acting in sections was often average and spotty.

A Yorkshire Tragedie, although it was not intended to be, was a real farce and one of the funniest things I have ever seen. This was so mainly because of the direction of Ian Calder, who is British, and his "hamish" acting. He was full of noise and gesticulation and evidenced very little believability of characterization and actions. Because of his comic antics it was virtually impossible to pay much attention to anyone else in the play. No wonder the Africans laugh at tragedy. When it's presented in this manner anybody would laugh.

Modern Ghanaian Theatre at the University

On November 23, 1967, Janie, the children, and I went to the Commonwealth Lecture Theatre of the University of Ghana to witness two student productions by the Drama Division of the School of Music and Drama.

The first play, *Refund*, is an adaptation of the original play by Fritz Karinthy. The Producer was Daniel Boaten. The Stage Manager was Fred Akuffo-Lartey and the Assistant Stage Manager was Christina Ampah. A former pupil of a secondary school comes back to the school to demand his tuition fees which he paid during his school days eighteen years ago. The pupil is to be reexamined and is to get his tuition fees back if he fails the examination. The staff decide not to fail him, and propound theories to prove the pupil right though he answers wrongly. He passes with a distinction in every subject and is outwitted.

I had a difficult time tuning in to and understanding the language of the players despite the fact that the play was performed in English. The players have not learned to communicate from the stage and need much work on voice and speech production. They have not yet learned to listen, nor have they learned to build a character. Truthfully I had expected to see something a little more African in character and less Western in form and character. The adaptation of the play did lend itself however to the Ghanaian energy and style, and most of the players seemed to be able to relate to the experience of a Ghanaian school situation. Obed Ababio, as Owusu, the former pupil, gives evidence of being the best potential as an actor from among the cast of players. Joe Dankwa, as the history master, also bears watching. Though the play was rather enjoyable the direction was static and on the whole the acting was spotty and uneven.

The second play, *Scenario*, by L. Du Garde Peach was produced by Charles Flynt. The stage manager was Patience Addo and the assistant stage manager was Rowland Harrunah. This farcical comedy, set in a producer's office, exposes the phony nature of Hollywood approach to film making. This is shown by the producer's attitude towards his artists, the author, his own assistants, and the motion picture business. I think the first mistake in this play was in its selection inasmuch as the experience of the "Hollywood scene" is far removed from the experience of the Ghanaian players. Consequently all through the evening the players were hamming it up instead of taking the germ of an experience close to themselves and then creating an experience which can translated and communicated to an audience. In my opinion, this particular play had very little connection with the lives of Ghanaian people. It was far too Western in character and form. The players tried to make a go of it, but they too, just as the actors in the first play, were very limited in theatre technique. Both the communication and the characterizations were poor. The director, Charles Flynt, also tried to make a go of it, but he too was limited; first with a play that wouldn't work, and secondly with limited instruments of action and creativity, his players. On the whole it was a tired show, boring, uninvolved, uninspired, and removed from the realm of the experience of both the actors and the audience. And as I left the theatre, I reflected on the question, "Where is the celebration when the experience and the form best suit another culture, and especially when it is communicated in the 'borrowed language of the oppressor'?"

Modern Ghanaian Theatre

On December 1, 1967, Janie and I went to see *Mother's Tears* at the Ghana Drama Studio. The play was presented by The Ghana Playhouse under the auspices of the Institute of Art and Culture and produced and directed by Kwaw Ansah. Kwaw Ansah, also the playwright, is a young Ghanaian who works in television and movie making for GBC. Ansah studied theatre techniques in America (New York City), where I first met him several years ago.

The play takes place in a fishing suburb of Sekondi (Ghana). Amponsa, an illiterate fisherman of rather unique character, takes a relatively young and beautiful wife, thus becoming a husband of two wives at the age of sixty. The conflict stems from Amponsa and his only son, Antobam, a scholar. It is highlighted when Antobam's mother, Araba, the elder wife, resents the advantages she has lost by the presence of the new spouse, Adoma. The conflict is resolved however by Antobam himself who realizes that no matter how hard Amponsa is, he is his father. At this point, Antobam also becomes convinced that "a crab does not beget a bird," and that it is the very blood that gave him (Antobam) birth that has also swollen his father's veins to become what he (father) is. In a real sense, the play examines polygamy in Ghanaian society and the role of the father in the family.

The Dance Ensemble of the Accra Drama Group was featured in the play. Unfortunately the drumming, dancing, and music were not directly connected to the play. Consequently it appeared as an aside rather than as an integral part of the drama. The play which presented an examination of an aspect of Ghanaian life provided an interesting evening in the theatre. However, here again, on the whole, basic technique from the director and the players was missing. A concerted ensemble effort would have raised the evening's performance to a higher level of theatre. Some of the players however did manage to rise above the level of mediocrity. Gwendolyn Benyard, who played Araba, the elder wife, created an interesting, believable characterization with great involvement. She was also able to sustain this characterization throughout the entire play and thereby create and transmit an experience from the stage. Sandy Arkhurst, as the Mender, was very believable and had some high moments of creativity. Mary Yirenkyi, as Jesiwa, Amponsa's mother, created a good characterization of the old mother and evidenced the appropriate physical and emotional energy of the character. Samuel Manu, as Kufashew, the head-relative, had some very interesting moments.

The Celebration—A Ghanaian Festival of Arts

On February 14, 1968, I traveled to Kumasi to attend the Seventh Annual Festival of Arts at the Cultural Center in Kumasi. I shall forever hold fond memories of the trip by car with Kwabena Nketia and Bertie Opoku to Kumasi. The sharing of life's dramatic experiences with Bertie and Kwabena, drinking in the beautiful African terrain from Accra to Kumasi, learning about Ghana through the traditional and artistic insights of two of the visionaries of the national theatre movement, all helped to prepare me for the Arts Festival in which I would soon be immersed.

This festival was truly an African celebration of life, connecting both with the African traditions and the modern conventional modes of theatrical presentation. It was full of music, dance, theatre, and the play of life. Needless to say I was greatly impressed by the rich display of traditional music, dance, and theatre. Two celebrations of the festival, one an experience and one an event, however, both stand out in my memory. It is about these two celebrations that I wish to speak. One is the adaptation of the play *Antigone* and the other is the musical program, a concert, by the School of Music and Drama from Legon.

Dr. A. A. Y. Kyerematen, Director of the Cultural Arts Center in Kumasi, had adapted *Antigone* for a Ghanaian audience. The play was presented in Ghanaian style and used as its language Twi, the language of the Ashanti people. The emphasis in the play was on court life in African style rather than on Antigone and her personal dilemma. As the play opens, the King and his court enter, Ghanaian style with children; and the greetings were also in Ghanaian style. I liked the use of Agoo which brought about an audience response and empathy and vibration. The expressions Yoo, as well as ei, ei, which is surprise, so what, shout, etc., ei, ei, ei, look out, etc. were also used to great advantage. I particularly liked the King's attitude (Service Odoi), bearing and sense of authority. He had good stage and audience presence and gave evidence of talent and theatre technique. I also liked the bearing and stage presence of most of the players. They all seemed relaxed, with just the proper amount of energy for their characterizations. Though at times they appeared to be too casual, they seemed to be enjoying what they were doing, and as a result they involved the audience and evidenced believability in respect to their actions. The blocking was good and the arrangement of the people on the stage was most effective which was no easy task since there were twenty-three people on the stage at one time. The dramatic experience would have been even more effective however if we had seen a sense of urgency and concern in respect to what's at stake in the play. For example I missed a real connection and relationship between the sisters (Ismene and Antigone). I also would have enjoyed a stronger relationship between the King (Creon) and Antigone. The son (Haemon), however, did create and establish the proper attitude, bearing, and relationship in respect to his father and Antigone. As the play ends the body lies in state, uncovered as the chorus sings. All through the play, music, drumming, dance, and mime had been interwoven with the basic actions and characterizations in the play, making for a total creation or celebration of life experience.

Though the performance was played in Twi, a language which I do not speak (although I am studying it), I understood the play and enjoyed it immensely. The audience's response to the play was very enthusiastic as they participated from time to time in the celebration themselves. All throughout *Antigone* I mused, They've opened up the play and really made it African. In fact, it is possible that *Antigone* plays even better in Twi than many of the English versions which I have seen. For after all the experience is connected with the traditions and life-styles of African people. And the style is African, which I imagine is similar to what the Greek people were doing in style at Antigone's moment of time.

The Concert of Instrumental Music by the School of Music and Drama of Legon featured in its program the Atenteben Ensemble, Guitar Ensemble, Xylophone Music, String Ensemble and Flute Trio, and the School Orchestra, and Music by and with Kwabena Nketia. The Atenteben Orchestra is a merger of two groups each of which toured Europe successfully in the summer of 1965, one to the Commonwealth Festival of Arts in London, Cardiff, Liverpool, Glasgow, Manchester and the other to West Germany, East Germany, Hungary, Poland, Czechoslovakia, and Russia. The leader of the group was William Amoaku, a former student of the School of

Music and Drama who had just joined the staff as instructor in Atenteben and Drumming. The school orchestra is a young orchestra consisting of players from one to three years' experience. This was their second engagement outside the university campus. Four months earlier they had given a successful concert to a large audience made up of students at the Ada Training College and the general public at Ada.

The performance by the Atenteben Ensemble featured music composed by Kwabena Nketia and Dr. E. Amu. The Atenteban flute, a Ghanaian instrument, when used in ensemble performances, produces rich melodious sounds. I particularly enjoyed the performance and was greatly impressed by the compositions of both Nketia and Amu. Although Ghana is a country of guitar players, few of the musicians play from music. The guitar quartet showed how authentic Western music could also be played by performing selections from Handel and others. Kakraba Lobi played "Work and Happiness," a popular selection appreciated and enjoyed all over Ghana. Kakraba is one of the best known xylophonists in Ghana who was discovered at a Kumasi market by Professor Nketia and was taken to the University. He toured Eastern Europe and Russia with the School of Music and Drama in 1965 and was twice in Germany in 1966 with Professor Nketia and played to a capacity hall in Israel in June 1963. Kakraba is one of Ghana's most versatile and ingenious performers. His music is a treat to any ear. Needless to say, I enjoyed his music at the festival. In the years that followed I was to learn to know the man and the artist and his music.

The concert of instrumental music was a dramatic event with interspersed experiences. It too was another approach to the Ghanaian celebration of life.

A Ghanaian Celebration in the Theatre

On March 5, 1968, Janie, the children, and I went to the Arts Centre in Accra to see *The Lion and the Jewel* presented by the Arts Council of Ghana. The play was produced by George Andoh Wilson and featured the Ghana Dance Ensemble under the direction of Albert Mawere Opoku (Bertie Opoku), who choreographed the show.

The elders say that "If you try to look into the eyes of a dead person, you see a ghost." Sidi, the village belle in *The Lion and the Jewel*, has this kind of confrontation. Sidi, a young girl of the village of Ilujinle, is very much loved by a young school teacher, Lakunle, in the same village. Sidi, however, in all seriousness and with all the pride of the tradition of the village, refuses to marry Lakunle because he is not prepared to pay the bride-price. To Lakunle the idea of the bride-price is "A savage custom, archaic, degrading, humiliating, unspeakable, redundant, retrogressive, irremarkable, unpalatable." And as the story progresses you wonder if Lakunle is a man of words or action.

The big chief—Bale Baroka, Lion of Ilujinle, who has several wives, lives in this same village. At the age of sixty-two, he still wants Sidi. Using the same trick he had used to get all his wives, Baroka sends his elder wife—Sadiku, to persuade Sidi to come to dinner. Sidi however refuses to attend the dinner. She already knows that a young girl never enters the Lion's house and comes out unscathed.

Losing the first round, Baroka decides to make-believe that he is impotent, and tells Sadiku. Sadiku, who is very happy to learn of such news, pretends she is very sorry. Immediately she goes to tell Sidi and they both rejoice over the news.

Later, Sidi decides to go to Baroka's house to tease him. Baroka pretends not to notice her. He is busily engaged in his daily exercises and does not have time for women. But Sidi is soon to learn that Baroka's plan has been worked out with great precision. That was when she saw the ghost.

In my opinion this is one of Wole Soyinka's most theatrical plays in which he gives witness to the celebration and the total creation of the African's art. As I watched the celebration my thoughts went back to 1964 and Wole Soyinka. Yvonne Walker, of AMSAC, and I had gone to Kennedy Airport to meet Soyinka and take him to his hotel. At the hotel we had a spirited provocative discussion about Africa, theatre, and people. I had already been impressed by Soyinka's skills and talents in writing, but after our meeting and the conversation I was even more impressed by his sharp wit, intelligence, and perception. Soyinka is certainly one of today's leading lights in the world of theatre.

I enjoyed this play very much because on the whole it was well written and well produced and generally speaking the Playhouse Players were able to exist on the stage in terms of an experience. I also liked the directorial concept in which Wilson and Opoku collaborated and shared their expertise in the process of the total creation. Although this marriage was a good one I think it would have been far better with more of an integration of the word, the dance, and the music on the stage. The players need stronger direction in respect to coordination between the dance-performers and the other performers in order to bring about a unified ensemble experience upon the stage. Of course much of this must come from the players themselves who must understand the nature and the concept of African theatre in respect to the need for a unity of art forms in the total creation. This calls for a complete performer who embraces first the concept and next the need to train the instrument in such a manner that it will be able to create and sustain this total experience in a shared manner on the stage. The mere idea of a specialized dancer, a specialized musician, or a specialist in the mastery of the word will give way to the unity and completeness of the performer who is able to synchronize the vocal life with the physical, emotional, and intellectual life of the character in order to produce the experience necessary in the total creation. The player will be an embodiment of his culture and an exemplifier of his art forms, and when he finds a good play such as *The Lion and the Jewel* he will have a happy successful marriage.

The Ghana Playhouse was formed in May 1963 to help promote theatre in Ghana. It is a voluntary organization whose aims are to generate wide interest in theatre and to encourage artists. They are doing this through production of plays, poetry readings, and drama workshops. The group is also interested in establishing music halls and organizing variety shows. In short, the Ghana Playhouse is out to infuse the theatre spirit into the general public. Thus far, since its formation, the group has been able to present five plays: *A Raisin in the Sun, The Day of the Lion, Deep Are the Roots, The New Patriots, and The Lion and the Jewel.* The Ghana Playhouse is international and opens its doors to anyone who has an active interest in theatre.

Kofi Yirenkyi strikes me as being a dedicated theatre-maker with talent, skill, and imagination. As Lakunle in the play, I felt he understood his character and possessed an instrument upon which he could play this particular experience. I also felt that he used imagination and daring in order to implement his actions. I would like however to see him trust his work and his inner experience and not force or make it happen. His work will affect his behavior, and in turn he will have a more relaxed, involved, and believable characterization. As a result his character will have even more involvement and vibrations with the audience. He will not be "playing the role," he will become the role. Generally speaking, Phyllis Quarshie was effective as Sidi, and Joe Akunor was effective as Baroka. In fact I found Joe Akunor much better playing the role of Baroka, than he was as Charlie Adams in *Moon on a Rainbow Shawl*. He seemed to be more involved and connected with Baroka as a character than he was with Charlie Adams. And the communication of the experience was better in as much as he was able to merge his vocal life (he has a beautiful voice) with his physical and intellectual life. Gwendolyn Benyard played Sadiku, head wife of Baroka, and was very good. I enjoyed her as I have in her previous performances in other plays. From the beginning of the play to the end she was immersed in the process of creating, embellishing, and sustaining her character and communicating the experience of that character to the audience.

Ghanaian Theatre in the Making

On September 1, 1968 Janie and I went to the opening of The Arts Centre Theatre Season. We saw three Ghanaian one-act plays presented by the Ghana Institute of Art and Culture and produced by G. Y. D. Lurd-Kekey and N. K. Hoedzie. Lurd-Kekey studied theatre techniques at the Moscow Art Theatre and is an actor and director-producer. Hoedzie is a graduate of The School of Music and Drama at Legon. The plays were performed by The Arts Centre Drama Company which was formed on May 1, 1967. The group consists of twenty boys and ten girls selected from the various regions of the country, who are being trained in all fields of the theatre including the following subjects: acting, stage lighting, stage designing and construction, traditional drumming and dancing, speech, poetry, mime and movement, theatre history, theatre business administration, and judo. This particular production directed by their tutors was the result of three months' vigorous training and is their first public appearance.

The three plays were experimental in both form and content and appeared to me to be still in their raw form of development. For example, *Crackpot* by Saka Acquaye strikes me as being very Western and not very African. Jack and Willie are friends. They both saw active service in the Burma campaign during the last war. Both of them unfortunately suffered from a mental disease and were once mental patients at the Asylum. The question is, however, were they cured? "B" has lodged a complaint to the police about a man who has been wooing her on the telephone anytime the husband Jack is away on business. The police mount a big search for this mysterious caller and after many unsuccessful attempts, suspect Jack and arrest him. "B" tries in vain to persuade the police to free the husband. Despite "B" 's efforts Jack is taken away, which leaves "B" in great confusion. Eventually however the Crackpot exposes himself and we learn the truth about who was really cured.

Papa by Patience Carboo-Sumney examines a slice-of-life situation of a frustrated mother and her child abandoned by a callous husband who lives in a world of self-disillusionment and hypocrisy.

Lonesome-Rose is a light comedy springing from a situation in a game of chance. Fondo's ticket has won seventy-five thousand new cedis on African Football Pools, but loses this large sum of money to his employer, Miss Opoku, Headmistress of Kindergarten School.

In my opinion neither *Papa* nor *Lonesome-Rose* is well developed and they both examine content of little significance. Both plays are more Western in form and content than African. Generally speaking, all three plays suffer from mediocre acting and directing, but especially the acting. The players need to learn to listen on the stage, to become involved in the action of the moment, to develop concentration and control. And above all they need to concern themselves with the use of the word in respect to faulty melody, sense meaning and word emphasis. The plays and the players both suffer from the lack of specific actions which are necessary for characterization and story development. Related to the problem of actions is the problem of unnecessary anticipation in respect to speaking and listening by the players. On the positive side of the ledger, however, the company is eager, interested, and desirous of learning theatre technique, and especially the ability to communicate and express themselves in the language of the theatre. Also, both directors, Lurd-Kekey and Hoedzie appear to be dedicated to the theatre and possess the theatre background and talent necessary for the development of such a company. In the future I would hope to see the company perform theatre in the vernacular language as well as in English and the borrowed word.

A Ghanaian Celebration in Dance

On Monday, September 30, 1968 Janie and I went to see a special performance by the Arts Centre Dance Troupe at the Arts Centre in Accra, in aid of the YWCA. I had seen this troupe perform before. In fact I had taken the children to see them in an outdoor performance on a Saturday afternoon. At that time, despite intermittent rain, we thoroughly enjoyed ourselves. The afternoon had been an occasion for celebration. Ghanaians had come in this spirit to enjoy themselves, and many people entered the performance area to participate along with the regular members of the troupe. To-night however was an indoor performance at 8:00 P.M.

The program-celebration was divided into two parts. Part One began by a demonstration on drums by the female members of the group. This was truly "a moment of women's liberation" and the drumming performance was most enjoyable. Next was a "Fontom-from Dance Suite." This is a celebration of a warrior's dance of Akans, believed to be originated from Akwamu. It is said that a hunter went hunting and heard a sound of waterfall. He went home and prepared a drum to suit the sound he had heard; hence the dance was started. It is danced during the performance of funeral rites, festivals and on other important occasions. "Adzogbo," which followed, is a fetish dance of the people of Dahomey. It is danced during the performance of the fetish and on special occasions. I enjoyed especially the ritual aspects of the dance. Next came the "Madedji," which is a recreational dance from Jongu district in Volta Region, usually danced for enjoyment and during funeral rites. The "Krashie Dente" is another fetish dance. It comes from the Krashie District in the Volta Region and is danced during the performance of the fetish. The last dance before the intermission was the "Ada-Kete," which is a moonlight dance for Ada youth in the Eastern Region. Young men and women gather in the evening to do this dance when the moonlight comes. As I watched this dance I recalled the beautiful music of James Bland, America's outstanding composer and minstrel man. I began to hum his melody, "In the Evening by the Moonlight."

After the intermission, Part Two began with an "Ashanti Adowa." The Adowa is a dance which was invented by the Ashanti women. During the warring days of the Ashanti nation, women gathered together in the evening and played and danced to express their moral support for their men. Today the Adowa is also danced during festivals. I particularly enjoyed the spirit and energy of this dance which is recognized and appreciated throughout all of Ghana. The Ga women have a recreational dance used by them during fishing seasons. They also dance it during festivals. The dance is the "Ayika," which was next to follow. Then came the "Tokoe," a dance from the Ada district in the Eastern Region. This dance is used when young men and women are getting married. It is also used however as a recreational dance. The "Sebre" is a Lobi dance of work and happiness from Lawra district in the Upper Region. This dance is used to invoke the gods and ask for prosperous harvest. Both the music and the dance are enjoyed by both performer and audience, and the Sebre ranks among my favorite dances. Next came a popular dance, "Kpalogo," one of the latest West African recreational dances created by Gas. This is an enjoyable dance both to watch and to perform. It is usually done by young men and women. The final performance of the evening was an "Yewe Dance Suite," a powerful fetish dance from Anlo District in the Volta Region. It is performed in the main by the members of the fetish cult. It includes many variations and the drum rhythm dictates the pace and style of the dance. The dancers gave evidence of talent, technique, and a connection with their traditions. Our evening at the Arts Centre was a most exhilarating experience in which we were not merely spectators but participants so to speak in the exciting celebration in dance.

Yewe, a fetish dance from the Volta region (*Arts Centre, Ghana*)

International Theatre in Ghana

On October 4, 1968, Janie and I went to see *Six Characters in Search of an Author* at the Arts Center in Accra presented by the International Drama Group in association with the Arts Council of Ghana.

Six Characters in Search of an Author, written by Luigi Pirandello in 1921, is considered a classic of modern theatre. It has been successfully translated into many languages and is considered to be of universal significance. The play examines aspects of communication such as the noncommunication among people thrown together by chance, the inability to shake off one's destiny, and definitional difficulties and frame of reference difficulties wherein humans often feel that hell is other people.

A company of actors is rehearsing a play when six people dressed in black make a sudden and mysterious appearance. An odd group, a father, a mother, a stepdaughter, a son, a young boy and a little girl. They bring with them a drama . . . the story of their lives . . . an unfinished play, telling how the author who called them into being has refused to provide a conclusion to their lives. Each is tormented by a passion which consumes him. With the father it is remorse, with the stepdaughter, revenge, with the mother, sorrow, and with the son it is contempt for the rest of them. Only the small children have nothing to say. But ironically enough they innocently pay the price of the adults' obsession with their own emotions. *Six Characters* is the precursor of works such as Beckett's *Waiting for Godot*, Sartre's *Huis Clos*, and Pinter's *The Caretaker*.

The play was produced by Toni Walter who used a mixed cast of expatriots and Ghanaians. For me the evening didn't work at all. It never seemed to get off the ground. I attribute this to the director and the players and their inability to involve the audience in the experience provided by the playwright. On the whole, the cast lacked even a clue of working together as an ensemble group. There were few character-connections by the players and certainly not enough involvement or concentration in respect to meaningful or believable player-actions. One actor did however make me pay attention to the stage and the play and keep me from going to sleep.

He was Paul Danquah who played The Producer. Paul gives evidence of good stage presence and a combination of talent and technique. Paul, the son of the late Dr. J. B. Danquah, is a lawyer by profession, but in my opinion could also be an actor by profession if he chose to be. Frances Sey who played the Step-Daughter had some interesting moments on the stage and shows promise as an actress. She is a recent graduate of the School of Music and Drama.

Six Characters in Search of an Author may certainly be of universal significance, but for me, this particular production missed the mark and merely cast a fleeting shadow in the direction of anything that might be called a Ghanaian experience in the theatre.

A Celebration in Music—An Evening of Soul

On October 10, 1968 I went to the Arts Centre in Accra to witness a presentation by The Arts Council of Ghana. The program was billed as A Choral Night with the Dama's Choir. Ishmael Adams is the director of the Choir. The American guest conductor was Jester Hairston. Ishmael Adams is one of Ghana's most talented choir directors, while Jester Hairston, gifted Afro-American composer, singer, and director, has been a movie actor and composer for many years.

This coming together of the Black American Jester Hairston and the Ghanaians through the Dama's Choir provided a rare treat for music lovers. For me it was a real night of "soul." This was indeed a unique celebration and a memorable moment of theatre. The air was filled with electricity brought about because of the vibrations between Jester Hairston and Ishmael Adams and the members of the Dama's Choir. And the audience was at one with both the evening and the performers. The music, written mainly by Jester Hairston, and Ishmael Adams, was pleasant to hear and see performed. Part One of the program started with "Camp Meeting Tonight" followed by "Oh, Rocka My Soul" which is a very spirited rhythmic number. Next came a variety of numbers showing the versatility of the Dama's Choir. For example, "Now Is the Month of Maying" by Ernest A. Dicks was a song filled with harmony. "Singing in the Rain" by Franz Joseph Haydn was a selection for three girls, while "My Bonny Lass, She Smileth" by Thomas Morley was for three men. Jester Hairston's "Go Down in the Lonesome Valley" received an enthusiastic response from the audience, but when he followed it with his song "Free at Last," the house actually began to rock. I wondered how he could top his selection "Free at Last" but he did with his "Mary's Boy Chile," a Christmas number made popular in America and in England by Harry Belafonte.

Part Two of the program opened with Hairston's "Poor Man Lazarus" which is a rhythmic moving number. It was followed by Hairston's "You Better Mind" which puts Ishmael and Jester singing together more than in some of the other numbers. The two of them performed along with the choir as though they had all been working together for years. Hairston's "Goin Down Dat Lonesome Road" is a mood piece and was excellent for the audience participation with the whistling and snapping of fingers. Hairston's "Gossip, Gossip" is a fun song and was also enthusiastically received by the audience. Next came the Ghanaian folk songs all sung in the Ga language. First was Saka Acquaye's "Yee, Yei Yee" ("Twin's Song") adapted from the folk opera *The Lost Fishermen*. And this was a natural for both the choir and the audience. Ishmael Adams' "Nyontsere Le Edse" ("Moon Song") and "Lose Duade" ("Village Cassava") were both pleasing to hear and see performed. But it was his "Se Mi Ni Oya" ("Farewell Song"), so popular with most Ghanaians, that brought enthusiastic vocalizing from the audience. It was now time for Jester Hairston to come forth with another of his numbers and he did so with his "God's Gonna Build up Zion's Wall." This was followed by I. Adams' "Go and Sin No More" which is a very moving number. The evening was afraid to end when Jester Hairston captivated both the choir and the audience with his "Amen," an audience participation number. Encore after encore kept us there singing and enjoying the celebration through music. But finally realizing that even the best must come to rest, the night ended.

A Ghanaian Celebration in Theatre

On Thursday October 31, 1968, Janie and I and the family went to see a request performance of *Odasani* ("Everyman") at the Ghana Drama Studio.

The play examines everyman's conflict in respect to how he will answer his God when Death calls. Odasani (Everyman) is a name for the human being. In this play, which is a Ghanaian interpretation of the ageless play *Everyman*, it is a prosperous young man who bears that name and, in bearing it, stands for all mankind.

Death calls him, as Death will call all men, and we see the story of a man caught unprepared and what he has to go through before he is able to face his end.

The play is set forth in four parts. In Part One we find companions at a drinking bar. Odasani walks in ready for fun, and proud to display his wealth in treating everybody. The thought of death has not even entered his mind. In Part Two Odasani decides to move the party from the bar to his home. On his way to get his car, he is confronted by Death. At first he takes the entire matter as a joke. When Death orders him to go and give an account of his life before God, Odasani finds himself unprepared and greatly afraid. In Part Three we find Odasani learning the bitter lesson that he must travel his Death-journey all by himself. No one is prepared to become Odasani's substitute. His drinking companions, relatives in the family house, his wives, all forsake him. In his moment of crisis he learns that his wealth is the most useless of all things to him. In Part Four, finally, all alone, Odasani becomes self-contained and turns his thoughts inward. Agonized he is led to grace through repentance.

The play was written by Efua Sutherland and performed by her Kusum Agoromba company of players. It was produced by Sandy Arkhurst and the sets were designed by John Kedjani. Kwamena Ampah and his musicians (guitar, drum, flute) have provided excellent music which becomes an integral part of the story line, the conflicts and the actions of the play. In fact the music opens up the story, sets the mood, helps develop the situation and gives the chorus an opportunity to participate in the action and comment on the development of the story. Thus the music adds another dimension to this particular celebration. Unfortunately however this production of *Odasani* has great needs with respect to its acting and its directing. The Kusum Agoromba company has not yet mastered sufficient basic acting technique to enrich the play or bring it alive. There are few solid characterizations among the players. They have life but it is not theatrical life. Consequently the play lacks spine; the production lacks spine, and the direction lacks focus. Even the staging or blocking needs to be improved, for generally speaking you can't see the players, especially when an action or a development in the story is being highlighted. Each picture on the stage should be easily seen and understood and connected with the basic actions of the play. This makes it easier for an audience to retain its involvement regarding the major experience of the moment. This particular play requires a strong player for the role of Odasani. The role cries out for a talented player with technique who can create and develop this major character in the play. For it is around the fate of Odasani that the audience focuses its attention. And it is also around Odasani that the players focus their attention. Odasani generates the energy of the experience and controls the spine of the play and the celebration. It is around this character, Odasani, that the director should attempt to orchestrate the major score of the play and choreograph the actions and movement of the celebration. In my opinion it is essentially for this reason that this production misses the mark. Peter Amoah, who plays the role of Odasani, has not yet been able to fill this character. His physical, intellectual, emotional, and vocal life have not yet all come together to form the essence of Odasani.

On February 20, 1969 Janie and I and the family went to see this same play, *Odasani*, at the Ghana Drama Studio. And this time the Kusum Agoromba players had "put it all together," so to speak. Sandy Arkhurst, the producer, had given us a good production of the play. And what had happened between October 31, 1968 and February 20, 1969? In the first place the producer had tightened his play and now there were definite connections between the experience of the celebration, from the director to the players to the audience. The players had better involvement and seemed more connected with the basic actions of the play rather than "putting on an act" or playing an idea. The blocking and placement of each player was logical and made more sense than it had in the previous production. But more than anything else I think it was Kofi Yirenkyi who made it possible for this production to rise to its high level of performance. Kofi Yirenkyi played the role of Odasani, and by all standards, he was the outstanding player of the cast. Kofi, a graduate of the School of Music and Drama, is a talented and sensitive actor. He became an embodiment of his culture and an exemplifier of his arts. He was the experience on the stage, making it possible for the audience to share the experience in the midst of the celebration. *Odasani* is played in Twi, the language of the Ashanti people, rather than in English, Ghana's borrowed language.

Ghanaian Theatre at the University

On December 19, 1968, Janie and I and the children went to the Commonwealth Lecture Theatre of the University of Ghana to witness two student productions by the Drama Division of the School of Music and Drama.

The first play, *The Pot of Chicken Soup,* was an adaptation of *The Pot of Broth* by W. B. Yeats. In this adaptation, an old hungry beggar makes a selfish, stingy, and greedy village woman believe that a stone he has can produce a pot of chicken soup, "akpeteshi" and palmwine. He outwits the woman by using her own chicken and ingredients for preparing the soup.

The beggar takes the pot of chicken soup away, leaving the supposed magic stone behind to provide the woman with another pot of soup. The producer was Adriana Panou-Gaba. The stage manager was Kofi Nipah, and the assistant stage manager was Jones Kyei. Though I enjoyed the play it was obvious that this was a student production. This was so essentially because of the uneven acting and directing. Fred Akuffo-Lartey, who played A Beggar, showed the most promise of the three players. However, both Christina Ampah as Mame Abena and Chris Tackie as Paa Kojo also gave evidence of promise as potential actors and theatre-makers. All three members of the cast, however, need direction. They need to be taught how to exist in terms of the characters on the stage. They need to learn basic theatre technique and they need guidance from professional directors of the academic professors or lecturers in addition to the guidance they are receiving from the student directors.

The second play, *The Shepherds of Trom*, is an improvised adaptation of the Wakefield Second Shepherds' Pageant from Everyman and medieval miracle plays.

It is a moonlit night and the shepherds, Issa, Maama and Yarro swing into the storytelling mood after a hearty meal.

Gruma, the sheep-stealer, intrudes and is invited to pass the night with the shepherds. He cunningly exploits the situation to steal a sheep. Christmas is in the air and he must celebrate it in a big way. The theft is cleverly concealed by Dede, his wife, but the sheep betrays them.

Gruma is promised a sound beating the next morning but he is miraculously saved by an angel who announces the nativity in which Gruma's house becomes the birthplace of Christ.

Franklin Akrofi was the producer. The stage manager was Osei-Wusu, and the assistant stage manager and prompter was Lucy Osei. The acting in this play was similar to the acting of the players in the first play. It was often spotty and uninvolved. The players need to learn to listen and they also need to learn how to communicate honestly and with believability from the stage. I feel that the student directors could profit greatly from professional directors from the university who would serve as models of excellence for these student productions and in a sense still enable the student to "do his own thing" as a director. Obed Ababio, as Gruma The Sheep-stealer, stood out among the players and appears to have a good flair for stage presence and theatrical awareness.

The National Orchestra and Choir—International Music

On January 29, 1969, Janie and I and the children went to the Goethe Institute, where, in cooperation with the Arts Council of Ghana, they presented The National Orchestra and Choir under the direction of Philip Gbeho.

The evening concert began with the playing of the national Anthem which was composed by Philip Gbeho. The selections for the evening were all Western and included the works of Handel, Beethoven, Bach, Mendelssohn, and Geoffrey. In the first part of the program, Haydn's "Achieved Is the Glorious Work" and Mendelssohn's "Be Not Afraid" were most enjoyable. Handel's "Water Music" was not melodic and technically attractive, but his "Zadock the Priest" was an excellent mood piece and for my ears and eyes was the most enjoyable selection in the first part of the program.

In the second part of the program Beethoven's Symphony No. 1 was well performed and appreciated by the audience. Of the selections performed by the choir, Handel's "Hallelujah Chorus" was the best. Handel's "Behold, I Tell you a Mystery" was a showpiece for the male voice of R. Armah. Generally speaking, the male voices were far superior to the female voices in the choir. To my ear the female voices sounded shrill, off pitch, and tight, while the male voices were well focused, melodious, and pleasing. After Handel's "Worthy Is the Lamb and Amen Chorus" the Orchestra concluded the evening's performance with the playing of the National Anthem. The members of the orchestra all handled their instruments well along with the appropriate interpretation and mood of each selection.

Philip Gbeho, the conductor, is also director of the Music and Arts Council of Ghana. He is a warm personable man who spoke often of the "rich exciting days of Ghana." And I thought to myself, "Here is a man who feels that he is now being 'passed by.'" From this point of view he reminded me of Professor Sterling Brown, one of the giants of literature and especially Black Literature in America, who is virtually unknown by many of the new young Blacks of today.

Philip Gbeho was born in 1905 in Keta by the seashore. He went to the Catholic Mission School in 1911. Later he became a choir boy and in 1918 became a solo singer in the church choir. Later he ran away every Saturday on foot to Lome, a distance of twenty-five miles, to practice on the harmonium.

In 1925 he entered Achimota Training College as a teacher in training. He completed his training in December 1928 and took appointment as a teacher in the Catholic School, Keta in 1929. He was recalled to Achimota as a Music Master in 1938. In 1954 he became the chairman of the Interim Committee of the Arts Council, charged with the duty of combing the country for evidences of indigenous culture. In 1957, he won the Ghana National Anthem competition. From 1949 to 1952, he studied at Trinity College of Music, London, and graduated in this College as Teacher: G.T.C.L., L.R.A.M., L.T.C.L., etc.

The Celebration—A Ghanaian Festival of Arts

On January 31, 1969, Janie and I traveled to Kumasi to attend the Eighth Annual Festival of Arts at the Cultural Center in Kumasi. That evening we went to see an Eastern Region Performance of Joe de Graft's play in English, *Sons and Daughters*, by the Koforidua Amateur Drama Group. Nic Hoedzie, who also played James Ofosu, was the producer.

The play examines an aspect of the role or position of the father in Ghanaian society and his relationship to his children. James Ofosu, father of George, Kofi, Aaron, and Maanan will accept no advice from his children, from his wife Hannah or his brother Fosuwa on choosing a profession for his children. He will only listen to and accept advice from his friend, Lawyer Bonu. He wanted Aaron to be an engineer and Maanan a lawyer—"Ghana's first lady lawyer" as he puts it. But Aaron and Maanan would not agree with the father on the professions chosen for them. In fact, Aaron wants to be a painter instead of an engineer and Maanan wants to be a stage dancer instead of becoming a lawyer. The father even went as far as accepting Lawyer Bonu's proposal to make Maanan work with him in his office. Maanan was obviously unhappy with Lawyer Bonu and with his expectations of her. Hannah tries to persuade her husband to listen to her and to his children, but to no avail.

De Graft's *Sons and Daughters*, an old standard of Ghanaian playgoers, looks at modern Africa by examining a conflict between a father and his children. The basic clash ignites around the fact that the father, James Ofosu, has chosen professions for his children. The play itself has many theatrical flaws in it, being more of a literary piece than a dramatic one. The playwright invites many dead spots and "trucks to run through" by stopping and starting the action on the stage time after time. He reduces the involvement on the stage by leaving one character upon the stage doing nothing, except wait for the other character to return. Unfortunately most of the characters are not fully drawn or developed to the extent that the playwright is able to bring about believable clashes from them except in a melodramatic manner. Moreover, the language of the play is so British, and somewhat Victorian. Also, the characters make speeches but rarely if ever do they converse with each other. As a result of this rather stilted style of language the characters become stock characters who find it difficult to "live" on the stage. The playwright needs to deal more with theatrical terms for his characters and let them breathe the life of actions which is the heart of theatre.

The relationship and conflict between Maanan and Lawyer Bonu is, in my opinion, the pivot around which the play eventually turns and brings about the orchestral clash between James and Lawyer Bonu. For this reason, I believe that the play should be staged around this dramatic situation and crux. However, this production appears to have been staged around James. (I might add here that all of the productions of this play that I have seen in Ghana have been staged in this manner.) From the director's point of view, I feel that this staging is a mistake. I believe that the play should be staged around Maanan. Such a production would demand different actions and involvement from the actors and result in a "different experience" on the stage.

The Koforidua Amateur Drama Club appears to be a serious and enterprising dramatic group with a perceptive director. However, when the actors learn more about the basics of acting technique and theatre, they will certainly be able to stage better productions. Some of these *basics* include *listening* on the *stage*, *speaking* and *communicating* with one another on the stage, and becoming *involved* in the *characterizations* and the *actions* of the play. A mastery and control of these basics will enable the players to establish meaningful relationships between characters and serve as the theatrical medium between the playwright and the audience. Outside of Nic Hoedzie who played James Ofosu, the father, the acting was uneven and amateurish. There were trucks running all over the place. There were very few connections among the players, and the actors had very little sense of involvement or creation of reality. They gave evidence of excess mannerisms, and there was far too much bunching on the stage. Nevertheless the play is a melodrama and the audience loves it.

A Ghanaian Celebration in Theatre

On Thursday February 27, 1969, Janie and I and the family went to the Arts Center in Accra to see *The Dagger of Liberation* presented by the Voice of Germany Club (Accra) and The Ghana Theatre Club, under the auspices of The Arts Council of Ghana.

The Dagger of Liberation by Sebastian Y. Kwamuar is a historical play about the revolt and the escape of the Ewes from Notsie in Togoland where they were enslaved for years by King Agokoli, noted for his tyranny.

The play derived its title from a sacred old dagger which was used by most of their heroes and now in custody of Togbui Adeladza II, Paramount Chief of Anlo.

Notsie is a town east of Agu between Lome and Atakpamo in Togoland. There is today in Notsie the remains of the historical wall said to have been built around the town by King Agokoli. Its height was originally seventeen feet and about twenty-eight to thirty feet thick and takes about half an hour to walk around.

The strategy of the revolt and the manner of escape of the Ewes from the mighty walls of Notsie has and remains a source of great inspiration and admiration by the Ewes and of great curiosity to the world.

The celebration began with African drumming by six male drummers. The dance ensemble (four males and four females) began to perform an Ewe dance. The curtain opened and the narrator, in African storytelling style, began to tell us the story and involve us in the experience of the evening. We see a court scene and immediately become involved in the drama of the liberation struggle of the Ewe people. Throughout the celebration in the midst of the struggle for liberation we see and hear music, drumming, dancing, and the word all coming together as a volcanic eruption caught in the middle of the culture of the Ewe people. We are witnessing a total creation. And I find myself asking the question, "Just who would you have direct this play? Would he be the musician, the dancer, or the master of the word?" And in time of course I find the answer for myself. He should be a theatre-maker, schooled in the culture of Africa and trained in the art forms of African theatre. For his job is to put it all together in an integrated manner with a complete experience to be shared by performer and audience. And certainly he must be able to work with the drama as well as the players and shape the experience through his players in such a manner that the audience will demand participation.

I enjoyed the evening. I thought that the performance was fairly well acted and I liked the directorial concept of the producer. Generally speaking I felt he was able to bring together through his players a happy marriage of the appropriate life and energy of the characters as we followed them moment to moment in their liberation struggle. On the whole the physical life of the characters was in concert with the vocal and emotional life of the characters providing both involvement and believability. I was especially pleased with the attitudes of the old men and I liked the dance of possession before the liberation. The men's preparation for war was animated and interesting, and in a sense it reminded me of a shadow boxer preparing for the big bout. I do think however that most of the players still need quite a bit of vocal training, for most of the voices had a breathy quality which in my opinion did not enhance their roles or add to characterization. I would also like to see the players strive for an inner experience in their characterizations and not make the experience so external. I liked the acting of William Okai as the narrator, storyteller, and Emmary Brown as Akpini. Godwin Lurd-Kekey, Secretary General of the Ghana Theatre Club, was the technical adviser for the production and Emmary Brown was the producer. I think the playscript is fairly well written and merits publication. It certainly depicts a segment of the history of the Ghanaian people, and for that reason alone, I think it is significant. The play is written and performed in Ewe, the language of the Ewe people.

Godwin Lurd-Kekey informed me that the Ghana Theatre Club has decided to concentrate on Ghanaian plays as a means of encouraging Ghana's young writers. The Club, an association of playwrights, producers, technicians, stage and screen actors, actresses, and dancers was formed in October 1961. Its stated aim was to select and produce both tried and untried dramatic works and to cooperate with the various cultural and artistic bodies. Above all it hopes to instill the love of the theatre in Ghanaians.

A Ghanaian-Nigerian Theatre Celebration

On February 28, 1969, Janie and I went to the Ghana Drama Studio to see The Free-Lance Players production of *Song of a Goat*. The play was produced by Nicholas Teye, and the stage manager was David Iyanda.

The Song of a Goat is one of John Pepper Clark's early tragedies, based on a cleansing sacrifice—a pre-dramatic ritual. The story is about an Ijaw fisherman and his wife. Having had his first and only son, Zifa has become impotent but clings to the wife even though society dictates that such a man should hand over his wife to the next of kin. For five years the wife has been waiting with the hope that the husband will get back his "strength." Desiring to have more children, she becomes restless and bitter. Eventually she lures her husband's younger brother into committing adultery.

A prophetess of the house, an aunt, forewarns of the impending doom which is to follow. Zifa, learning of his wife's unfaithful act, disappears into the sea. Meanwhile his brother, wishing to escape the wrath of Zifa, hangs himself. *The Song of a Goat* is a good play which makes an excellent piece for theatre in the hands of competent players and a good director. The characters are well developed and the theme connects itself with the traditions and culture of the Ijaw people in Nigeria.

As I watched the performance my mind went back to 1963 and I remembered it as the year in which I helped a Nigerian theatre group in New York City stage *The Song of a Goat* for AMSAC. I recalled their theatrical energy and connection with the play. The players were committed to a good production; they understood their own culture, and they possessed the necessary technique with which to fill the experience. As a result their celebration in the theatre was a successful one. Unfortunately I cannot say the same thing for this production by the Free-Lance Players. The group certainly appears to be committed to the development of the National Theatre Movement in Ghana. Several of the members of the group are graduates of the School of Music and Drama at Legon. They came together with the aim of bringing good theatre to Ghana, and tonight's performance celebrates their first anniversary as a group. Although Mary Yirenkyi, as Ebiere, Shanco Bruce, as Zifa, and Paddy Anipong, as Masseur, all impressed me as having potential to become good actors, on the whole the play was labored. The acting of the cast was labored; the direction was labored; and consequently the play came through to the audience in the same manner. The players have not yet mastered the basic acting techniques. They must learn to listen and to communicate with one another on the stage. They must learn to exist on the stage in terms of the life of the character. They must learn to let the work on the stage affect the behavior of the character and strive for more inner experience thereby minimizing excessive externalizing. I would like for the players to examine different approaches to old age and not merely suggest old age by being bent over and by using a lot of unmotivated gestures. Let the players examine motivations for their actions and they will gain more involvement and believability in their characterization. It would behoove the stage manager to work for better scene changes, because technically the scene changes were very poor, and truck after truck ran through the performance. I kept asking myself, "What emotional experience am I supposed to feel and when? What big moment have you saved?" I never found it. And consequently I missed the impact of the shared experience in the celebration of the evening. The play-script is good enough but it needs more and better technique from the players before it can be transformed into exciting theatre. The play was performed in English, the borrowed language of the Nigerian people.

A Night of Ghanaian Theatre

On March 8, 1969, Janie and I and the family went to a soirée and a night of Ghanaian theatre at the Ghana Drama Studio. One of the plays we saw was Efua Sutherland's *Ananse and the Dwarf Brigade*. The producer was Sandy Arkhurst and the set was designed by John Kedjani. The music was by Kwamena Ampah and the students.

Ananse, one of Ghana's favorite folktale characters, is liked by children and adults alike. This play is based on one of the Ananse stories.

Ananse goes out in search of a place where he can make a farm and keep it secret from his wife and children. Finding a suitable place very close to a sacred grove, he selects the site. Thinking he can get away with his own interpretation of the custom which forbids farming so close to a sacred grove, he begins working but suddenly finds himself surrounded by dwarfs.

He is surprised to find that the dwarfs don't behave like the terrible creatures they are said to be. They seem to be so cooperative, so willing to work hard for Ananse that very soon he is letting them do all the work and calling himself lucky to have arranged his affairs so nicely. However he was not as clever as he thought he was, for the dwarfs are not fools. In the end they punish him in the worst possible manner by ruining all the crops just when they are ready for harvesting.

This play looks at the many facets of Ananse and through him examines the idea that rarely do you get something for nothing. The play is set forth at the beginning in a storytelling fashion with Ananse being at the center of the action and the conflict. Ghanaian traditions also become a part of the play through the use of the dwarfs and the children and by examining the husband-wife relationship in Ghanaian society. Sandy Arkhurst plays Ananse and in my opinion he creates and develops an interesting characterization. He works well with the other players on the stage, especially the children who play the Dwarfs and the members of his family. He has good stage presence and has learned to harmonize his stage movements with his stage actions, thereby managing to keep a good rapport with his audience. As the play opens and we find Ananse trying to get lost, I should like to see Arkhurst work more with the reality of the situation, and thereby make better use of his energy, both his physical life and his vocal life. When he begins to sing "Nobody Here but Me," I should like to see him enjoy the moment more, and listen to the music and hear his own voice and then let it affect his behavior. Towards the end of the play in the "snooping scene" between Ananse and his wife, Arkhurst is in rare form with good energy and theatrical life. He seems to be enjoying the scene. I too enjoyed it. However the scene would have been far better if he had put more work on the "hitting aspect" of the scene and endeavored to make it real rather than suggesting it. The spider's web was used to good advantage at the close of the play. This was an interesting production and the use of the music with the children and the chorus opened up the play and moved it closer towards the nature of a celebration and a total creation.

A Soul Concert from Liberia

On Tuesday night March 18, 1969, Janie and I went to the Great Hall at Legon to hear a concert by Miss Louisa Sherman, daughter of Mr. G. Flamma Sherman, Liberian Ambassador in Ghana. The program was under the sponsorship of the University of Ghana Law Students Association. Louisa, with the backing of the GBC Orchestra, gave Ghanaians a glimpse of her singing and theatrical talents.

Introducing a show, based mainly on the new soul and beat music, Louisa Sherman demonstrated her ability to hold and communicate with an audience. And as I watched her and listened to the beat, I was struck by the fact that her voice was pleasant, and that her movements and gyrations were in keeping with the music. However, in most instances, the GBC Orchestra was so loud with its background music that I could rarely ever tell whether Miss Sherman could or could not really sing. However, there is no doubt about the fact that she is already a budding performer, revealing both instinct and ability for imitation, which is certainly an asset for a performer beginning a career of singing and entertaining.

For example, Sammy Davis Jr., who started in show business at the age of three, learned to imitate many performers before he found his own style. As a tap dancer, Sammy imitated the world's greatest, the late Bill Robinson. He also received excellent guidance and training in the performing arts from his uncle and his father as a performer in the Will Mastin Trio. And now, forty years later, he commands respect throughout the world.

Another example of an early imitator is Ray Charles, "Mr. Soul and Blues" himself. Charles, in his early years, imitated the late King Cole, and his early records, which are now collector's items, reveal this fact. A few years later though, when Ray began to discover himself, he moved into the "rhythm and blues field" and later began to command the stage as "Mr. Soul and Blues."

In most of Miss Sherman's renditions the background music was too loud. Certainly, she needs the beat but once in a while the audience needs to hear and understand some of the lyrics. Let her remember that James Brown has a great variety of sounds and gyrations and displays many facets of his versatility, but always, even in his rendition of "Say It Loud," he gives you some "soul singing" and lets you know that he actually can use various levels and registers in his singing. When Miss Sherman sang "Yesterday," a John Lennon number made famous by the Beatles, the audience did get a chance to hear her voice. From this song she revealed a pleasant voice with the promise of an interesting range which should enable her to handle both low and high registers. Miss Sherman moves easily and often, like a perpetual ball of energy, demonstrating good physical life. If she wishes to become a top-notch artist it would behoove her to strive for better breath control and support, and also to learn to keep her throat open and her resonating cavities relaxed and free in order to insure proper placement of her tone.

Miss Sherman has "somebody else's sound" at the moment, and gives evidence of having been greatly influenced by such artists as Aretha Franklin, James Brown, the Beatles, the Supremes, and others. But she does have a real "feel" for the beat. In a number entitled "Say It Loud . . . I'm Black . . . and I'm Proud," Louisa was joined by a group of dancers who simulated the "soul" dance. They were all lively and pleasing to watch, but the most interesting member of the group was a little girl who appeared to be only three or four years old.

The Celebration and the Total Creation

On Wednesday night, March 19, 1969, Janie, the children, and I went to the outdoor theatre at Commonwealth Hall, University of Legon, to witness the theatre from Ola Rotimi's Nigerian company. Over six hundred students, teachers, and friends of the theatre from Accra sat from 8:30 until 11:30 to enjoy an evening of real African theatre. The Ori Olokun Players of the Institute of African Studies of the University of Ife, Ife-Ife, Western State of Nigeria, due to transportation problems had arrived in Ghana a day late. But the performance rendered on Wednesday night was well worth waiting for.

The play, *The Gods Are Not to Blame*, an adaptation of Sophocles' tragedy *Oedipus Rex*, is presented in terms of modern theatre, using the staging techniques of ethnic African drama. The tragic flaw in the central character, a man caught in a dilemma from which he cannot escape, shows man struggling against the overwhelming forces prevalent today in African society, much as they were in the Greek days of Sophocles.

On the whole, the players gave a good performance and celebrated the experience in the play. The major characters were easily understood, heard, seen, and believed. They were involved and immersed in an experience. They all appeared to have the desire, the awareness, and the need to communicate this experience to the other players on the stage. The players' involvement set up a circular response between the player and the audience. I also witnessed a different kind of audience behavior from the behavior I had often seen in Ghana and in other parts of Africa. This audience, though participating in and enjoying the performance, became a part of the dramatic experience to such a degree that they would not tolerate any distractions from other members of the audience who felt the need to "talk or be loud." From time to time some of the members of the audience felt it necessary to "shush" those few loud members of the audience and ask them to keep quiet. The players had been trained to listen to one another, to talk with one another, and to move easily and freely upon the stage as their characterizations dictated. It appeared to me that they were merging their talent with their technique and also that they were enjoying themselves. They were enjoying the experience—either through the pain of the enjoyment or the laughter of the enjoyment, but always through the dramatic experience. In time, the audience seemed to be as one with the players as the magic of the celebration of African theatre permeated the air through a total creation of the music, the mime, the dance, and the dialogue.

Ola Rotimi himself introduced the play as a storyteller-performer and covered the early years of the oracle and the play. Through his skillful dramaturgy, also at the very beginning of the play, he introduced art elements of African theatre such as mime, music, dance intermingled with the prose and poetry. The pictures on the stage through the choreography of a crowd scene and a battle attack with its aftermath created an overall mood of suffering, foreshadowing that which was to follow. Interspersed throughout the play were moments of comic relief communicated via proverbs and character elements of the players such as the "court jester type" or others who gave you just enough factures of laughter to make you wish for more.

When I interviewed the cast and the director-playwright, I was not surprised to learn of the talent, dedication, and commitment of many of the members of the company. The group struck me as being quite democratic in its structure and format as it cut across class, educational, and professional barriers. The company, comprised of teachers and students from the University and interested people from the community impressed me as I watched them strike the set after the performance. I witnessed an ensemble approach which gave little evidence of a "big-man complex" from any member of the company. Their actions seemed to flow from a true trooper spirit and a healthy realization of creative cooperation. I learned from Rotimi that he had studied theatre in America where he took his B.A. from Boston University and majored in directing and playwriting. Continuing his studies, he took his M.F.A. from Yale University where he majored in playwriting. At Yale he wrote the play *Our Husband Has Gone Mad Again* as a final project for the degree. I had heard of this play before from a fellow member of our society, Broadway Society of Stage Directors and Choreographers, Jack Landau, who had entertained hopes of staging the play on Broadway.

Femi Robinson, who played the King, the major character in the play, and I might add, a most demanding role for any actor, is a graduate of the University of Nsuka, Eastern Nigeria. He is employed by the University of Ife where he works as a technician. When I asked him about his acting technique and his approach to his role, he smiled and replied in a modest manner, "I don't have any particular approach, it just comes naturally." Upon further inspection however he talked about his acting experiences at the University of Nsuka and especially his roles in *King Kong* and *No Strings.* As I listened to him speak, it was evident to me that he loved the theatre and was committed as an actor. And I learned that "what comes naturally" as an actor has been a part of his life for at least nine years.

Yinka Aujorin, who played the Queen, is a school teacher in a teacher training college in Nigeria. Her husband teaches at the University of Ife. Traveling with her were four of her five children, the youngest of whom is one. And of course the children are also in the play. So Yinka has a dual role, first, her life role as mother to her four children, and secondly, as Queen in the play.

I asked Rotimi how he manages to hold on to such an enthusiastic group of players. He told me, "Our students want to act. But of course we don't have a Drama Department yet, but this doesn't stop them from acting. And besides there are no academic demands on them from the point of view of drama. They do however have their other studies in the University. And of course the other members of the company also have responsibilities aside from our theatre troupe. So there are some sacrifices."

It appeared to me that Yinka Aujorin as the Queen, and Femi Robinson as the King were good models for the other actors on the stage, and that the two of them also worked quite well together. Yinka created a carriage and walk that was truly "Queenly," and she was able to sustain her attitude and physical life throughout the play. The audience applauded her enthusiastically for her portrayal of the Queen. Femi Robinson, as the King, handled his vocal life in a very professional manner and his spoken English was intelligible, believable, heard, and understood. In fact he "suited his action to the word" in such a manner that he made his role look easy, though in truth it was a very demanding role. Generally speaking, some of the minor characters were not consistently audible or sustained in character portrayal. There were also some production flaws in respect to staging and communication but, on the whole, the production was a good celebration. The use of music and dance was good, and the lighting and staging were consistent in respect to the mood and the tone of the play. Also the sets were attractive and appropriate.

Ola Rotimi, a Research Fellow of the Institute of African Studies and the author of *The Gods Are Not to Blame*, is a playwright of many talents, who gives evidence of marked ability in his use of rich language and his skillful interweaving of African proverbs in a poetic prose style fully blended in traditional African beliefs. The theme of the story of Oedipus Rex is followed closely by Rotimi, but at the same time *The Gods Are Not to Blame* becomes a completely different play, with the music, the energy, and the rhythm couched in African theatre forms.

The dramatic experience is very similar to that witnessed and felt in the Greek version, but the energy, the "soul," the vibrations are not the same, for in this play the mores and beliefs are African —for example, such beliefs as in Ifa, the oracular deity; Sango, the God of Thunder; Ogun, the God of Iron and War, and, of course, the wisdom of the African ancestors. Moreover, Rotimi's use of the richness of African culture adds new dimensions in respect to meaning and character portrayal. Proverbs such as, "A toad likes water but not when it's boiling." "I am the butterfly who calls himself a bird." "Can a cockroach be innocent in a gathering of fowls?" and "We are close friends like he-goats and cocoyams" are used in the right place by the right characters at the "correct" moment of time in the drama.

Moreover, dialogue such as this between the King and his Queen: "When will you return, my Lord?" "When you see me, Woman, you see me," captures the spirit and energy of characters who are truly African.

In my opinion the play is an African play set forth in universal terms. And the production was equally a genuine experience in the theatre—in African theatre, easily understood by Africans though spoken in English—played by Nigerians for a Ghanaian audience. Yet this was theatre also easily understood and enjoyed by a Western audience. It was truly a celebration, an eruption of the art forms caught in the middle of the culture of its people, and a total creation.

Ghanaian Theatre and the Celebration

On March 25, 1969, Janie and I went to see *Foriwa* at the Ghana Drama Studio. The play was produced by Sandy Arkhurst and performed by the Kusum Agoromba Players, and written by Efua Sutherland.

Based on a story, "New Life at Kyerfaso," written by Efua

Sutherland in 1959, the play inspects the relationship between change and tradition in an African town. It explores the attitudes, the communication, and the actions that bring about this change.

This is a "slice of life" story about modern Africa, caught in a conflict between traditional and modern life. It is a good story with a good message; however, as a play, it needs more. A play needs a dramatic situation with strong characterizations which bring about variety and contrasts on the stage. It needs basic conflicts and dramatic revelations in the midst of the poetry and the celebration of life.

The plot unfolds mainly through the actions of four people, Foriwa, Ohemaa, Labaran, and the Postmaster. Foriwa is the daughter of the Chief of Kyerefaso, who has been trained as a teacher and must decide whether she will remain at home and try to bring about change or continue teaching away from home in another town. Her mother, Ohemaa, Chief on the Stool of Kyerefaso, troubled about the state of the town and its lethargy, decides to break tradition to help bring about change. Finally, there are Labaran, a university-educated "stranger" who has come to Kyerefaso to live, and the Postmaster, a retired owner of a bookshop, who works with him in bringing about the change.

The Kusum Agoromba Company, one of Ghana's newer developing professional companies, unfortunately has not yet developed its theatre technique to the extent that it is able to lift this play from the page to the stage. Generally speaking, the actors lack the basic technique to achieve a meaningful characterization of their roles. Most audiences expect to believe the characters in a play, and to understand WHAT and WHY the character is doing WHATEVER he is doing on the stage. In other words, the *actions* of the players should illuminate the theme of the play and, at the same time, make the audience feel and understand a direct relationship between the conflict and the characters in the play. Moreover, the actor's theatrical life should be three-dimensional, embracing believable vocal, physical, and emotional life. The actor or the director should never split or dissipate the focus of attention on the stage. He should never stop and start his action, but should try to maintain a "continuous flow" of the dramatic experience and the music of the theatre. For the director cannot afford to lose or confuse his audience for a split

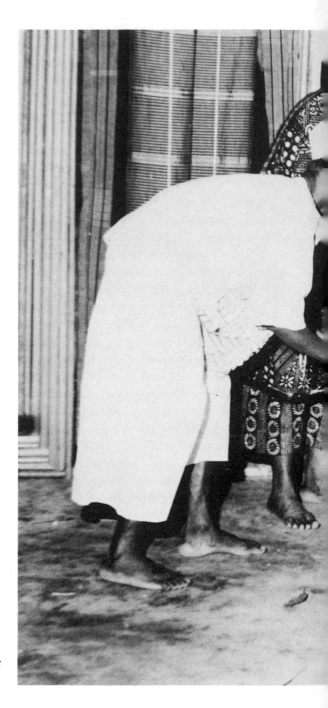

The Gods Are Not To Blame
(Osun Photo, Ghana)

second; he must always try to capture and hold their attention upon the "line of focus" on the stage. He cannot afford to present three or four sight lines at the same time.

The actor, however, must create the *reality* before he can respond to it. For example, the draughts players at Kyerefaso should have played their game and enjoyed it. After creating this reality by actually doing the act, they could then fill and enlarge the scene by employing theatrical life. Instead, the actors hammed it up and tried to show off or steal the scene. Consequently they destroyed the meaning of everything else that was happening on the stage at the time.

Despite the fact that *Foriwa* is presented in the vernacular language, Twi (Akan), the play remains static. But language is only one aspect of the theatre; the playwright and the director must use the many other elements to take hold of the audience.

I do think however that the play and the company deserve more of a turn-out than the sparse audience which attended the performances. The Kusum Agoromba Company is one of Ghana's newer developing professional companies producing plays as their major occupation. If it is to fulfill its potential it needs encouragement and support. And since people make up an audience, people need to support the theatre movement.

A Ghanaian Celebration in Folk Opera

On March 29, 1969, Janie, the children, and I went to the Arts Centre in Accra to witness *The Lost Fishermen* presented by the Institute of Art and Culture. The play was directed by Saka Acquaye, author of book, songs, and lyrics. Featured was the Dama's Choir directed by Ishmael Adams, also director of music and assistant director of the play. Nic Hoedzie was the stage manager.

Saka Acquaye examines cultural conflicts, along with other matters, as well as the relationship of the chief to his son and the members of the tribe. He also experiments with language and communication for African theatre inasmuch as he presents his dialogue in English, while retaining the lyrics in Ga. Music, dance, rituals, regalia, and the dramatic form are integrated.

The Lost Fishermen concerns itself with a group of fishermen who disobey the gods of the sea and go out fishing on Tuesday, a day they are to observe strictly as religious holiday. As a consequence of their folly, they are caught in a storm, and eventually drift away onto a haunted island, inhabited by a group of stranded women who have lost their husbands earlier on this island.

In this current production Saka Acquaye has introduced new cinematographic effects through the use of lighting and a screen which aid the exposition and help get the play off to a good start. However, in my opinion, after the appeal of these new effects has worn off, the effects become a distracting element. For better coordination of these effects and a fuller use of the actions of his players, the director should let the storm begin with the singing and music behind the curtain. Then with the drawing of the curtain, he should gradually bring into focus the struggle of the men against the storm and the sea. At the same time he begins to diminish the effects of the storm. I think this direction would heighten the struggle and involvement of the fishermen. Directorily, at the outset I would focus attention upon the fishermen in the play with the hopes of compelling the audience to become interested in their outcome and future. After hooking my audience I would strive to maintain this focus of concentration throughout the play, making the necessary adjustments as the actions of the play dictate. This production however does not control the crux of the play in this manner. And herein lies one of the major weaknesses of the production. Also one of the major weaknesses of the structure of *The Lost Fishermen* lies in the fact that the original conflict and clash of the play "thins out" in the second act. The emphasis is then shifted to the life on the island and the actions and involvement of Koshi. Thus the relationship and conflict between Kotey and his father, Amaso, the head crew, and chief of the village, is weakened and diminished, while the major emphasis is thrown upon the women of the island through Koshi and her actions. Also, theatrically speaking, the use of the gods, and the extra dancers who appear upon the island at various times, is not always clear or justified or integrated in a unified way into the total creation. The players weaken the dramatic intensity of the play by failing to use the dancers in a dramatic sense during the celebration on the island. This celebration scene could erupt into heightened dramatic moments if staged differently and performed by the players with more involvement and stronger and different relationships.

The Lost Fishermen is indeed a "celebration of life" and a total creation in folk opera form, utilizing music, dialogue, mime, dance, and ritual. I found it both interesting and entertaining to listen to and to watch. Though the music and the dance were well presented and performed, the acting technique of the players still needs much polish. Since the player is a theatrical medium he must *communicate* a specific interpretation and characterization based on specific actions to an audience. This creation places great demands upon an actor. It demands great concentration, involvement, and the sustaining of a specific character on the stage. This is especially true in the celebration of life form of theatre. It follows then that the more believable variety of contrasts and clashes we have on the stage, the more involvement and enjoyment we will get from our audience. Consequently, since The Lost Fishermen Company is also emerging as one Ghana's professional companies, it too must continue to develop its acting technique in order to bring about a closer unity in respect to the use of music, dance, ritual, mime, and dialogue in the celebration and the total creation.

Towards the end of the performance I had a question regarding language. Saka uses Ga for the lyrics and English for the dialogue in the play. However in the last act, the Chief speaks in Ewe. If the Chief is a Ga chief, would he not normally speak in Ga, especially since he sings in Ga and his sons and the other members of the crew all sing in Ga? What is his reason for speaking in Ewe? Is the intention a dramatic point?

Generally speaking Ghanaians really enjoy music and dance. I gathered that they were very pleased with the celebration of *The Lost Fishermen* as it played nightly to an audience of over one thousand people. On several occasions people were turned away at the door because no more seats were available.

A Ghanaian Celebration in Dance

On April 3, 1969, Janie, the children, and I went to the Arts Centre in Accra to witness the Ghana Dance Ensemble in a benefit performance for the Cripples Aid Society, promoted by the Insti-

The Lost Fishermen (Arts Centre, Ghana)

FEAR WOMAN

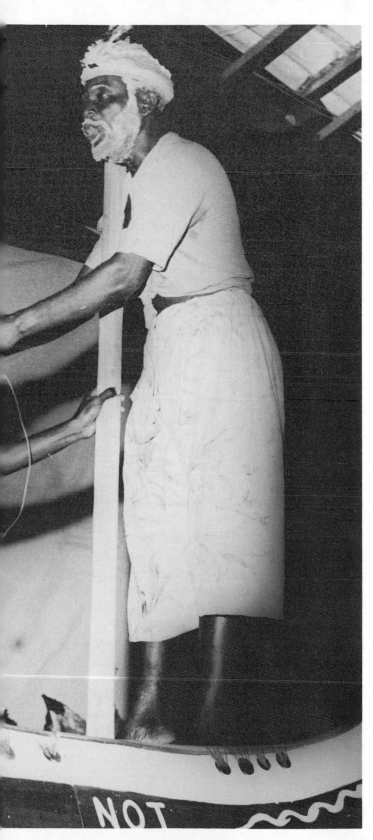

The Lost Fishermen
(Arts Centre, Ghana)

tute of Arts and Culture. Bertie Opoku presented his Ensemble in a variety of dances from various regions of Ghana and West Africa. I had seen this Ensemble dance many times before and had always enjoyed their performance.

The program-celebration was divided into two parts. It opened with the Akan Ceremonial Dance Suite in four movements. First came the "War Dance of Harassment" followed by the "Victory Dance of Achievement" in the field. The third movement included the "Victory Dance" of narration on the return of the Warrior during the celebrations of victory in which the dancer asserts his supremacy. The Suite ends with the Kete, a favorite court dance of the Asantehenes.

All throughout my stay in Ghana Bertie Opoku had "schooled" me regarding the nature of the dances and their relation to tradition and Ghanaian life-styles. Therefore, for each celebration dance-drama to which I gave witness I found myself remembering my conversations with Bertie. So tonight, as I swelled with pride re-garding my new-found perceptions on Ghanaian traditions and life-styles, I thought to myself, "Kennedy, you're not doing badly as an 'outside-insider' member of the family.' " And needless to say the Ghanaian audience seemed to be at one with the performance of the evening.

Kete has always been a court dance for chiefs, Amanhene, Abrempon and members of the Royal Household. It is and has always been the favorite of the Asantehenes. This dance is noted for its courtliness and for the contrasts between the graceful move-ments of the women and the strutting display of masculinity by the male dancers. The full Kete includes Kete drums, voices and odoru-gya flutes. This is performed only for the Asantehene's private entertainment in the palace, where the Asantehene acts as the or-chestral leader, keeping time with a red covered rattle, which he uses as he dances with his wives. When dancing with the Queen Mother he guards her with a gun. Tonight's performance was an adaptation for the theatre but nevertheless it still reflected the spirit of the full Kete. My children especially enjoyed this Akan Ceremo-nial Dance Suite.

Ceremonial events like the Adae Festival, or a durbar, provide opportunities for festivities during which the people demonstrate their loyalty to local dignitaries or chiefs as fathers of families. Court dances are not exclusive to the chiefs and anybody on such occasions can dance, but usually only the best dancers have enough confidence to face the audience of dance experts. These groups of dances suggest the atmosphere of the court and the festive spirit of such ceremonial gatherings.

Next came an interesting "work" dance, the Kundum, a Harvest Dance. Then the Ensemble gave the audience a treat with the Kpanlogo, Ghana's latest development of the popular West African recreational dance, the Highlife. They followed the Kpanlogo with a social get-together dance, the Anlo Kete. Finally, before the intermission, the last group of dances presented were the Frafra Bima Dances which are most colorful and interesting to watch.

The second part of the program began with a "Suite for Donno and Brekete Drums." This Suite presents regal and spirited ceremonial and popular dances from northern Ghana. The changes in the rhythm of the dances require great control from the performers since smoothness must prevail within each change. Opoku has required and received from his dancers the appropriate control and smoothness. The rhythmic changes in this part of the dance-celebration provide variety and contrast within the framework of each group of dances. This provides the audience with an enjoyable and rewarding experience.

In this particular dance-set Opoku has increased the involvement of the dancers on the stage by multiplying (increasing) the solo dance by four in regards to the four young girls who pay respect to the chief. And in the "chase" aspect of the dance, which requires a relationship between the drummer and the girls, each girl has been able to create and sustain an individual character and relationship throughout the dance. As a result of this relationship, the audience becomes involved with both the girls and the drummer, who is trying to woo each girl through his drumming.

In the stick dance, also in this Suite, you can see and feel a definite relationship between the music and the movement of the dancers. And finally towards the end of this Suite, as the Chief dances with dignity leading his people off the stage, you can note and enjoy the contrast in the rough movements of the male dancers, as compared to the somewhat delicate movements of the female dancers.

In between the dance numbers Opoku employs the use of flute music played by three of the members of the dance troupe. In most instances, the music helped introduce the next dance by employing the thematic music to be used for that dance. I felt that this brief musical interlude between dances helped theatricalize the evening.

The "Akom" dance, with the Chief Priestess, performed by Grace Kotey, who is a Ga doing an Ashanti dance, was one of the highlights of the evening. Miss Kotey created and sustained both the physical and the emotional life of her character. Her trance segment of the dance, as well as her circling and pivotal turns in the Ntwaaho segment, and her spins and turns in the air in the Adaban segment, revealed her technique in respect to control, coordination, creation, and involvement. And by her movements and actions she was able to create and maintain a state of empathy with an enthusiastic audience.

"Akom" is the general name given to a series of dances performed by "Fetish Priests." This dance is used mainly as a means of releasing priests from trances into which they must fall in order to act as "mediums." The popular notion that priests "dance themselves into a trance" is false. However, the rhythm of this dance is such that it has been known to have diverse effects on people, according to their susceptibilities.

After an act of healing the priest walks around greeting people and dispersing powdered clay in the same manner that Christian priests use holy water. He acknowledges God who is the Spirit of the earth, the source of physical strength and material well-being. He also acknowledges the "four winds" which carry to him the words of God. He then begins the Ntwaaho, circling in a series of soutean pivot turns, to illustrate the perfection, wholeness and oneness of God. Then follows Adaban, a retreating and advancing movement of great power and fascination, combined with spins and turns in the air. Some of the dance motifs are "hotted-up" versions of secular and popular dances.

Next came "Three Eve Dances" which were virtuoso pieces. I and the audience thoroughly enjoyed the next dance, the Siki, with its flirtatious nature and its dancers strutting and bobbing up and down in their Ghanaian display of theatrical elegance. The Siki is a popular gay dance for social occasions.

The mood changed for the next group of dances which included the "Lobi Dance Suite." In this set the dancers display great agility, dynamism, dignity, and controlled inner strength. The physical energy and life of the dancers was often characterized by infectious abandonment in harmony with the fascinating rhythms. A tremolo of fast contraction and release is the special technique of the Lobi dances.

For the evening's celebration the Legon Dance Ensemble gave evidence of good control and involvement. It also demonstrated the use of proper attitudes and relationships in respect to player-involvement for each dance. And it was evident to the audience that Bertie Opoku has been able to theatricalize his dances and still retain their basic theme, mood, and structure.

The last dance, the "Gahu," was pleasant to watch, and I felt that it was most appropriate for the final number. Gahu, originally a Yoruba social dance, is an example of acculturation. It is a blend of the pelvic shift style of the Yoruba and a softer, lighter version of the Anglo torso contraction. Infectious gaiety and abandonment form the expressive keynote, with fun-poking at the pompous rich, and as a light-hearted gay dance, it leaves much room for individual expression and improvisation. The "tease" nature of the dance is entertaining and interesting. The girls teasingly choose one partner, but quickly run to another, accepting his advances. This continues until finally they do decide to pair with a permanent partner.

The vibrations of a special experience from each group of dances were transmitted to the audience by the performers through their talent and their technique, and their understanding of the nature of the celebration in dance-drama. And as I saw and heard it, from the audience's responses, the evening's celebration in dance-drama was a huge success.

Ghanaian-Nigerian Theatre—A Celebration

On April 25, 1969, Janie, the children, and I went to the Commonwealth Hall Amphitheatre of the University of Ghana to witness two student productions by the Drama Division of the School of Music and Drama.

The first play, *Jewels of the Shrine*, was written by J. E. Henshaw,

a prolific Nigerian playwright. To an older generation, youth ig-
nores the traditional love and respect that is due to an elderly
person. To youth, the old generation makes a mistake in thinking
that the ideal place for a young man is in the farm and a young
woman in the kitchen. This clash of generations is embodied in the
roles of the grandfather and the two grandsons in this play.

The play opens with a visit of a stranger to Okorie, an old man
who has suffered neglect from his two grandsons Arob and Ojima.
After this visit Okorie tells his grandsons that there are hidden
jewels on his farm. Immediately the grandsons go to dig up the
whole farm, but to no avail. Okorie then tells them that he himself
has dug up the jewels and upon his death will leave the property to
them. However they must take good care of him and show him
respect and love while he lives. Also, at his death they must give him
a decent burial.

The grandsons change their attitude towards Okorie. They
take very good care of him and give him the greatest burial any old
man has had in their village. However, as the play ends, they are still
waiting for their reward.

The producer-director was S. Kofi Nipah. The stage manager
was Alex Agyeman, and the assistant stage manager was Kwabena
Darkoh. I enjoyed the play and felt that this was some of the best
stage direction and acting that I had witnessed from the University
players. I thought that the acting performance by Fred Akuffo-
Lartey who played Okorie was outstanding. He seemed to understand the nature of this celebration of life through the old man's
experience, and he was able to merge his own talent and technique
in the creation of an effective characterization of Okorie. I reflected
upon his work and acting over the past two years and remembered
a particular performance in which he played the Beggar in *The Pot
of Chicken Soup*. At that time I noted that he showed great promise.
He has grown as a performer since then and has lived up to those
early expectations. He has now learned to listen, to communicate,
and exist on the stage in terms of a specific character within the
frame of a special experience. And now he is beginning to celebrate
and share that experience with his audience. The other players also
deserve mention since they too have begun to understand the idea
of mixing talent and technique in the creation of a specific charac-

Frafra Bima dance (*Halifax Photos, Ghana*)

Anlo Drum Ensemble (*Halifax Photos, Ghana*)

ter. R. Addo-Mensah played Arob; Joe Dankwah was Ojima; Christina Ampah was Bassi; and Judas K. Amoah was the Stranger. Joe Dankwah and Addo Mensah have stretched their instruments considerably since 1967 at which time they played the History Master (Refund) and A Man from the Jewelers (Scenario) respectively. The audience enjoyed the play; and my children enjoyed the play. They especially enjoyed Fred Akuffo-Lartey as Okorie. And I think he enjoyed himself tremendously, celebrating the evening.

The next play, *The Trials of Brother Jero,* was a treat for all of us including the players. Chris Tackie was the producer-director. The stage manager was Jones Kyei, and the assistant stage manager was Margaret Ninson.

This is one of my favorite short plays by Wole Soyinka. As the play opened my thought went back to 1964 and New York City at which time I helped a Nigerian theatre group stage this play for one of their productions at Columbia University. I remembered a special energy they had for this play and the good production they presented. Tonight's players also had a good production though their "Ghanaian energy" was somewhat different from the "Nigerian energy" in the play which I had witnessed earlier in NYC. The "Ghanaian life of each character" was different from the "Nigerian life of each character." Consequently the vitality and the music of each production played somewhat different scores. The total celebration however was very similar. Certainly there would be some difference because the physical habit patterns of the Ghanaians' speech, voice, and movement are not exactly like those of the Nigerians. But the experience from the celebration was similar and consequently the total creation through the word, the music, the mime in a specific characterization was communicated to the audience.

This play is a comedy in which Soyinka attempts to mirror for his audience some traits in human character. Brother Jero, a prophet, who lives by the credulity and stupidity of his community is (as a result of a curse by his mentor, the Old Prophet) nearly caught in his tracks, when Chume his faithful assistant attempts to murder him. Jero, however, is able to extricate himself from this situation through his ingenuity and so his day is saved.

In *The Trials of Brother Jero* Soyinka is satirizing religious sects in Nigeria. Dramatically he uses Jero as character and narrator. Obed Ababio plays Jero and provides his audience with an interesting characterization and, generally speaking, gives a good experience for the evening. Obed handles the transitions from narrator to character most effectively and is learning to use himself as the character on the stage. When he begins to trust his work a little more he will be even better in his characterization. He has certainly stretched his instrument through talent and technique since his earlier performances in which he showed promise as an actor. I remembered specifically his role as the pupil in *Refund* in 1967. In this play he evidenced stage presence but had not learned to listen and communicate with the other players nor exist in terms of a character. As Jero, however, Obed does exist as a character and also communicates and expresses a specific life generated by that character. I would like now to see him create his life completely and thoroughly before he begins to use it. He will then create another kind of energy for his characterization and begin to merge physical and vocal believability with his actions, especially as it relates to the moment-to-moment reality. His actor's work will affect his behavior more and he will develop a greater sense of communication with his audience and his characters.

On the whole I felt that the play was well directed and, here again as in the first play (*Jewels*), I thought the acting was fairly good and certainly some of the best that I have witnessed from the players. I thought the best performance of the evening were given by Obed, as Jero; D. A. Addo, as Chume; Susie Akuetteh, as Trader and Fat Mama; and B. Mohammed as Member of Parliament. Mohammed shows great promise and bears watching as an actor and a theatre-maker. My son, James, who is rapidly developing his perception as a critic, enjoyed both the *Jewels of the Shrine* and *The Trials of Brother Jero*. And as we left the outdoor theatre at Legon he remarked, "This was quite a celebration, and the audience was one of the best university audiences we've had." Janie and I both agreed.

The Use of Music in African Theatre

At this point in our sample of observations and impressions let us turn our attention to the use of music in African theatre. We know that music, like any other art form, may be treated from several points of departure. Music may be viewed from the composer's frame of reference or the ethnomusicologist's frame. It may be seen as a creative artist's or researcher's tool, or it may be viewed as a performing art and an applied art.

In the creation of and the development of African theatre, music, along with proverbs, rituals, regalia, and visual arts, dance, mime, and the tale, is one of the many variables. So in fact, all of these art forms may be viewed as variables in respect to the evolution and the development of African theatre. Therefore, through necessity, they lead us to a consideration of the basic question, "How might one best approach the study of African theatre?"

Universities in America, Europe, Africa, or elsewhere often offer M.A. degrees or Ph.D. degrees to students who submit theses on the plays and the significance of a particular African writer such as Wole Soyinka, John Pepper Clark, and others. While this approach is both valuable and meaningful, is it not at the same time purely a literary approach to the written play? Does it not bear little relevance to the "theatre of the particular experience" manifested by the germ from the play? Does it not relate more to drama and literature and less to theatre?

We do know however that the literary approach to the study of African theatre is a valid approach which in itself offers vast opportunities for research. This is true essentially because anyone looking into any aspect of African culture soon learns that the Yoruba society of Nigeria, though "African," is unlike that of the Ashanti of Ghana or the Mende of Sierra Leone. In other words, he learns that African societies are similar and yet different from country to country throughout the continent of Africa. Thus, in this respect alone, the study of African theatre presents a great variety of approaches either from an interdisciplinary point of view or from the viewpoint of a specialist's discipline.

Consider the need to examine the culture of a particular African country in order to understand its dramatic experience and its theatre. Do you call upon the cultural anthropologist or the sociologist to provide insights? Consider the need to examine the language and behavior of the people of a specific African country in order to understand its dramatic experience and its theatre. Examine the need to engage in research in the "language of African theatre." For example, find an African writer who works well in one of his own local languages as well as in a borrowed language such as English or French. Then examine the influence of this borrowed language on the state or development of African theatre in this country. Try to determine which "energy," in which language, best suits the style or character of that particular African country. Or, for example, what is the difference in the audience responses to a play presented in Amharic and that same play presented in English? Or a play presented in Twi and that same play presented in English? And what about the actors in these plays? Which language is the most "comfortable" and the most "usable" for the actor? Or which "music" best fits the "energy" of the dramatic experience? Do you call upon the social psychologist, the linguist, the communications specialist? Or should a team approach be stressed?

Another consideration would include an examination of the "nature and structure of African drama and theatre" in respect to the "integrated arts concept." Let the scholars in the areas of music, dance, mime, ritual, regalia, and the visual arts provide insights into this aspect of the study of African drama and theatre, and then collaborate with the theatre-makers and dramatists.

In the light of these questions and facts, then, is it not also true that the behavior, communication, and actions of the characters in African plays will vary from country to country and from tribe to tribe? And is this not especially true in respect to the "energy of the play" and the style and presentation? Certainly, research regarding the "character" and "structure" of African theatre is forthcoming. Is research, then, not also necessary regarding the "style" of presentation and acting as it relates to the "life-styles" of specific African groups or nations? What are the materials to be studied in order to arrive at the proper "technique" for the presentation of this African theatre? In Africa? Elsewhere? And what of the training program for this "total theatre"? (When we speak of "total theatre," we refer to African theatre which employs the use of the "culture concept" and the "integrated art-forms concept.") And what kind of training program will produce a "complete performer and actor"? (A complete actor is one who will be able to speak, sing, dance, mime, and so forth while creating a particular role or characterizing a specific person.)

Why not seriously investigate the richness of the culture of Africa to be used for the development of African theatre? Numerous research opportunities await the person who wishes to investigate the dramatic and the theatrical aspects of African rituals, festivals, and ceremonial occasions. Or consider researchers who might wish to tap the rich resources in the African oral traditions and begin to investigate oral interpretation and its relationship to the development of African theatre. Then, finally, when all of these facets have been explored and researched, is it not, at that time, also necessary to find a creative way to use this "found material" for the creation of African theatre?

Finally, what is to be the role or direction of music in the development of African theatre? Consider the ethnomusicologist or composer who wishes to investigate the use of music in creating African theatre. Just what kind of music must be written for the new African theatre? And how can the artist "root" his music in the old forms and still extend the medium?

I have posed several questions in respect to research opportunities in the study of and making of African theatre. Yet many questions remain to be asked. Many problems remain to be found and later solved. In the final analysis, however, all areas of drama and theatre in respect to African theatre and its development are yet to be truly explored. Both the technical and artistic areas warrant extensive and intensive investigations. Many discoveries are yet to be made. Production problems for the development of African theatre? African theatre histories in the various countries! African theatre criticism! The language of African theatre and African style and technique! In short, much general research for the African theatre-makers awaits the energy, inventiveness, and hard work of those persons interested in intercultural communication and the further development of African theatre.

I have presented an overview of problems and questions. Let

us now come back to the original issue of music. When will we seriously begin to look at the ethnomusicologist, who studies "music in culture," and the composer, in African societies, and *begin to examine their role and relationship to African theatre?* I think this is a most serious, pressing, and important question. I say so because African theatre is directly related to the culture of the people, and because we know that music is one of our most important art forms, used in the integrated arts concept of African theatre.

With hopes of focusing your attention upon this important area, I shall now include a very brief sample of observations and sketch a canvas of four people who I know who are addressing themselves to problems and questions regarding the use of music in African theatre. We have already mentioned Dr. Amu, Saka Acquaye, and William Amoako from Ghana who are interested in the use of music in the development of African theatre. So let us now look in on Kwabena Nketia, Evaristo Muyindo, Akin Yuba, and Mulatu Astatke.

Professor J. H. Kwabena Nketia is one of Ghana's leading ethnomusicologists, composers, and scholars. He is Director of the Institute of African Studies at the University of Ghana and also Director of the Ghana National Dance Ensemble. He has used his musical skills and knowledge in the development of the Institute and also in the molding of the dance performers of the Dance Ensemble. Nketia is also a composer of numerous songs and the writer of several books including *Funeral Dirges of the Akan People, Drumming in Akan Communities of Ghana, Folk Songs of Ghana,* and *African Music in Ghana.* As we can see he is both a talent and a scholar, but in my opinion, it is his perception and clarity of vision that make him one of the leaders and the visionaries in the African theatre movement. He seems to know how to ask the right questions, especially about relationships of art forms and the culture of African people as they both relate to the development of African theatre. And he is especially interested in the use of music in the development of African theatre. In this connection I should like to mention one instance in which he and I collaborated regarding the issue of music in African theatre. We wanted to collaborate on a piece that would be a celebration and a creation in African style using music, dance, mime, the word, and things connected with a

special experience. I had been working on a "Black Experience," a
piece based on Darwin Turner's poem "One Last Word," along
with some of my "Gospel Suite" music. When Kwabena came forth
with Ashanti music for a theatrical piece, we were "in business."
Our collaboration was called "Mourning Memorial" to depict a
special funeral mourning memorial experience for Ashanti people
in Ghana and also a special funeral mourning memorial experience
around the Gospel idiom for Black people in America. We were
trying to match "musical vibrations" and fuse a dramatic experience in a memorial occasion for the loss of a loved one.

Evaristo Muyinda is one of Uganda's most versatile and active
musicians. He started playing the xylophones at Nabbale in 1923 at
the age of nine, and since that time music has been a part of his
creative, busy life. In 1948 he began working as demonstrator at
Makerere College and part-time assistant at the Uganda Museum.
Since 1959, however, he has been working full time at the Uganda
Museum. Evaristo studied under the famous Temusewo Mukasa
and upon completion of his studies with Temusewo he taught in
several schools in Uganda. Evaristo is both a creator and an innova-
tor inasmuch as he usually makes his own instruments; he plays
twelve different instruments, and when he, the legend, dies, his
craft may die with him. This is especially true in reference to some
of his instruments, unless some young Ugandan musicians begin to
study with him. Muyinda has been recorded, and two of his most
famous records are "Omunya" and "Akayinja."

It was my good fortune in May 1969 to meet Evaristo Muyinda
and later to collaborate with him in the creation and the presentation of a show entitled *Prelude to Black Power*. I was in Uganda
checking out the "theatre scene" and I met Mrs. Zirimu, Producer,
School Broadcasting Service, Uganda, and also Producer of Ngoma
Players in Kampala. We had just finished doing a radio broadcast
and I told her that I would like to do a theatrical performance while
I was in Kampala. I wanted it to be a collaboration with some of my
African brothers. We talked about the idea over lunch at Mrs. Zirimu's home. At that time she suggested that she could take me to the
village and let me meet one of Uganda's legends. In the village I met
Evaristo, his wife, and his children. We discussed the idea; he liked
it and we decided upon a collaboration. Mrs. Zirimu, one of Ugan-

da's leading dramatists, served as our interpreter for the rehearsals of the production.

In a cooperative venture between Ugandan dramatists, me, and USIS, Evaristo and I staged a successful production of *Prelude to Black Power* at the USIS auditorium in Kampala before a mixed audience of Ugandans and expatriots. For the celebration and the dramatic experience I had provided the dramatic poetry and prose in the Black idiom of Afro-soul. And Evaristo Muyinda had provided the appropriate traditional music of Uganda and he and I were the sole performers. But despite the barrier of language, since I spoke English and he spoke Luganda, we were able to celebrate in our communion of vibrations with each other as well as with the audience. And the members of the family had come together in a unique celebration.

Akin Euba, a young Nigerian composer, is a Senior Research Fellow at the University of Ife in Nigeria. A few years ago he served as a Research Fellow in Music in the Institute of African Studies at the University of Ghana. I met Akin in Ghana where we often discussed the use of music in the development of African theatre. He was searching for a new music, a new music that is distinctly African.

Akin Euba started his musical studies in London, but later became a student of composition and ethnic musicology at the University of California. In his early studies, he experimented in combining African and Western instruments to be used in the extension of African music. Recently, however, he has worked in terms of composing entirely in the African tradition itself—trying to develop new forms within it. Now he uses African instruments, writes in an African style, and utilizes African processes of performances. He is now "rooting" his music more in old forms and extending the creation. In experimenting in music for the Yoruba people from Nigeria he wrote a piece for dance-drama. It was called *Abiku*, based on a poem by J. P. Clark.

I recall with fond memories the occasion of the Eighth Annual Festival of Arts at the Cultural Centre in Kumasi in 1969. My wife, friends, and I had enjoyed the celebration and were now participating in the International Food Fair aspect of the evening. We were all enjoying a hearty meal. We talked about African music, dance, theatre, and other things. Akin spoke of his research in Ghana. "I feel a great need to extend my range in African music, especially as it pertains to the use of different African instruments. I must begin to learn to write for Ghanaian instruments, especially the xylophone and the drums." Akin is indeed extending his range and working closely within the dramatic field, using music and drama. He feels that this form has great possibilities, and that he should like to remain close to traditional music since it is directly related to the people. Along these lines, he has just completed "The Laughing Tree," a work for narrator, chorus, and an orchestra of Nigerian, Ghanaian, and Senegalese instruments. It is based on the story of the mischievous Mr. Tortoise, taken from Kunle Akinsemoyin's "Twilight and the Tortoise."

Mulatu Astatke, the youngest of our group of four using music in the dramatic experience for African theatre, is a young Ethiopian composer. Mulatu told me, "I was greatly influenced by the jazz played by the Black musicians I heard and saw during my brief stay in the United States. I think Duke Ellington was my strongest influence." Mulatu is currently experimenting with music for African theatre, both as background music and as an integral part of the dramatic experience. In a collaboration with Tsegaye Gabre-Medhin, Ethiopia's leading dramatist and Amharic scholar, he provided the music for the production of *Petros at the Hour*. As we have already learned, this production was enthusiastically received by the audience and the critics at the First Pan African Cultural Festival in Algiers in July 1969.

During my tour of East Africa I had the pleasure of doing a television show in Addis Ababa in May 1969 in which the music of Mulatu Astatke was used. We were able to match vibrations for a celebration in TV theatre. The show, which I wrote and in which I performed, embraced a combination of my own poetry and that of Langston Hughes. It became however, a "complete show" through the use of Mulatu Astatke's music, along with visual pictures and paintings of Africa. The program, *Rivers of the Black Man*, was produced by Ethiopia's promising young television producer, Abate Makuria.

CHAPTER
8
Technique in African Theatre

I *Language and Communication*
    wanted to look at the theatre technique in the midst of the celebration of life. I wanted to consider the in-depth problems and the possibilities of the links in the chain of theatre-making in Ghana. I decided however to isolate a single problem and then examine the relationship of that problem to the other links of the chain in the process of theatre making.

I chose the actor—the Ghanaian performer. I would look first at his use of language in the theatre and then examine his problems and possibilities in the overall process of communication in the theatre, both verbal and nonverbal. I could do this within the framework of my research and participant-observation studies at the University, the Ghana Drama Studio, and in the villages. My base essentially, however, was Ghana.

The problems of language and communication in the current Ghanaian theatre movement present a rather complex picture. Many of these problems are found within the process of theatre making just as they may be found anywhere in the world wherever theatre is made. That is to say that some problems arise from the process of creative cooperation in theatre making which requires among other things the use of creative people, diverse audiences, creative materials, and various technical problems. In Ghana, added to these problems were others arising from tradition, from a country in transition, and from the great diversity of languages and dialects in use. This last element alone presents a major obstacle to theatre development in Ghana. The playwright, for example, must decide whether he will and can write in the vernacular, in English, or in both. The director must learn to handle both the symbols and the actions in the play through his players, whether these actions and symbols are written in the vernacular or in English or in both. The dancer and the musician must accommodate the player's need to use both nonverbal and verbal communication taken from the language used by the playwright. And the audience must perceive that which has been communicated.

Of all the links in this theatrical chain, however, the performer has perhaps the greatest challenge. With this thought in mind I sought to examine the role and responsibility of the Ghanaian actor in Ghana's theatre movement. Included in this examination would be an inspection of the actor's use of language and communication.[1] Fortunately Ghanaians from diverse disciplines had already opened the door to this important problem. I decided to examine some of their conclusions.

Professor Jones-Quartey examines the African audience response to words and actions and asks the question: "Why do our African audiences laugh at stage tragedy?" This very important question is yet to be answered. It is especially important from the actor's frame of reference since it invites another question, "What technique does the actor need to enable him to cope with this specific kind of audience reaction?"

Professor Jones-Quartey goes on to make another important observation regarding audience responses. He writes:

> Most typically African audiences watching drama characterize themselves by two different but related reactions: first they participate in the action—emphatically and persistently: second, they turn tragedy into comedy by laughing—laughing at tragedy.[2]

---

[1]Scott Kennedy, "The Use of Language and the Ghanaian Actor's Technique," Institute of African Studies *Research Review*, Vol. 4, No. 2, 1968.
[2]K. A. B. Jones-Quartey, "Tragedy and the African Audience," *Okyeame*, Vol. 3, No. 1, December 1966, p. 50.

Now the desire of the audience to participate in the action is of course in keeping with the participatory nature of African theatre. In respect to the laughter, however, I might suggest that skill, technique, and involvement in characterization probably have much to do with the acceptance or the rejection of the drama as truth and as tragedy. In other words, bad technique and performance must of necessity affect the audience response. This is especially true if serious intentions on the actor's part regarding tragedy are demanded by the script but not fulfilled by the player.

Saka Acquaye writes:

> It takes the Ghanaian about twenty of his most impressionable years to get to understand Western culture, in an effort to secure a position for his material needs . . . it is not easy to find any Ghanaian who can express himself well in English who has not (at the same time) lost something of his personality.[3]

The question then is how does the Ghanaian retain his own African values and personality and also master expression in English. How does the African *performer* learn to deal with a multilingual language situation in the theatre where he is often forced to work in "a borrowed language of a foreign dominator or oppressor"?

Dr. K. E. Senanu, Lecturer in English at the University of Ghana, poses a basic language problem for the director and also the problem of theatre training for the actor. He writes:

> The question is how to handle a script like *The Lion and the Jewel* so that the verbal communication dovetails smoothly into the dance-spectacle, and the dance becomes an organic part of the total production.[4]

Senanu poses a hard question for the director. He asks, in fact, how can the director get the players to communicate the total life of the characters—a total life which includes the vocal life, the physical life, and the emotional and intellectual life of the character. And certainly this question also raises a serious problem for the

[3]F. Saka Acquaye, "The Problem of Language in the Development of the African Theatre," *Ghana Cultural Review*, Vol. 2, No. 1, p. 28.
[4]K. E. Senanu, "Thoughts on Creating the Popular Theatre," *The Legon Observer*, Vol. 2, No. 21, October 13–26, 1967.

actor. After all, in the final analysis it is the actor who must acquire the ability and the technique that will enable him to communicate a total characterization on the stage which includes vocal, physical, emotional, and intellectual life.

Another writer, Professor J. H. Kwabena Nketia issues a direct challenge to the playwright, director, and other persons in the theatre movement when he writes:

> The artist has similarly something to learn from the use of language symbolism in the visual and performing arts, while linguists can gain some insight and understanding into linguistic structures, into language and culture, language and social behaviour from analysis of African materials. . . .

> Modern African states must therefore follow a multi-lingual policy which allows for the use of dominant African languages (each in its respective area) side by side with a world language. Opportunities must therefore be provided in schools as well as in mass literacy campaigns for the study of an African language alongside a world language. . . .

> If we need French and English both for communication with the outside world and for gaining access to Western scientific and technological knowledge, we certainly need our own languages for gaining access to African civilizations and humanism, to the treasures of the African past in which we can re-discover our identity, our spiritual awareness, our sense of pride and our dignity; our sense of pride and our dignity overshadowed in the colonial past.

Nketia feels that a multilingual policy is necessary and justifiable in Africa. He suggests that opportunities be provided in schools for this policy. He thereby opens the door for bilingual or multilingual programs of learning through the arts, for theatre making, and total-creation programs. Speaking of the vernacular languages, he continues:

> These languages were used not only for ordinary social intercourse but also for entertainment, for judicial purposes and for the rituals and ceremonials that characterized the African way of life. . . .

> If we find our languages inadequate, it is because we have
> not contributed anything to them. We have not been able to
> re-create them in the light of the new experience that we have
> acquired, because we have not tried to communicate with our
> own people in our languages.[5]

Nketia makes a special call for the use of vernacular languages, "our own languages." He has also suggested that rich areas in research and creative possibilities remain untapped, especially for dramatic and theatrical experiences. He therefore sets the stage for a bilingual approach to creativity which would appear to be a normal and natural approach to theatre making in Ghana. A bilingual acting company would certainly provide a built-in research and training program for educators, dramatists, and theatrical producers alike. It would offer opportunities in schools for the study of an African language alongside a world language where the students could use the African language for gaining access to African civilizations and humanism. They would also participate in the process of rediscovering their identity and a sense of pride and dignity.

It is true that such a bilingual company would place great demands upon the actors or performers in the company.

As we have seen, concerned Ghanaians in the theatre movement agree that a complex language and communication problem does exist. Let us now focus attention upon relationships and consider language, speech, and communication with the actor in the driver's seat.

Language is an *expression of life*, and theatre mirrors life. The language of the theatre involves both verbal and nonverbal communication. It involves the use of symbols as well as the use of actions. But since the *language of drama is speech*, not pure literature, proper voice and speech production are essential to the actor. And this is especially true for the African actor, since he is more often than not dealing with oral literature. And the *essence of oral literature* is *speech*. Oral literature only *comes to life through performance*. The language of drama is that which is spoken and heard, that which

[5]J. H. Kwabena Nketia, "The Language Problem and the African Personality," *African Humanism—Scandinavian Culture: A Dialogue*, Copenhagen, August 13–23, 1967.

speaks both of sound and sense, of rhythm and rhyme, of words and music and action. It is that which *shows* the *behavior of a player*, communicated through his actions, thoughts, and feelings to an audience.

Speech, according to Benjamin Whorf, is "the best show man puts on," while language, according to John Carroll, serves two major functions, namely: (1) As a *system of responses* by which individuals communicate with each other *(inter-individual communication)*, and (2) As a system of responses that facilitates thinking and action for the individual *(intra-individual communication)*. So we see that the actor is among other things a speech man and a man of communication inasmuch as he deals with both the inter-individual communication as well as the intra-individual communication in his art.[6]

The Actor

The actor deals in *theatrical terms* and must *communicate* this *language of life* to his audience. Therefore the actor's life must be four-dimensional, that is, vocal, physical, emotional, and intellectual—*a four-dimensional theatrical life* depicting a character in a particular situation of life's dilemma at a given moment in time. Consequently, the actor must learn to work with the subject of theatre, *i.e.* life; and his instrument of theatre, himself. Moreover, he must understand the process of communication and the psychology of an audience. It also helps if he understands the nature of stimulus and response, theories of learning and memory, and the importance of sensory perception and learning through the senses. In short, the actor must understand and use *the language of symbols* in order to take the play and its characters from the page. But he must also understand and use *the language of actions* in order to place the play and its characters on the stage. Since much of the work of the actor embraces language and communication, it follows then that voice and speech production, movement and mime, and the use of any other skills that deal with verbal and nonverbal communication are essential to the actor's training and discipline.

    [6]B. L. Whorf, *Language, Thought and Reality* (Cambridge, Mass.: M. I. T. Press, 1956). J. B. Carroll, *Language and Thought* (Englewood, N. J.: Prentice-Hall, 1964).

The actor is the theatrical medium. Marshall McLuhan concludes that, "The medium is the message," because it is the *medium* that *shapes* and *controls* the scale and form of human association and action. Now inasmuch as the actor is the theatrical medium, it follows then that theatre companies should pay more attention to the actor and his needs because the key to any company is the actor. He is the one who interprets the play for the audience. He explains, expounds, or translates. He reveals meaning. He acts as an agent between two parties in a bargain. The bargain in the process of theatre is an *experience* shaped from the ideas and emotions *generated by the actor.* The task then for the actor is to search out or find the experience; understand the experience; and then communicate that experience to an audience. The actor therefore is one of the most important forces in the dramatic experience. *He is the connecting link between the experience and the audience.*

Of all the theatrical elements the actor is the closest to the audience. This is true in most theatres whether they be European, Asian, or African. The actor turns the play into theatre. Through him the ideas and emotions of the play are most readily communicated and expressed. His magnetism and power are felt most by the audience. The actor's role becomes even more important in African theatre however because of his *special player-audience relationship* in respect to contact, rapport, empathy, and vibration, and the *participatory nature* of the *celebration* in the *experience* of *a total creation.*

In African theatre, *the actor controls the celebration and the creation.* He is the *"sharer of the experience,"* not the "dispenser of the experience." He is always in immediate touch with his audience as they share the experience with him. *He is the embodiment of his culture. He is the exemplifier of his arts.*

Our participation-observation studies all seemed to point naturally towards a bilingual approach to the theatre movement. We therefore decided that the bilingual approach would be our point of departure in theatre making. We would use "that borrowed language, English," and our own language, Twi, one of the vernacular languages; we would use them both at the Ghana Drama Studio and also in our classes at the University. In time the conclusions in our experiment underscored the justification for a bilingual or multilingual approach to theatre companies in Ghana and probably throughout most of Africa.

Our conclusions however were gradual and came to us in stages. We first discovered that the following facts were significant to our experiment.[7]

The actor must learn how to use his own instrument—himself (his body and voice and mind) as a medium for his art. He must also learn how to take a character from drama along with a dramatist's comment on that character, and find the dramatic experience. Using his own inspiration, talent, and technique, he must then learn how to express and communicate that dramatic experience to an audience. He must learn how to share that experience. The audience in turn translates the experience in their own terms and "feeds back" to the actor.

After our initial discoveries we then proceeded to examine these findings in the light of a training program for the Ghanaian actor.[8] We began to stress the importance of the use of the actor's language in the development of his craft, especially in respect to technical training and skill in his art. We soon realized however that the African actor should not be trained in isolation, as is often the case in Western training programs. We felt that the *integration of the arts concept* should be stressed. In other words, all facets of the actor's skills and art should be *interrelated in the training program,* facets such as acting technique, voice and speech production, music, dance, mime, and other skills of the African actor. The actor should be trained in *basic communication* which stresses both verbal and non-verbal communication *from an African frame of reference,* based on tradition, culture, and *his modes of expression and communication.*

The training program should be designed to emphasize the importance of THE LIFE and THE BEHAVIOR of the ACTOR on the stage in relation to his communication, his expression, and his culture. His ACTOR'S LIFE should always include a combination of the vocal, physical, emotional, and intellectual life of the character. In other words the actor should be trained to communicate and express

[7]Scott Kennedy, "Ghanaian Producers for Radio and Stage—Similarities in Training Programs," Institute of African Studies *Research Review,* Vol. 5, No. 1, 1968.
[8]Scott Kennedy, "An Approach to African Theatre," Institute of African Studies *Research Review,* Vol. 5, No. 2, 1969.

himself through his thoughts, his actions, and his movements. We therefore set about to design exercises for the integration of this African "total-life training" for the African actor.

The focus of this particular aspect of our experiment centered around the ENERGY and the ACTIONS of the actor stemming from his *expression* and his *communication*. The design stressed exercises including the specialized techniques of dance, voice, speech, mime, music, and basic acting. We sought however to integrate and synchronize those exercises in a unified manner. The training program focused upon creating "a complete performer"—a performer who is always ready and able *to celebrate life* on the stage and to involve himself in *a total creation* in a *people-oriented manner*.

Our training program revealed many discoveries and conclusions for those of us involved in the experiment.[9] Let us consider some of the discoveries.

The actor develops a better acting technique as he improves in the use of his language. Though the potential for acting technique is rich and varied, the *concept of African theatre,* and "the *idea* of theatre" in respect to the discipline of the craft in Ghana and the professional acting technique must be encouraged and supported by the actor. Both the *concept* and the *idea* in training programs are slowly being developed within the consciousness of the theatre-makers in Ghana.

In the training program a definite need exists for the "tune-in" process in respect to the use of language in the theatre; the "unlocking" process should go hand in hand with the "tune-in" process. Actors must become much more aware of the importance of the use of language in the theatre; they must also be taught to "dig deeply" for the dramatic experience in the literature of life. The director must show and teach the actor the difference between *the literary approach to the theatre* and *the theatrical approach to the theatre.* The actor is much more "at home" and "comfortable" when using his first language than he is with the borrowed language of English. Consequently a method must be designed to transfer the physical habit patterns used by the actor in his first language to his use of

[9]Scott Kennedy, "A Bilingual Approach to Theatre Development in Ghana," in Gilbert Ansare, *Ghanaian Languages* (Ghana: Ghana Publishing Corporation, 1969).

English and of other languages. Actors should be encouraged to use their vernacular languages first in theatre companies along with other languages.

Technique

TECHNIQUE is the actor's tool for the creation, re-creation, and sustaining of a role. Often the amateur actor can create beautiful life on the stage, but it is spotty and erratic, and rarely if ever sustained. Technique enables an actor to sustain a role. The theatrical process therefore must find a method that enables the actor to do this—*create life and sustain life*. It must also *create conditions that make it possible* for the actor to produce "good tone" (voice and speech production) and "believable life."

Many ingredients go into acting technique. They include, among other things, attitude, stage presence, audience presence, the use of objects (image-objects, imagination-objects, people-objects, and inanimate-objects), relationships to places, persons, and things; communicative need, or intention or action (WHAT he wants, WHY and HOW he wants it; WHAT and WHY and HOW he wishes to communicate it—through storytelling-drama, dance-drama, or ceremonial-drama, or a combination of these or by some other means; ability to characterize, impersonate, interpret, perform, and BECOME an EMBODIMENT of the ACT (doing) and an EXEMPLIFIER of the EXPERIENCE—BEING.

The actor's job demands that he possess the proper ACTING TECHNIQUE coupled with talent and specific cultural insights and knowledge of art forms which enable him to depict the specifics of a character, a culture, a communication, a people, a given circumstance, for a PEOPLE.

The actor's life on the stage carries with it a certain *energy* stemming from the specifics of the character depicted on the stage. The ACTOR'S ENERGY is dependent upon a number of aspects and ingredients. They include language, voice and speech pattern, intention, action or communicative need, attitude, and numerous variables in the personality and culture of the character being depicted or portrayed. PERSONALITY may be viewed as the sum total of the individual involving his actions, reactions, and interactions.

CULTURE is one's way of doing things, or the life-styles of a specific group of people.

The Ghanaian personality and culture transmit a myriad of shades, varieties, and nuances blending into a unified whole accepted as Ghanaian and as African. Yet we know that the Ewe traditions are both similar and dissimilar to Ashanti, Ga, Fanti, Dagboni and other "nation-group-tribes" comprising Ghana. The physical habit patterns in the production of the speech and voice in the language of Ga are somewhat different from those in Ewe or Twi or other Ghanaian languages. In other words there are specific physical habit patterns in each Ghanaian language. Also the physical movement patterns in each group vary from group to group. Consequently the TOTAL ENERGY of one group is dependent upon the physical habit patterns from his voice, speech, movement, and language; in other words it is dependent upon his vocal life, physical life, emotional life, and intellectual life which merge to reflect or depict a SPECIFIC QUALITY OF ENERGY.

A broad training program for the development of players and company staffs must be launched; and much more time should be spent on developing actors with "a discipline for the theatre." The University of Ghana (Division of Theatre Studies, Dance and Music) and the Ghana Drama Studio should provide this training base and should try to bridge the communication gap between the academic and the processional theatre in Ghana. Traveling theatre companies must be taken all over Ghana and especially to the villages.

Stronger relationships should exist between theatre forces such as the Arts Council of Ghana, the University of Ghana (Theatre Studies, Dance, Music) the Ghana Drama Studio and other theatre groups. Moreover, both private enterprise and the government should be encouraged to help finance this theatre development in Ghana. Outside financial support through foundation grants and scholarships should also be sought.

Specific theatre audiences must be created and developed. The Ministry of Education should be encouraged to support the program, especially as it relates to audience development within the schools and the language program; Ghana Broadcasting and Television should also be encouraged to support this movement and step up the use of programs created from the companies. Churches in Ghana should also be encouraged to support the program, especially as it relates to audience development within their own congregations.

Teamwork is essential in company development, and consequently, the theatre forces in Ghana must learn how to work cooperatively for the good of the total development of theatre in Ghana. They should strive for unity in purpose and concept despite the fact that they may not have uniformity in respect to company development, creativity, or training programs.

The bilingual approach to theatre is a sound approach and this particular concept of theatre is important and necessary for theatre development in Ghana. It provides opportunities in schools for hearing and seeing an African language alongside a world language. It provides opportunities for Ghanaians to become more aware and appreciative of their own vernacular languages. The use of African languages helps the actors and also the audiences to rediscover their identities and a sense of pride and dignity overshadowed in the colonial past. They also become more aware of the bilingual or multilingual nature of communication in Ghana and learn to appreciate the importance of the use of both vernacular languages and English. No doubt translators will be provoked into making translations of plays into English from the vernacular and vice versa. Language attitudes and habits in Ghana will be changed in a positive sense, and theatre companies will gain a rich experience from their multilingual work.

Ghana stands prepared to root its theatre in the culture of its people. At the same time it is prepared to break loose from its old educational ways and find new sources and ideas of inspiration stemming from African-centered concepts and humanism. It is prepared to find new and exciting ways of engaging youngsters in language activities. Being cognizant of the process used in acquiring a language, wherein speech readiness precedes reading readiness; reading readiness precedes writing readiness, which in turn precedes the complex language skills, the Ministry is beginning to place an early emphasis on oral communication and the speaking of languages. It stands prepared to revamp its entire system; to take from the rich African oral traditions; to mechanize the system if necessary and use communication experts. It stands prepared to change language attitudes and habits in Ghana and at the same time produce giants in the creative and performing arts where language is so important.

Although our bilingual experiment provided us with discoveries and revelations it also gave us problems and questions. For example, in keeping with our major concern for the actor, we found ourselves struggling with the questions, "What is the task of the African actor or Black actor as an artist in the contemporary Black world? Why does he play such an important role in the shaping of his Black world of today and of tomorrow? What are his *problems* and his *possibilities?*"

The Dream

The Black actor is the MEDIUM and the MESSAGE. He is a maker of VALUES. By *profession* he is an *actor*, but by *destiny* he is a *shaper* of *images* and a *maker* of *values*. As such, he is faced with many problems.

He is faced with the problem of being plagued by *stereotypes* and *myths* about Black people in Western civilization. He is faced with the problem of *adjusting* to a *technological age* of *the mass media* in the highly competitive modern world of today and tomorrow. He is faced with the problem of *preserving* and *re-creating* the *old traditions* of Africa. He is faced with the problem of *creating new forms* and *extending* his *traditional art forms* in new ways for African people throughout the world. And finally, he is faced with the overall problem of a culture conflict in a "continent with peoples in transition."

How then does he cope with these realities and these problems? And in a real sense, how does he as an artist confront the myths of society? How does he *become* an *embodiment* of his arts and an *exemplifier* of his culture in order to play his role and accept the task that destiny has thrust upon him? For example, what is his POWER as the MEDIUM and the MESSAGE in plays, movies, television? In *The King Is Dead?* In *Shaft?* In *Ain't Supposed to Die a Natural Death?* In *Theodros?* In *Petros?* In *The Palm Wine Drinkard?* What is his power as a *fool*, as a *clown*, as a *hero?*

The Black actor must not only learn the art of the intrepreta-
tion, the characterization, and the creation of a role, but he must
also be able to express and communicate that LIFE—the life and
experience of the contemporary Black world from the stage.

Since he is an actor, HE IS HIS OWN INSTRUMENT. He carries his
own instrument with him upon the stage or wherever he goes.
Therefore he must understand the KEYS OF HIS OWN INSTRUMENT in
order that he may play and communicate the proper music or life
of the experience he is sharing. Consequently the Black actor must
strive to gain insights in respect to SELECTION and EMPHASIS. First
there is the selection and emphasis in respect to knowing his own
instrument and being able to play the proper keys on that instrument. Secondly, there is the selection and emphasis in respect to the
use of the OLD and the NEW, the ethnic and the theatrical, the rituals
and the roots, the African and the non-African. And certainly he
must be aware of his need to communicate to all groups of African
people; to the masses, including the literate, the nonliterate; the
urban and the rural; the educated and the uneducated. But at all
times he must strive to link tradition to his art; to wed the past to
the living, and at the same time to embark upon new creations and
discoveries as well as to reinterpret the old. In so doing, he will
always be desirous of keeping abreast of new methods and techniques regarding presentation and theatricality. At all times however he will seek to keep a constant view of the values of his society,
for in the final analysis he will strive to keep his creative roots
embedded in the soil of his culture. His artistic modes of thought
will forever be linked to a communion of vibrations and a communal communication within a true community experience.

Before the Black actor, however, can connect with his role in
society and accept his task as a shaper of images and a maker of
values he must recognize specific realities and he must accept certain responsibilities. He must recognize a reality of the problems
which include proper frame of reference, attitude, skills, knowledge
and expertise in many areas. He must accept the responsibility of
using his skills, his knowledge and his expertise in helping to shape
and mold the contemporary Black world of today and tomorrow—
of actually playing his role as a shaper of images and a maker of
values.

How then can he begin to play this role? How does he begin the journey towards the realization of his task? To begin with he must gain and acquire knowledge and *understanding of the arts of Africa* and of *the Black world.* He must discover the *essential characteristics* and *relationships* of African music, dance, drama, literature, art, sculpture, rituals, and the arts of the Black world. In short, he must learn to know and use the *language of African theatre and the related arts.* Before doing this however he must discover and evaluate the *drama of the life of African people.*

After the discovery of this rich African drama of life he must then strive to develop his instrument and his ability to use his "found materials" in the creative process of making Black theatre. He must place this theatre within the grasp of the masses of African people throughout the world. Eventually it will rest alongside Asian theatre and Western theatre within the sphere of world theatre as a universal expression of man.

Drama on the page only gives the player a MINOR score. The player, however, in order to fulfill the communicative cycle and circular response must play the MAJOR score, that score of "life" interpreted and created by his own instrument—that MAJOR score taken from his own life's experience. Today's Western man, because of the nature of his circumstances and existence in a highly complex competitive society and his life-styles is usually "uptight" or rigid. He expects to play everything by a *creative rule of interpretation* and consequently finds it very difficult to engage in the *"spirit" of true improvisatory creativity, of a creation within an interpretation.* On the other hand, because of his circumstances, life-styles, the nature of his existence, and his mode of expression and communication, *African man is usually improvisational in his creation.* He is less "uptight" or rigid. He seems to have a *natural instinct for the "major" score.* He possesses the necessary "time-space" and "looseness" to fill the gap between the major and the minor score. He finds it easy to engage in the "spirit" of true improvisational creativity of a creation within an interpretation.

Therefore in most instances the Black actor can be an interpreter as well as a creator at the same time. He must however, like the jazz performer, *learn to compose within the framework of his interpretation.* Striving at all times to be true to the score of the universal and the Black experience he must first understand and work with the minor score in order to fill the major score. And the greater his talent, creativity, discipline and technique, the easier it is for him to improvise and fill his major score. This is especially true if he is RICH as a human being; if he is a SHARING human being, willing and eager to give witness to a celebration of life and a communion of vibrations—willing to examine his survival experience. On the stage he mirrors his experience from life. If within the framework of his unique circumstances from life he has struggled to SURVIVE or to LIBERATE himself, he must dare to learn how to share this experience on the stage. He must be prepared to DIE a little on the stage, much as he has done every day in his life. He must be prepared to be played the fool, to walk the tightrope between sanity and insanity, framing man's inhumanity to man within the soul and the spirit of his African genius. He must die in order to be born. He must stretch his craft, his instrument, and his vision. He must create a theatre within a world where mankind is important. He must dispense information and images designed for some use by the community of man. He must be modern man and merge his humanism with his technological expertise. But he must never merely possess scholarship and creativity without humanistic roots and a vision of man. He must search for a vision of a new man. And within this search he could dream. So he began to dream.

He dreamed. He dreamed that Mother Africa had made him the original man. And as such all things could stem from him. He was universality. He dreamed. He dreamed that Mother Africa had given him a unique instrument. And so he began to KNOW his own instrument, to keep it tuned and sharpened and in good physical and mental condition. He began to discover the notes and the keys of his instrument. He began to search for the best way to play his instrument. However, unlike the African xylophone, the bamboo flute, and other instruments with set keys for set melodies, he discovered that his personal instrument was forever growing, stretching, developing, unlocking, and remaining either tuned or untuned. Soon he learned that the process of growth lay within himself and his own experiences—within the range of his own instrument or being.

He dreamed. And within his dream he learned that he became obligated to play his instrument in human terms and the universality of the human experience. But above and beyond that dimension he learned that he had to take from the "richness of his own unique Black experience." He forged the embellishments of that Black experience upon the core of the human experience. And in so doing he began to create from the roots of himself. He began to embark upon an entirely new experience for and in the theatre.

He dreamed. He dreamed that he played and he played. He played his instrument with honesty and with sincerity using his inner experience and his Afro-soul, for they were inseparable. And soon he became the embodiment of Black theatre and the dramatic experience, couched in the misery, the music, and the mirror of that Black experience. And he began to see himself not only as an artist, but as an exemplifier of African theatre. And from within the music of his own rich theatrical experience he became an *embodiment of his own being*. His cries were different; his expression was different; his responses were different, for he was different. And then he saw the parade, the carnival, the celebration. And they were there too. They were all there doing their own thing.

There was Duke Ellington at his piano. A master of the materials and the technique for his instrument, the piano, he was applying his own uniqueness through his medium of jazz, a new creation. And he had it, a new sound, and a new experience, which people called jazz. There were others, so many he could hardly see them all. Duro Ladipo and his company; Okot p'Bitek, Evaristo Muyindo with his unique musical instruments; Robert Seramagna and his company; Wole Soyinka and his company; Efua Sutherland and her company; John Pepper Clark, Saka Acquaye, James Ngugi, Tsegaye Gabre-Medhin. And then he heard the sound. It was Miles. Miles Davis had teamed up with Dizzie and Louie and they were having a "blowing good time." And they blew his mind through their own unique technique and experience in a universal mold of the jazz idiom. And then the chorus began to sing. He had never heard anything like it. Bessie Smith, Billie Holliday, Dinah Washington, Ethel Waters, Aretha Franklin, Mahalia Jackson, Lena Horne, Paul Robeson, Roland Hayes, Jimmie Rushing, Billie Eckstein, Ray Charles, Harry Belafonte, Sammy Davis, James Brown. He couldn't see them all. But out there in front was the Jackson Five with Michael leading the group. And what a sound it was. He had never heard anything like it before. And then he heard Marian Anderson, Leontyne, and Matiwilda. He couldn't take it anymore. He didn't know what to listen for. But he dug it, all of it coming together— the spirituals, the blues, the gospel, the jazz, the soul. It was a new sound all right stemming from the richness of the Black experience. New dimensions and new forms in the area of new creations. He dreamed.

He dreamed about the rich possibilities for the Black actor. And he saw them all waiting in line. There was Canada Lee, William Marshall, Ossie Davis, Sidney Poitier, Bill Cosby, and Ivan Dixon in a line stretching into a sea of Blackness. There they were all waiting to create a unique presentation through Black theatre based upon the Black experience—waiting to accept the challenge. They had all witnessed the Black experience manifesting itself in the music of the spirituals, the blues, the gospel, the jazz, and the soul. They knew now that it was also possible for the *Black experience to manifest itself through the celebration*, the total creation, the theatre. They began to use themselves and their inner power to find a way to express themselves in a unique manner, in a new form, in a new total creation with all of its dimensions. As instruments of action, energy, and creativity; as actors engaged in the cultural thrust of theatre they began working to help bring about a SPIRITUAL CONSCIOUSNESS of humanity, a reawakening, a revolution.

Resting between evolution and revolution, between annihilation and liberation they must confront and destroy the fallacious myths and stereotypes about Blacks. They must help deniggerize the Black man. They must replace the old Negro-African man of yesterday with the new contemporary Limbo Black of today and tomorrow—that new Black man couched and caught between survival and liberation, resting between Black consciousness and Black reality. They must place this new LIMBO BLACK squarely in the minds and the hearts of Blacks and non-Blacks throughout the world. They must be the embodiment of African theatre, the connecting link between the people and the play; the medium and the message —the REVOLUTION. And as such, they must demand relevant theatre, a theatre of change, a theatre of revolutionary change.

African theatre itself is basic communication, and as such it must be a dynamic, communicative, and expressive force, a total eruption of the art forms which pricks man's inner experience and provokes the totality of his sensory perception. African theatre, in its current stage of development, must be both evolutionary and revolutionary. It must be a connective link of the life process and the people. It must begin to bring all groups together on a common human plane, transcending the barriers of class, status, and religion, embracing and connecting cross cultures and solidifying the core of man's strivings for freedom, equality, and being.

This ever-evolving African theatre must strive to address itself to the needs of the people. It must be a theatre *from* the people and *within* the people; orchestrating the cries and the soul of the people. It must be a theatre of art *for* the people, rather than art for art's sake. And as such, it must utilize the African culture concept which stresses a direct relationship between the culture and the people, the behavior and the act, the act and the actions.

It will of necessity rely heavily upon the integrated arts concept of theatre which utilizes all available verbal and nonverbal forms of communication for a "total experience" in theatre. Thus, by its very nature it becomes *a theatre of change*, a theatre of examination, inspection, discovery, confrontation, and *revolution. Revolution is its raison d'être.*

Black Theatre and African People

Black American theatre and African theatre are blood brothers. They both have their own unique dramatic consciousness which is more African than European, a dramatic consciousness coming out of the genre of the experience of these people who are called African people or Black people. African theatre springs from a unique cultural traditional experience, while Black American theatre stems from a social experience and expression. Both theatres however have a common heritage link and utilize similar modes of expression and communication. African theatre—Black theatre, or theatre of the contemporary Black world—must be perceived from a cultural, a social, and a dramatic-theatrical perspective. It must not merely be perceived from a "fine arts" or art for art's sake view.

To be "Black" in America is to be revolutionary—to seek self-determination. It is to set one's own frame of reference and definitions. It is to understand that as a Black American, you are more "African people" than European people. Such thinking by Blacks in America is both frightening and revolutionary to the average white American. It is also revolutionary "to do your Black thing" in respect to ethnic drama or theatre. Woodie King Jr.'s act of producing *The Black Quartette* was revolutionary. Melvin Van Peebles' *Ain't Supposed to Die a Natural Death* and *Sweet Sweet Back's Bad Ass Song* were revolutionary. For "doing the Black American thing in Black Theatre" is to step out of the role or image prescribed by the white American for Blacks, whether the play is *The Dutchman*, *A Raisin in the Sun*, *Blues for Mr. Charlie*, *Funnyhouse of a Negro*, *Simply Heavenly*, or *Mulatto*. And of course the Black image from Africa or anywhere else in the contemporary Black world as depicted in *The Palm Wine Drinkard*, *LeRoi Christophe*, *The Lion and the Jewel*, and *Kongi's Harvest* is certainly new for most Americans.

Much of our learning is dependent upon our vision, our perception, and our images. Our attitude and behavior are usually created or influenced by images. Images of the Black man in western civilization have been marred by distortions, omissions, and a faulty frame of reference or definition. For example, consider the omission of the Black cowboy and his contribution to the development of the West in most history books. And pause to remember the comic buffoon or the docile Christian slave in plays, movies, and history books. And yet Theodros, Petros, Chaka, King Menelik, Malcolm X, and Dr. Martin Luther King were not niggers. They were universal men—African people. Yes, images of the Black man have been marred by the creation of myths or stereotypes, or the blatant use of overt and covert racism.

Black theatre smashes this fallacious "Nigger-Image." In America, Amamu Baraka (LeRoi Jones) epitomizes this "Blackness" of the "revolutionary Black writer" through his actions and in his plays, *Revolutionary Black Plays* and others. From both Africa and America, Tsegaye Gabre-Medhin's *Theodros* and *Petros at the Hour*, Dr. J. B. Danquah's *The Third Woman*, Duro Ladipo's *Oba Waja*, and Amamu Baraka's *The Slave* and *Slave Ship* all give the lie to those fallacious stereotypes. In a real sense they help deniggerize the Black man.

And yet the average white asks the question, "Why Black Theatre? Why not just American theatre? When you speak of Black theatre, you speak as a racist." How naïve of this white American. Especially when he should know that there was never any "true American theatre." There was nothing but white American theatre shaped in the white image. White American theatre with white European values and a perpetuation of the myth of white superiority. Today's Broadway scene still seems to reflect this image, and a good example is the musical *1776.*

Who created these damaging stereotypes of Blacks? Who is guilty? Among others, the white American writer is certainly guilty. For example, historians Henry Steele Commager and Samuel Eliot Morison reduced the Black man to a caricature represented as "Sambo" or "Mr. Zero." In their Pulitzer prize-winning textbook *The Growth of the American Republic,* they wrote, "As for Sambo, whose wrongs moved the abolitionists to wrath and tears, there is some reason to believe that he suffered less than any other class in the South from its peculiar institution [slavery]. Although brought to America by force, the incurably optimistic Negro [sic] soon became attached to the country and devoted to his white folks."

White playwrights also lost little time in establishing in their plays numerous stereotypes such as: (1) *the buffoon:* a comic, ignorant type; (2) *the tragic mulatto:* a product of miscegenation, excluded from both groups; (3) *the Christian slave:* a docile worshipper of his white master and his immortal master; (4) *the carefree primitive:* an exotic, amoral slave; and (5) *the Black beast:* a villain who seeks equality with the white people.

For years Blacks were denied their existence as human beings. They were stripped of their cultural heritage and enclosed in an invisible wall. They were robbed of their rich resources. They were literally erased from the "world of theatre." Blotted out! Only to be used to dot the i's and to cross the t's as the whites saw fit! The theatre belonged to the white world and the whites shaped it and controlled it. They never entertained a thought that the Black man could be an integral part of it. The white man's mind was forever at work with his stream of consciousness permeating his white world. And as far as his Negro was concerned . . . *"I want you, and I will use you! You must be shaped to be like me! But you can never be me. You can never be equal to me."* So the Black man was, in Paul Lawrence Dunbar's words, "To wear the mask that grins and lies/But let the world dream otherwise." This was true in everyday life, and it was also true in the world of the theatre. And whenever the Black man was "used" or "misused" by white theatre-makers Black directors were never called in to score or to orchestrate the "true cries of that specific dramatic experience." *Green Pastures, Porgy and Bess,* and *Lost in the Stars,* among a host of others, are examples both on the stage and in the movies.

Black theatre had to reemerge at this particular moment of time because of the white world's resistance to the Black man's culture and existence. It also came at this particular time because of the Black man's desire to stage a last attempt to communicate in human terms with the white man, thereby establishing a workable white-Black relationship.

Today's Black theatre advocates are examining a new aesthetic. They are setting up new frames of reference in respect to "their art." They are starting a "New Dialogue." They are setting forth their own definitions and examining SELF: the Black man and his relation to himself, his society, to everything. The new dialogue is not necessarily a dialogue of exclusion so far as the white man or anyone else is concerned, but it is certainly *a dialogue of inspection.* It is therefore a therapeutic dialogue for everyone, but especially for the Black man. And it is a "new ball game" for the white man. It is a dialogue addressed to Black people, but by circumlocution, it is also a dialogue inviting the white man and others to inspect these new Rules in this new Game—with the rules now set by Black people. Though the game may be very similar to the old game, the frame of reference is now being set and decided by the Black man —the Afro-American.

In terms of Black theatre, the themes are Black themes. The dialogue and the dramatic experience are Black. The themes may address themselves to Black-white relationships, the jazz experience, religion and the church, the folk experience, double consciousness, Black life-styles and the substance of Black life, or many other subjects or issues. A few examples of the plays are Ernie McClintock's production of *El Hajj Malik, The Life and Death of Malcolm X*, Lonnie Elder's *Ceremonies of Dark Old Men*, Ed Bullins' *Clara's Ole Man* and *In New England Winter*, James Baldwin's *The Amen Corner*, J. E. Franklin's *Black Girl*, Melvin Van Peebles' *Ain't Supposed to Die a Natural Death*, and my own *The King Is Dead*.

The visionaries of the Black theatre movement in America are taking a hard look at African Studies and Black relationships. Such an inspection of African Studies usually brings about a positive relationship between the Afro and the African. It also brings about attitude-relationship changes between the Black man and the white man both in America and in Africa. In time, the Afro by inspecting his own "roots" and examining his relationship to Mother Africa gains a better self-image. Thus he reduces for himself some of his self-hate and replaces it with a certain degree of self-love and self-determination. He discovers his "manhood," and as a result, gains much more respect for himself. Using his added knowledge and understanding of the needs of Africans and Black people around the world, he is able to articulate his message with much more clarity than ever before. And in the long run, he therefore establishes a better dialogue for and with all persons concerned, but especially among Blacks throughout the world.

6
Memories–From Dakar
to Algiers

From Dakar to Algiers is a distance of less than two thousand miles by air. It would be hard to measure this distance for me however in terms of my African memories. It would also be hard to measure this distance for African people in terms of their recognition and their acceptance of being African or Black and the implications of that situation.

In 1966 Dakar, Senegal was host for the First World Festival of Negro Arts. In 1969 Algiers, Algeria was host for the First World Pan African Cultural Festival. The cities, Dakar and Algiers themselves, helped set the stage for the climate of each festival, for both were ideal settings for international gatherings.

On May 25, 1857, the Commandant Superieum of Goree and dependencies, Capitaine de Vaisseau L. Protet, reported to the Government of the Second Empire in Paris: "I have the honor to inform you that I have raised the French flag over the small fort which we have constructed in Dakar." This French flag, flying over an uncompromising African fishing village, marked the birth of Dakar. From 1902 to 1959 Dakar was the capital of the Federation of West Africa. Since 1958 it has been the capital of Senegal.

Today DAKAR, capital of the Republic of Senegal, one of the largest cities in Africa, is the administrative center of the Senegalese Government. Here in this "French city" still suffering from French colonization, one may first view Dakar as another "little Paris."

And yet the rhythms and the smells of Africa permeate the city, for the African traditions and cultures have not been destroyed. The African personality struggles to be seen and heard, often reflecting itself through the Senegalese writers, many of whom are immersed in the negritude movement.

Dakar, in appearance and character a modern European rather than an African city, at the time of the Festival had a population of over five hundred thousand. Now, six years later, Dakar, one of the most densely populated cities of Africa, has a population of nearly one million. Though Wolof is Dakar's major African language, Fulani and Mende are also spoken; and many of the people also speak French. Dakar, often called the Gateway to West and Southern Africa since most commercial planes and ships from other parts of the world call there en route to other parts of Africa, has one of the largest seaports in Africa. Her airport is of international standard and possesses the capacity for any aircraft in use in the world today. The beautiful University of Dakar, Senegal's only university, is situated in the city. Majestic modern buildings and the attractive boulevards add to Dakar's beauty.

My memories recorded vivid Festival image-impressions of the sights and sounds of Dakar—with its many poets, writers, artists, and musicians—with its beautiful Senegalese women, elegant in their normal everyday dress. Here I was among members of the family of African people. Here I was also among ten thousand visitors from four continents who had come to immerse themselves in the dance, folkloric, and theatrical performances; in the exhibits of painting and sculpture, and the everyday life of Dakar. Also I was among people in an atmosphere of brotherhood and warmth. And certainly there would be many more things for us to do each day than was humanly possible. There were four daily showings of festival films (over one hundred fifty films related to Black life were entered for jury consideration), poetry readings (I would read my poetry along with Langston Hughes, Yevgeny Yevtushenko, and others), boat excursions to the Island of Goree (that infamous slave depot), bus excursions to the Senegalese interior, jazz concerts at Camp Marin, dramatic presentations at the new Daniel Soreno Theatre and at the Daniel Brottier, two different dance and drum ensembles performing simultaneously in the Place de l'Indépendance, traditional dancing by National troupes at the Stade Amitié, traditional art at the Musée Dynamique, contemporary art at the Palais de Justice, and parties, receptions, parades, and parties.

I sharpened my sensory perception in order that I might better view the multicolored life teeming in the market places. Pass along the attractive streets such as the Avenue Roume, Avenue de la Republique, Avenue William Ponty, and the Place de l'Indépendance, and enjoy the cosmopolitan nature of Dakar with its beautiful hotels of international standard and its restaurants offering a great variety of cooking: African, European, and Asian.

Dakar is noted for its many cultural activities. The Daniel Sorano theatre, situated right in the center of the city, is a twelve-hundred-seat theatre and has an ultramodern stage with the capacity for all kinds of cultural productions. Dakar's Dynamique Museum is perhaps the first modern gallery in Africa. It is a museum which provides education in the arts, and also allows for cultural exchanges. Here the works of Senegalese artists and artisans are housed along with the works of foreign artists.

All over Dakar I sensed a *recognition of the roots* by members of the African family who had come "home" to discuss direction. The three founding fathers of negritude, President Léopold Senghor, Aimé Césaire, and Léon Damas were there to connect the festival with the past. Some of the members of the family had decided not to appear for one reason or another, but the Festival would flower and blossom without them. To be sure there would be disagreement, definitional difficulties, conceptual meanderings. But what family among humans has uniformity of frame of reference or direction? But after all as a family they are unified by their roots. So the family of African people had gathered on the soil of Dakar to "give witness to negritude." And the establishment had come as if to say, "We are saying it is so—we are the exemplifiers of our culture and the embodiment of its arts. And if we, the people, are not, then tell me who is."

From Dakar to Algiers! Try to measure that distance in terms of African people and their needs and their attempt to redefine themselves while liberating themselves. While liberating themselves from both the outside enemy oppressor and also from themselves, often their own enemy. A shadow cast itself over my shoulder as I caught a glimpse of this distance from Dakar to Algiers for African people around the world. As I sneaked a peek through the window of the eyes of Africa's attempt to liberate itself from her colonial mentality and her slave mentality. There was the image in terms of the huge task of deniggerizing the nigger whether he be dressed in the clothing of the slavemaster or in the clothing of the colonial master. There was the image in terms of the quiet quest and a striving to cope with the problem of neocolonialism in Africa and the neoslavery condition in America and elsewhere in the world of African people.

Certainly Dakar to Algiers focused upon Black people's needs and aspirations. Dakar stemmed from the negritude movement and was a a reinterpretation and a reclaiming of the spirit of African man and his cultural soul. It was a self-awareness, a realization, a recognition. It was a recognition that Blacks must begin to deal with the realities of being Black and all that Blackness means.

Dakar was the *recognition and an acceptance by* the *patient* of the *mental illness* in his *first stage of the cure.* It was a recognition of the problem and the ability to state it. It was a recognition of the nature of the duality of the mental illness, that is an illness imposed by outsiders and oppressors and also often a self-inflicted consuming mental illness brought upon the sick person himself through his own self-hate and his denial of his own worth and dignity and pride.

On the opening night of the Dakar Festival, Dr. Léopold Senghor, President of Senegal and principal architect of the Festival, told the audience that its purpose was the "defense and illustration of negritude—the elaboration of a new humanism which this time will include all of humanity on the whole of our planet earth."

Aimé Césaire defined negritude in this manner: "Negritude is the mere recognition of the fact of being Black and the acceptance of this fact of our destiny as Black, of our history and of our culture."

Léon Damas put it this way: "The festival is particularly important for Africans who know now that they are not alone in their continent. They know now what we are doing on the other side, and can learn from us. In some ways America's heritage has grown richer than the source. So, you see, we can do something now not only in a 'Cameroon' way or a racial-African way, but in a universal way. The problem is no longer racial, but social and economic. That is the new significance of Negritude. These are the aims of the festival."

Aimé Césaire is convinced of the underlying unity of all Negro peoples. He believes that the implications of the festival transcend a simple reassertion of the common bond between Black people. He considered questions of negritude such as: Where is it going? What are the cultural trends that may be transforming the Black world? Can the restless activity of the festival be given purpose and direction?

He felt that the festival represented a confrontation of all aspects of the Black world, which has an internal unity. Superficially, the traditions of negritude are lost in the US, in the Antilles, and in Brazil, where they have been cut off by slavery. In the bourgeois elites of these areas, the common bond of negritude has been superficially lost. "These people are terribly formal with each other, they are too correct and less instinctive; in rising they have paid a price. But this can change."

Has negritude changed? "It is not the negritude that has changed in the last ten years, but the historical situation . . . Negritude has been seen as a force for political change. Since the realization of Black African independence, negritude has necessarily assumed more ethical and moral implications. It must direct the evolution of Africa. It was a political weapon, but it can how have a broader emphasis. Negritude is a philosophy which shakes itself free, which unites, which makes a synthesis of the traditional and the modern."

Césaire saw an immediate need for another festival and he said: "The next step after this festival is another festival as soon as possible, perhaps in two years. This festival anticipates the future of African unity. The power of renewal is the strength of the cultural."

The Algerian people will tell you, "The soil of Algeria is hard, intractable; the people take their image from this soil. Today our main challenge is to gain from our land a higher living standard. The new Algeria feels most acutely the need to cultivate a national identity which proved so costly to acquire. We are a people trying to achieve a national destiny in a language alien to ourselves."

Algeria became independent in July 1962. The National Council of the Algerian Revolution (CNRA) had met in Tripoli in June of the same year to approve the future government's program. On September 15, 1963, Ahmed Ben Bella was elected to the Presidency of the Algerian Republic.

The Army coup d'état of June 19, 1965, ended the Ben Bella regime. Since that date, the Revolutionary Council has been the Supreme state body. Its current chairman is Colonel Houari Boumedienne, who also acts as Premier.

Algiers is Algeria's great city—modern with a large commodious harbor protected by breakwalls, and a population of about 950,-000 people. Algiers by appearance is also a modern European city rather than an African city. And although the French also left their stamp upon Algiers, like Dakar, it too is struggling to assert its own identity. This terraced city of Algiers climbs from the blue waters of the Mediterranean up the slopes of the coastal hills. Long break-waters shelter an extensive artificial harbor. The buildings rise glistening white from the edge of the water, mounting steeply up the slope of the coastal ranges that wall it all around. High office buildings face the waterfront, but behind and to the west lies the maze of the casbah, teeming with its Arab-Kabyle population. Algiers, Mediterranean in character, resembles European cities on the north side of the sea.

This city of Algiers built on the ruins of the Roman port of Icosium—known as El-Djazair in Arabic—gave refuge to the Andalusians, chased out of Spain because they would not bow to the Spanish domination. They appealed to the Turks, commanded by the Brothers Aroudj and Khair-Eddine, also known as the Brothers Redbeard. They were the ones who managed in the years between 1517 and 1529 to chase the Spaniards out of almost all the towns of Algeria.

Today the people in Algiers say to you, "The aim of political culture in Algeria was to give the people the possibility of once more finding their artistic and intellectual tradition. It was essential both to retrieve and re-create the works of the past, to disseminate them widely and to foster modern creativity whose sources of inspiration are authentically rooted in the national souls."

It was evident therefore that for a country as politically involved as Algeria, information and culture would be indissoluble. In endeavoring, immediately after independence, to fulfill its vocation of national culture, popular culture, and "engaged" or involved culture, the culture of Algeria was truly started off on the right track. In November 1962 the five theatres then existing in Algeria were nationalized and a national theatre company, the Algerian National Theatre or TNA, was formed. The Algerian theatre, which belonged to the people and had first shown its paces during the revolution, quickly acquired its own repertory, actors, and public.

If Dakar was a recognition of the roots, a recognition and an acceptance by the patient in his first stage of the cure, then Algiers was certainly an extension of the cure, an extension of the recognition and self-determination. It was a *coming together* of the *roots and the revolution.* It was a realization and a recognition that African people must begin to deal with the realities of liberation. And that they must begin to evolve a positive plan of action leading to that liberation. It was a recognition of the idea and the concept of unity, if not uniformity, stemming from the idea of an Organization of African Unity—of African people of all shades and colors, sharing a commonality of experiences. Algiers stemming from a direct call from the OAU sought to examine the relationship between culture and communication, and revolution and liberation. Algiers was an extension of the recognition and acceptance by the patient of his mental illness with the aim and view of finding a way to cure that illness.

In his inaugural speech, President Houari Boumedienne, Chairman of the Revolutionary Council and Head of the Government Acting Chairman of the OAU, stressed both unity and liberation as he welcomed the African people and their friends: "Algeria is happy to welcome the First Pan-African Cultural Festival on behalf of our entire continent . . . We should not forget to what an extent this first Pan-African Cultural Festival is concerned not only with our values and sensitivities but also with our very existence as Africans and our common future. By the same token it takes a further step forward in the continuing struggle against all forms of domination. We naturally admitted that freedom, nationhood, personality and finally universal dimension were but the product and origin of culture." In speaking of culture Boumedienne examined its relationship to freedom and concluded that culture must become an instrument for liberation and further development. "Culture in its widest and most complete sense is what enabled men to order their lives . . . The preservation of our culture saved us from the attempts to make us peoples without a soul and without a history; our culture preserved us . . . Culture, which is the cement of our resistance, the source of our oneness, the reason for our right to a universal hearing, the basis of our personalities, and a weapon in our struggle for liberation is also for Africa one of the essential elements in its development and social progress. In the name of man, his rights and acquisitions, we refuse to accept a false destiny, cultural underdevelopment and the disguising of mind, heart and soul as we refused to accept both slavery and racialism. This festival was a duty for us and a debt of gratitude owed to our fathers who preserved our personality. The First Pan-African Cultural Festival must be seen as a united African tribute to its own cultural and artistic foundations, and to its characteristics of structure and expression. We want and *must make our cultures into an instrument for our final liberation and further development.* Culture in general, and in particular our own, will no longer be the basis of injustice or domination, but rather the instrument of a greater understanding between human beings."

Mr. Diallo Telli, Secretary General of the OAU, has already stated that the Festival will certainly be one of the Organization's most judicious and boldest initiatives, as it will materialize Africa's victory over the alienating and depersonalizing forces that have assailed it for centuries. It exemplifies the determination of all the Organization members to bring the combat for freedom to its conclusion. He also proclaimed that: "The wager, which was the initiative for OAU to organize the first Pan African Cultural Festival, is being won. It constitutes the most hazardous initiative of African Unity since its creation. What is here and now certain, is that all who dreamed of the rehabilitation of Africa on a cultural and artistic level will have an exceptional opportunity to meet and exchange points of view, to know and appreciate each other better, and to work out a basic plan more than in the past, as was done on a political level in 1963 in Addis Ababa, the real bases of solidarity and unity of the continent, the governments and the people of Africa."

The Zimbabwe People's Union, engaged in a liberation struggle, saw culture as the nearest thing to its people, and concluded that Africa is best served when expressing its own from its own. They spoke of culture in these words: "Like any other society, Zimbabwe culture is expressed in every walk of life—in song, dance, social relationships, architecture, religion and so on. Our religion is ancestral belief. It is based on the fact that the source and transmitter of life, in essence, is the point of reference for a guide in all problems which confront life . . . Culture is a dynamic expression. It does become a way of expressing appreciation or rejection of a national event. The nearest thing to a people is their way of life, their culture. . . . The Zimbabwe people today are engaged in a liberation struggle. The struggle is to reject foreign impositions in our systems and concepts of culture. The struggle, in a positive sense, is to salvage our culture, live by it and preserve the aspects we consider consistent with progress in this dynamic world. . . . It is our considered view that Africa is best when expressing its own from its own. This is the great necessity of fostering our culture as the basis of our lives and personality."

The Congo-Brazzaville delegation saw the festival as a confrontation and a new era in which African people must strive to liberate the continent of Africa. They spoke in these words: "Africa has proved beyond question that even while enslaved, even transplanted to other continents, even during her struggle for liberation, she will never slacken her cultural and artistic production. It is thanks to her stories, her songs, poems and dances that she managed to survive, to resist, to fight, finally to free herself . . . Culture is not a collection of encyclopedic information pertaining to such and such a region, but the organization of knowledge enabling men to act and behave in such a way as to work toward a better life and a fuller understanding of each other. Culture is life. It is quite wrong to claim that it turns its back on life. . . . From art and culture a man can draw the strength to live and to fight for the highest ideals of mankind. . . . This Festival and this symposium are not just a meeting, just an excuse for festivities. They constitute a confrontation, the moment for emulation and perhaps also for an international soul-searching with a view to a fresh departure . . . In 1969, we have met to celebrate our more or less close connection with the African continent and our common option and efforts to obtain entire possession of the lands, oceans and rivers of this continent. As from now we will no longer be able to define ourselves by race or by any other physical characteristic but by geography, and above all, by our common determination which is the best basis for national and international unity. . . . The exchanges organized today by this festival on a Pan-African basis should become a permanent feature of bilateral relations between African countries . . . As President Marben Ncouabi said, "The Aim of our culture is not to lull our friends with fairy stories, nor to boast of our art or civilization—in a word, our knowledge of human sciences. It has a more important part to play, namely to awaken in the African a sentiment of striving for the national liberation of the continent."

Zambia called for a recognition of the magnitude of the task of the OAU in trying to find a common platform for people with such diverse backgrounds. Mr. Peter Chanda, Zambia's Minister of State, proclaimed, "For this paper I have taken Culture to mean a people's way of life in its widest sense. . . . African culture does not mean living in past glories, or living in isolation as to what goes on around the world. . . . Let us preserve our past by all means, thereby retaining our identity, but we should not in the process retard progress, nor ignore some of the useful influences that we may come across during our contact with other nations. . . . With the exception of the First Festival of Negro Arts that was organized in Dakar, Senegal in 1966, no other African nation has ever received such a large number of artists from so many African countries . . . The member states of the Organization for African Unity even though within the broad homogeneity and similarity, culture show marked differences from one another. This will make us be aware of the enormous task that the Organization for African Unity has before it, which is to try and find a common platform for people with such a diverse cultural background. . . . One major factor that can bring about the success of the Organization for African Unity *is the respect for one another's culture.* . . . The success of the Organization for African Unity first depends upon the stable internal and realistic policies of its own member countries."

The delegation from the Cameroons stressed the relationship

between culture and Africa's direction. They proclaimed that the role of African culture was one of unification and hence liberation. They set forth their communication in these words: "So, for us, the identity of our people defines the identity of our culture, and the authenticity of the one is inseparable from the authenticity of the other. . . . The African personality cannot be grasped when the observer or research worker, even if he is African himself, is haunted by the European, American or Asiatic model of mankind. We are convinced that African culture is and only can be that created, assimilated, experienced and transmitted by the peoples of Africa. . . . So the role of African culture seems to us to be one of unification and hence liberation. . . . We have therefore come here to Algiers to rejoin all the peoples of Africa, since African culture expresses the life of our peoples. These peoples have taught us to sing of mother Africa, to sing her wishes and her praises to struggle that she may be free and die that she may survive, to bring her finally together under the auspices of African unity."

Yes Algiers was similar to Dakar, but yet at the same time it was different. For now the family had first addressed itself to unity via the OAU and then set for itself a mandate to examine the relationship between communication and culture, control of self and cooperation, and finally liberation.

At first it seemed as though this was a playback of an old record, as though we had heard and played this music before at the Dakar Festival. But my wife, Janie, and I were not in Dakar, we were in Algiers among African brothers and sisters.

A Ghanaian brother was speaking, "Theatre in Africa may be found all over the continent, but real African theatre is pretty hard to come by. I for one had hoped that the Festival could have given up more African theatre, especially more of it in our own African languages." And then a brother from Sierra Leone chimed in: "But tell me my friend, what is real African theatre?" And such was the beginning but not the end of our discussions on African theatre and the theatre presentations at the Algiers Festival. They were discussions which were to continue at parties and after-hour gatherings throughout our stay in Algiers.

Although the First Pan-African Cultural Festival in Algiers is now a part of history, the discussions of African theatre, its role in the liberation struggle and the use of African languages will continue for years to come. But in Algiers the theatre-makers did arrive at some conclusions. A consensus proclaimed: "African theatre may be as rich and as varied as the culture and the art forms throughout the continent of Africa. And certainly African theatre may be found in the African languages as well as in the Western languages. The theatre may address itself to the roots of yesterday or to the problems of today. It may spring from a traditional mold or it may challenge or stem from a conventional base. It may be filled with the rich ingredients of African music, dance, mime, ritual poetry or prose; or it may be 'straight dialogue and conflict' based on modern methods of theatrical presentation and communication." We also agreed therefore that it was only natural for the festival to reflect a wide diversity among theatrical presentations. For example, Nigeria and Ethiopia, though miles apart in respect to the form of traditional or conventional African theatre, both nevertheless exemplified African theatre in respect to theme, content, character, and their connection with African history or tradition.

Nigeria's presentation of Tutola's *The Palm Wine Drinkard* stemmed from a classical traditional mold. Based on Tutola's classic story, and played in Yoruba, utilizing the art forms of Nigerian music and mime, in African style, *The Palm Wine Drinkard* gave the Algerian audience a rich folk opera in African theatre. Unfortunately however this particular production at times was marred by scenes of spotty acting and disjointed direction. Despite these weaknesses, the end result was an example of good African theatre.

Tsegaye Gabre-Medhin's *Petros at the Hour* was Ethiopia's drama selection for the Festival. *Petros* is an example of African theatre from a classical-conventional mold. Tsegaye presents his "dramatic experience" in straight dramatic form, through the eyes of three characters caught in conflict. *Petros* is a historical play set during the period of the Italian invasion of Ethiopia at the time of Italy's brief domination of Ethiopia. Tsegaye makes good use of mime and music, though using them sparingly, merely to highlight specific aspects of his drama or sometimes as a backdrop. Played in Amharic, Petros depicts a universal tragic figure who could certainly be likened to Becket or St. Joan of Western theatre. The music for the play, written by a young Ethiopian composer, Mulatu

Petros at the Hour (*Tsegaye Gabre-Medhin, Ethiopian National Theatre*)

Astatke, tends to open up the dramatic experience and invite the use of mime and dance movements from the major characters.

Petros is a play about survival. Petros is the African man who who stands in the face of tyranny; like the Ethiopian Emperor Menelik, who stood against the British; like Chaka, the South African "Warrior-King," or like Dr. Martin Luther King, Jr.! They all said NO! to anti-man. The director, Tsegaye, through his talent and technique involved his players in this essential conflict of the play, "survival" in the face of tyranny. An essential conflict which was and still is the conflict of African man. The man who begs for his own food! The man who went naked to clothe others! The man who sees his wealth on "the other man." The man who sees Africa humiliated to give respect to the "other man." Langston Hughes spoke of the "other man" in his "Note on Commercial Theatre,"

Obra Ye Ko (Life Is War) (*Arts Centre, Ghana*)

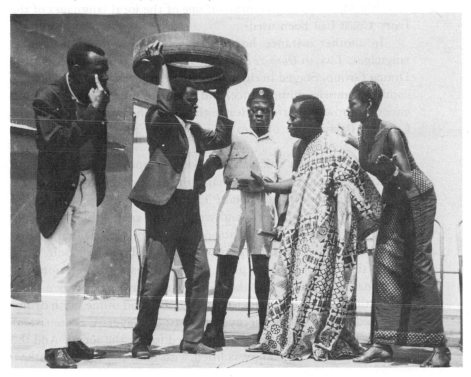

and he said, "You've taken my blues and gone. . . ." He also however spoke to African man in the same poem when he said, "but someday somebody will stand up and write about me . . . black and beautiful." Tsegaye Gabre-Medhin has written about African man—Petros, black and beautiful! Petros, who says no! Petros, who stands up against anti-man! Petros, caught in limbo between annihilation, survival, and liberation!

The Ivory Coast staged Bernard Dadie's *Monsieur Thogo-Gnini,* a brilliant satire on a "White-Black-Man" with a "Big-Man-Complex" who extends himself while taking advantage of his countrymen: who makes "small boys" out of his friends while corrupting the country through deals with European white masters. In this play Dadie gives evidence of his poetic and dramatic talent. This was a good production since the acting and the directing were uniform and of a high caliber. As I listened to the performance in French however a thought entered my mind about the language of the play. Would this play have come closer to the African core of "the Big-Man"—Thogo-Gnini—if one of the local languages of the Ivory Coast had been used?

In another instance, however, Ghana did use one of its local languages, Twi, in *Obra Ye Ko* ("Life Is War") by the Ghana Brigade Drama Group. Staged in the style of the Concert Party, *Obra Ye Ko* combined music, mime, dance, and drama to give the Algiers audience a glimpse of African theatre through Ghanaian eyes since the Concert Party style of theatre is perhaps the most African of Ghanaian theatre.

Obra Ye Ko is a story about goodness and evil, kindness and ingratitude. Set anywhere in Ghana, the play, a comedy, tells of the treachery of Yaw Bronya, son of Twinto who, having been helped out of the throes of poverty and want, turns against his own benefactor, Kodyo Abebrese. E. Kitson Mills, Director of Ghana's Brigade Workers Drama Group, produced the play while Bob Vans, writer and director of the play, presented his interpretation in a style characteristic of popular Ghanaian drama. This was a good production which made a lavish use of music and mime, with drumming and dancing. The energy of the cast of players was consistent with the style and characterization called for by the script. And the language, played in Akan, was filled with both humor and pathos.

L'Exil d'Alboury ("The Exile of King Albori") by Chak N'Dao from Senegal won the gold medal for the theatre. This was a good drama, beautifully staged and well acted. The production utilized to great advantage spectacle, lavish costumes, music, dance, and mime and depicted a unique dramatic African experience in African theatre in the French language. Once again however the question shot through my mind. Would this play have come closer to the African core of the exile of the King if it had been staged in one of the local languages of the Ivory Coast?

Make no mistake about it, the theatre-makers did discuss the language problem in the making of African theatre. We all admitted that we were desirous of seeing more African theatre staged in African languages. Aside from Nigeria with its Yoruba; Ghana with its Twi; and Ethiopia with its Amharic, most of the plays were staged in French. Algeria made use of a bilingual situation by using French and Arabic in the staging of its production. Notwithstanding this, French was the major language used in the Festival although this was a Pan-African Festival. Nearly all of the synopses and bridges for the plays were presented in French. On the other hand, the symposiums held at the Palace of the Nations had translations in several other languages. In regards to the language problem in making theatre our theatre-maker discussants concluded that the writer should use the language with which he is most comfortable. If it has to be one of those borrowed languages let him use it; by all means make theatre dramas. On the other hand, communication in local African languages whenever possible should be greatly encouraged. May the artist be provoked to write in his first language and let us hope that his first language is an African language. And if the writer is bilingual or multilingual then he will no doubt translate his play into one of the Western languages for consumption outside of his own country. There was major agreement on one basic issue among the theatre-makers. We all felt that a great need does exist for people to understand and accept African theatre in many forms, in many styles, and in many different languages. We were united in our agreement on the need for a concept of African theatre stemming from an African frame of reference, but also in agreement that it would be foolhardy to think of uniformity of approach regarding style and presentation. And we were looking for models and standards of excellence in respect to technique in all areas of theatre-making.

This covert search for the raison d'être of African theatre appeared at the Palace of the Nations in the discussions as well as within the dramatic and musical presentations in the theatres and streets. And the spirit of revolution hung heavily upon the city of Algiers. Also permeating that spirit was Black Beauty, Black Pride, and the Black Experience. The Black Experience—not the color, but the depth of the human experience and the commonality of the suffering, deprivation, and direction of those oppressed who had been caught within the institutions of colonialism or slavery. This very soul and the experience beneath it opened the way for a common language and a common articulation. The Black Experience— the depth of the cry from the soul of the experience which created a special kind of energy, exhilarating and penetrating! Caught in the middle of an African explosion, crossing barriers through inter-cross-cultural communication. Coping with the language barrier through the art forms and a common experience. Bringing together the sorrow, the pain, the cries of humiliation, of determination in a creative search, in a struggle for equality and freedom for the peoples of the Third World.

This special point of reference gave rise to a program called *The Black Experience* at the Salle des Actes, July 30, 1969 in Algiers. This unique presentation brought together through common "language" several African countries including Ethiopia, Haiti, Black South Africa, Ghana, Sierra Leone, and Black America.

I hadn't been in a South African prison like Dennis Brutus, but I had known the size of an American jail, so I too was "tuned in" to the cries of one of his poems written especially for this occasion. Dennis read:

STOP

I ASK YOU TO THINK FOR A MOMENT.

STOP

NOW

STOP THINKING OF OTHER THINGS.

THINK ONLY OF THIS—

OF PEOPLE DYING

DYING BY THE GUN
THE BOOT
THE FIST.

THINK OF THEM
THE PEOPLE WHO ARE NOT FREE
AND WHO WILL GIVE THEIR LIVES
TO BE FREE.

I wasn't South African, but I was certainly a part of this particular experience. So I listened as he went on and on. I crawled inside the moment as I played my dual role as participant-actor and producer.

Pat Maddy, actor, poet, and playwright from Sierra Leone, read some of his poetry—strong, brittle, demanding, and angry. And all together the "orchestra" made its special kind of music. John Okai, Ghanaian poet and scholar in Russian literature. Félix Morisseau-LeRoy, Haitian author-producer, journalist. E. Kitson Mills, Ghanaian director of Ghana's Brigade Drama Group. Tsegaye Debachen, director of the Ethiopian Orchestra and Folkloric Group. Janie Kennedy, professional actress and Africanist in theatre and literature.

And through my own "Ballad for Dr. Martin Luther King," in a monotonous, endless way, the words rang out:

I done picked that cotton all day long.
I done picked that cotton all day long.
I'm gonna rest my bones and sing me a song.
I'm gonna rest my bones and sing me a song.

Well the Boss said, Boy you're big and strong.
Yes the Boss said, Boy you're big and strong.
You gonna pick mah cotton all day long.
You gonna pick mah cotton all day long.

PICK A WAY   PICK A WAY   PICK A WAY   COTTON
PICK A WAY   PICK A WAY   PICK A WAY   COTTON

WHAT A WAY   WHAT A WAY TO SPEND A DAY
TO SPEND A DAY

Came the White Backlash
Will they ever learn?
Came the White Backlash
Will they ever learn?

Soon the echo rang out
Burn Baby Burn! Burn Baby Burn!
Soon the echo rang out
Burn Baby Burn! Burn Baby Burn!

FREEDOM, FREEDOM, FREEDOM NOW!

FREEDOM, FREEDOM, FREEDOM NOW!

WHAT A WAY   WHAT A WAY   TO SPEND A DAY

TO SPEND A DAY. TO SPEND A DAY.

Shades of African theatre with audience-performer-participa-
tion made unique music as the Brothers and Sisters joined together
à la poetry of Langston Hughes

The night is beautiful
So the faces of my people
The stars are beautiful
So the eyes of my people
Beautiful also is the sun
Beautiful also are the souls of my people.

Ethiopia's playwright, poet, and Amharic scholar, Tsegaye Gabre-
Medhin, spoke of Africa's current dilemma and the need to look
critically at itself through his poem, "Prologue to African Conscience":

Tamed to bend
Into the model chairs
Carpentered for it
By the friendly phoros of its time

The Black conscience flutters
Yet it is taken in
It looks right
It looks left
It forgets to look into its own self.

> The broken threatens to return
>> Only, this time
>>> In the luring shape
>>> Of luxury and golden chains

>>> That frees the body
>>> And enslaves the mind.

I reflected upon the characters in the cast of players in Dakar and Algiers. In Dakar the establishment had come, while Algiers had seemed to appeal more to the younger generation. My memories recorded both Festival scenes and the members of the family from Africa, Black America, and elsewhere. Duke's music was still ringing in my ears. I had never heard him play or seen him perform better than he did in Dakar at the residence of Ambassador Mercer Cook and his wife. I could see Langston Hughes all over Dakar. He

Dakar Festival (Ambassador Cook, Langston Hughes, Mrs. Cook, Duke Ellington) (*U.S.I.A., Dakar*)

was the embodiment of the Rivers of the Black man, whether he was reading his poetry or interpreting the culture and the aspirations of African people. The line of characters was too long to see them clearly. But there was Fred O'Neill, President of Actors Equity, and his wife. Bill Greaves was busy making films and enjoying the festival at the same time. And there we were, Janie, Brother Joseph, and me, all drinking in the riches of Africa and relaxing on the beach after a swim in the ocean. Dr. Martin Jenkins, President of Morgan State College, seemed to have brought the college with him —Dr. Benjamin Quarles, eminent historian, Professor James Lewis, sculptor, and his wife; Richard Long, writer and stimulating conversationalist.

Superimposed upon the scene of Dakar was Algiers, with its atmosphere of revolution. The established leaders of the OAU were there, and members of the younger generation of Black America came. Eldridge Cleaver, fired with imagination and energy, reflected upon the scene, while Stokely Carmichael talked about Nkrumah and Ghana and a land base for African people. Archie Shepp played the new music of revolt, while Don Lee and Ted Joans shared their poetry. Dennis Brutus and Alex La Guma from South Africa shared poetic vibrations; Morrisseau LeRoy, a veritable ball of energy, was caught between the theatre of Ghana and Senegal.

This superimposed picture of the two festivals dimmed and my eyes tried to catch a glimpse of the future. My eyes tried to visualize the next festival in Nigeria. Yes, Nigeria has issued a call for a Festival in 1974, and the Chairman of the International Committee, Chief Anthony Enshoro, is busily engaged with the demanding details and the pressing problems of our next Festival. In the meantime my search continues while I reflect upon the question, "What does the future hold for the African people and the gathering of the family in Nigeria in 1974?"

Part Three

Picture Impressions

First Impression

Africa

Africa!
I will be missing you
When the rain comes down
again this year
renewing its contact
with the earth.

I shall miss
the sound and sense
of your raindrops.

And no longer
will my body
be in tune
with the eternal rhythms
of the rains
torrential downpour.

Nor will I sense
the vibrations

of the universe,
nor smell
the sweet fragrance
of your cool clean earth.

Africa!
a land where pollution
is rarely ever heard of
and never truly felt.

I shall miss
the luxury
of your rhythms
of life.
especially
during
the rainy season.

the luxury
of being trapped
indoors.
or the luxury
of being completely
surrounded
and
covered
by rain
outdoors.

and feeling
the large drops
pounding
upon my
near-naked body.

I shall miss
your harmattan
and its dry heat.

Africa!
your harmothan
could never

be as cruel
as devastating
as the hot-humid heat
of New York City
in mid-August.

Africa!
in my dreams
I shall forever
embrace you.

seeking to renew
my connection
with the universe.

Ox cart, Addis Ababa (*Scott Kennedy*)

Oh
how I long
to touch
your wet earth
or your hot desert
with my bare feet.

My feet ache
for your contact.

My feet cry out
to be removed
from these new
mod mad shoes.

But they are trapped,
together with their

Pyramids and sphinx, Cairo (*Scott Kennedy*)

owner
in the
modernity of time
and the
madness of progress.

trapped
in their own
trappings.

Oh
how my legs
long
to run
naked
in the sun
      and the sand.
to stroll
leisurely
along the beach.

to dip in your ocean.

My eyes
begin

To sharpen
themselves
trying hard
to gaze
across
the ocean.

at the palm trees
and the beauty
of your world

My eyes
lost
in your
wide open spaces.

I search
I strive
I seek
to breathe again.

to let your
clean crisp
air
gently
open
my nostrils.

to breathe deeply
of the air
not yet
smoked
gassed
poisoned
polluted.

Africa!
I do
miss you.

Your lover
wishes
to embrace you
again.
to be
contained
by your
being.

Second Impression

Ghana

GHANA
    you touched
    the energy
    of my SOUL.

YOU
    bid me
    enter
    your rhythms
    and
    your cycles
    of LIFE.

YOU
    made me
    feel
    at HOME
    with
    your BEAT
    and with
    my own
    basic
    primitive self.

YOU
    made me
    LISTEN
    to the
    beat
    of my
    HEART

and LEARN
to hear it
in relation
to NATURE
and the
LIVING.

YOU
placed me
in touch
with
the OCEAN
and
the SKY
and made me
feel closer
to my WORLD.

YOU
CONNECTED me
with
the UNIVERSE.

Third Impression

How African?

HOW AFRICAN
IS
the African

Who has lost
his
surrealist appetite

Who has lost

his
pulse beat
    for the rhythms
    and cycles
    of life.

Who has lost
  his
zest
  for a communion
  of vibrations.

Who has lost
  his
    improvisational
    looseness
    and
    his SOUL.

HOW AFRICAN
  IS
he then?

Fourth Impression

Answer?

AFRICAN MYSTERIES
    MAY
still
lie
HIDDEN
      inside
      the
    AFRICAN
      definition

of MAN
and his
UNIVERSE
and
the
AFRICAN
frame
of reference
and his
RELIGION.

Fifth Impression

Question Period Again!

WHERE
are
the African
theatre histories
those
hidden mysteries
of Africa?

WHY
have
they
not yet
been written?

OR
have they
been
covered up

OR
eaten up
by those

big
driver ants
in
East Africa

OR
destroyed
by
an oppressive
nation
a
conquering
tribe

ARE
those African
theatre histories
still locked
within
the guardians
of tradition itself
locked within
the DRUMMERS
the PRAISE SINGERS
the TRADITIONAL RULERS
and their officials

HANGING
somewhere
in LIMBO
within
the ORAL TRADITIONS

PERHAPS
the oral traditions
are now
the only
LIVING
  AFRICAN
    HISTORIANS!

Sixth Impression

Ethiopia

ETHIOPIA
  stretched
  forth
  her HAND

To carry me
  through
  three thousand
  YEARS
  of her
  ANCIENT
  ANTIQUITY
  to
  the moment
  of
  her
  MODERNITY.

ETHIOPIA
  opened
  my EYES

And bid me
  ENTER
  the dark recesses
  of
  her WOMB

That
  I
  might DISCOVER

the ESSENCE
of
my HERITAGE.

ETHIOPIA
tickled
my EARS

That
I
might HEAR
the MUSIC
of
my BIRTH.

Seventh Impression

My Children in Africa

Africa
treated
them
differently.

More
like
a
real mother.

Africa
embraced them
showered them
with
her mysteries.

gave them
a new

zest
for nature
a new
feel
of the universe.

Africa
let them
romp
and
roar.

let them
hang suspended
between
modern conveniences
and
a bit of
the bush.

Africa
let them
see
the sacred grove
with
the Royal python

let them
see
the spitting cobra
the green mambo

let them
live
to tell the story
to nourish new images
to recall the memory.
Africa
treated

them
differently.

NO!
  She
    was not
    their
    step-mother.

Africa
was
the real thing.

Africa
was
their beginning.

Africa
was
their Mother!

Eighth Impression

Discordant Notes in the Orchestra

Do you really hate me
  Deep down within your heart?
    Or is that just a feeling
    That got its start
    Back in those early years
    When your parents said

        HATE THAT MAN
        BECAUSE HE'S BLACK!
          OR
            He was born a Jew.
            His clothes are shabby.

He's not fit for you!

Do you hate me
   Because of my SKIN
   Because of my RELIGION
   Or my pleasant GRIN?

Do we not LAUGH
   as you laugh
   and CRY
   as you cry
   feel PAIN
   and SORROW

Sheila in school, Kwabenya (*Scott Kennedy*)

and GRIEF
when we DIE?

Do we not WORK
        HOPE
        and TOIL
        and STRIVE
        for SUCCESS
        and HAPPINESS too?
  Are we not HUMAN
the SAME as YOU?

Do we not PRAY
    to the HEAVENS above
    to the GOD of all MERCY
    for FAITH
    and for LOVE?

Do we not WORSHIP
    a GOD as YOU do?
    and PRAY for forgiveness
    and SALVATION too?

WHY DO YOU HATE ME?
        perhaps
        you never really
        wanted to at all.
        It's just too bad
        it started
        when you were oh
        so very SMALL.

It's HARD to CHANGE you
        now though
But there's one thing
        you CAN do

DON'T BRING UP
    your CHILDREN
    to BE
    like YOU!

Ninth Impression

Go to Black!

(To the tune of "Nation Time" in
the "African People Suite")

And the WORD was given.
     GO TO BLACK!
An unconscious command
Understood by the masses
     GO TO BLACK!

Search out your ROOTS.
Discover your DIGNITY.
Command self-RESPECT.
     GO TO BLACK!

Cease that endless cycle
   Of self-denial
   Of self-hate
Recognize the link
   And the line
   Of your lost HERITAGE.
     GO TO BLACK!
Return to the SOURCE
Of your EXISTENCE
     GO TO BLACK!

Stop konking your HAIR
Stop the weekly ritual
And that painful ORDEAL
Of the fried-hair-weekend-EXCURSION.
     GO TO BLACK!

Throw away your SKIN LIGHTENERS.
Burn up your WIGS.
Find yourself.

Stop running from YOURSELF.
Be yourself.
    GO TO BLACK!
Speak for yourself.
Express yourself
Do your own thing.
    GO TO BLACK

Check your FLIGHT in COMMUNICATION.
Check out your FLIGHT in LANGUAGE.
Forget about the King's English.
Dig your own SOUND.
    GO TO BLACK!
Check it out.
    WHERE you're COMING FROM.
    And WHERE you're GOING
Check it out.
  WHO you ARE
  WHERE you ARE
  And WHAT you must DO
    TO BE YOU.
    GO TO BLACK!

Get Back
Go Back
Way Back
  To your own ORAL TRADITIONS
To your OWN CULTURE.
To your OWN HERITAGE HAPPENINGS.
Give WITNESS to your own
    BLACK EXPERIENCE.
    GO TO BLACK.

Get up
Set up
Your own
    FRAME of REFERENCE
Your own
    DEFINITIONS
Your own
    RELATIONSHIP
To YOURSELF
For YOURSELF

And with YOURSELF
Dig your BROTHERS
And your SISTERS
    For your own NATIONTIME.
      GO TO BLACK.

Change your SOCIETY
Challenge your WORLD
That denies you
Your own EXISTENCE
Your own DIGNITY and WORTH
Create your own AESTHETIC
Re-create from your own RICHES
Start from the ROOTS
      GO TO BLACK.

Examine the richness
Of your SURVIVAL SCENE
Of your CELEBRATION OF LIFE
Of your COMMUNION of VIBRATIONS
Of the MAGIC of your TOTAL CREATION
Pinpoint your LIBERATION
Dig what's about ME
      GO TO BLACK

Examine the Riddle of
    WHO am I
    WHERE am I
      and
    WHAT must I DO?
Of
    WHO is my ENEMY
    WHO is my BROTHER
And
    WHERE is my FAMILY

Seize the POWER
From the PEOPLE
From your ownself
FROM the PEOPLE
YOU are the PEOPLE
AFRICAN PEOPLE!
AFRICAN PEOPLE!
      GO TO BLACK!

GO TO BLACK!

WELL
  I feel so BAD
YES
  I feel so BLUE

  But it won't be LONG
  No, it won't be LONG

     Before I lose this VEIL
     And my EYES begin to SEE

     Before I lose this VEIL
     And my EYES begin to SEE.

Getting MYSELF together
       YEAH!   YEAH!

Getting MYSELF together
       YOO!   YOO!

     Cause it's NATIONTIME!
     Cause it's NATIONTIME!
     Cause it's NATIONTIME!

       And it ALL depends on ME!
       Yes it ALL depends on ME!

WELL
  I feel so GOOD
YES
  I feel so NEW

  Cause it won't be LONG
  No, it won't be LONG

     Before the NIGHT is GONE
     And the DAY belongs to ME.
     Before the NIGHT is GONE
     And the DAY belongs to ME.

Gettin it ALL together
       DIG MAN!
Gettin it ALL together
       DIG the PLAN!

     Cause it's NATIONTIME!

Cause it's NATIONTIME!
CAUSE it's NATIONTIME!

And the BROTHERS will be FREE
YEAH, man! YOU and ME.

YES, the BROTHERS WILL be FREE!

Last Impression

The Search

PART ONE: FIRST MOVEMENT

WHERE
and
WHEN

Does
one
BEGIN

THE SEARCH
for
Anything?

For LOVE
For HATE

For
the MEANING
of LIFE

For
your PHILOSOPHY
your political
religious
cultural
or
economic
LIFE-STYLE

I ask
myself
the QUESTION

    WHERE does it BEGIN?
        and
    WHEN does it END?

PART TWO: SECOND MOVEMENT

For
as many YEARS
as long
as I
could REMEMBER
I
had SEARCHED.

    Had
    it started
    When
    I made
    my debut
    at
    the age
    of six
    with
    a
    Paul Lawrence Dunbar
    POEM?

    Had
    it been
    in the middle
    of
    the many PICTURES
    I had snapped
    in my MIND
    of AFRICA
    over
    the YEARS?

    Had

it been
CONGEALED
in those years
in which
I
had
    imagined
    conceptualized
    created
        that dream-drama
        that celebration-creation
        of
AFRICAN THEATRE?

And
NOW
was I
to superimpose
this theatre
of my mind
  with AFRICA?

And
being AFRICAN
of
the first order
though
African
  second removed

Was I
  to reach back
  to my yesterdays
  to connect
  my todays
  and
  my tomorrows?
And
since
I
was AFRICAN
of
the first order

second
removed

I
knew
I
would enjoy
many DISCOVERIES
from
time's beginning.

BUT
would
they come
　through
　　my trained objective self
　through
　　my unfettered artistic self
　through
　　my Blackness and my Africanity
　　　OR
　through
　　ALL of ME?

And
would
I dare
to walk
the path
that makes
the artist
　hang
　on LIMBO
　　BETWEEN
　　　his freedom
　　　and
　　　his discipline
　　　　FOREVER
　　　within
　　　the realm
　　　of
　　　the discovery
　　　of

a new
EXPERIENCE?

PART THREE: FINAL MOVEMENT

The search
continues.

My search
for
African theatre.

My search
for
African man.
African people.

My search
for
the dialogue
and
the understanding
among peoples
of
the world
among
African
and
non-African
people.

Whenever
I see
a young
Black
child
raise his hand
in
a Black Power
salute.

Whenever
I see

a beautiful Afro and
colorful danshikis
adorning
shades of Black

Whenever
I see
my people
doing the bougaloo
my people
carriers of culture
shapers of soul

Whenever
I catch
a glimpse
of an
unfocused image
a distant
echoed vibration
an imitation
mimicking
the movements
the music
the madness
of
my people

straining
hard
in
the manner of
an ejaculation
to imitate
the soul
of
original man

trying hard
to grasp
the wisdom
of yesterday
and
the vibrations

of now.

Whenever
I
hear
the rain
beating
upon my rooftop

or hear
the cry
of thunder
as it walks
across the sky.

Whenever
I touch
the waters
of the ocean
and let its waves
wash me

Market scene, Cairo (*Scott Kennedy*)

back and forth.

I hear
Africa
calling.

I sense
its wisdom
and
its vibrations
permeating
the world
with its people
its theatre
its celebration
of life
everywhere.

I
make a note
I
write a melody
I
stand
READY
to give witness
to commune
with
the vibrations
and
the celebration
of life.

And
the search
continues

As
does life
with
its
enduring melodies
with
its
eternal rhythms.

Bibliography

Chapter 2

Bretton, Henry L. *The Rise and Fall of Kwame Nkrumah* (London: Pall Mall Press, 1966).

Ghana Ministry of Information. *Ghana Is Born* (London: Newman Neame Ltd., 1958).

Nkrumah, Kwame. *Ghana: The Autobiography of Kwame Nkrumah* (London: Thomas Nelson and Sons Ltd., 1957).

————. *Towards Colonial Freedom* (London: Heinemann Educational Books Ltd., 1962).

————. *Neo-Colonialism: The Last Stage of Imperialism* (London: Heinemann Educational Books Ltd., 1965).

————. *Africa Must Unite* (New York: International Publishers, 1970).

————. *Handbook of Revolutionary Warfare* (New York: International Publishers, 1962).

————. *Consciencism* (London: Heinemann Educational Books Ltd., 1964).

————. *Dark Days in Ghana* (New York: International Publishers, 1970).

————. *Class Struggle in Africa* (New York: International Publishers, 1970).

Chapter 3

Abraham, W. E. *The Mind of Africa* (London: Weidenfeld and Nicolson, 1967).

Abramson, Doris E. *Negro Playwrights in the American Theatre 1925–1959* (New York: Columbia University Press, 1969).

The American Assembly. *The United States and Africa* (New York: Columbia University Press, 1958).

Aptheker, Herbert (editor). *A Documentary History of the Negro People in the United States,* Volume 1 (New York: The Citadel Press, 1962).

———— (editor). *A Documentary History of the Negro People in the United States*, Volume 2 (New York: The Citadel Press, 1964).

Ardrey, Robert. *African Genesis* (New York: Dell, 1967).

Bachrach, Shlomo. *Ethiopian Folk-tales* (London: Oxford University Press, 1969).

Balandier, Georges. *Ambiguous Africa* (New York: World, 1969).

Beier, Ulli (editor). *Introduction to African Literature* (London: Longmans, Green, and Co. Ltd., 1967).

————. *The Origin of Life and Death* (London: Heinemann Educational Books Ltd., 1966).

————. *Art in Nigeria* (Cambridge: Cambridge University Press, 1960).

Betts, Raymond F. *The Scramble for Africa* (Boston: D. C. Heath and Company, 1966).

Biggers, John. *Ananse: The Web of Life in Africa* (Austin: University of Texas Press, 1962).

Brasmer, William, and Dominick Consolo (editors). *Black Drama: An Anthology* (Columbus, Ohio: Charles E. Merrill Publishing Co., 1970).

Brawley, Benjamin. *The Negro Genius* (New York: Dodd, Mead, 1937).

Breasted, James Henry. *Ancient Times: A History of the Early World* (New York: Ginn and Company, 1935).

Brown, Sterling A., Arthur P. Davis, and Ulysses Lee. *The Negro Caravan* (New York: Arno Press, 1970).

Budge, E. A. Wallis, *A Short History of the Egyptian People* (New York: E. P. Dutton, 1923).

Bullins, Ed (editor). *New Plays from the Black Theatre* (New York: Bantam, 1969).

————. *Five Plays* (New York: Bobbs-Merrill, 1968).

Cartey, Wilfred. *Whispers from a Continent* (New York: Vintage, 1969).

Clark, J. Desmond. *The Prehistory of Africa* (New York: Praeger, 1970).

Cook, David (editor). *Origin East Africa* (London: Heineman Educational Books Ltd., 1965).

Couch, Jr., William. *New Black Playwrights* (Baton Rouge: Louisiana State University Press, 1968).

Crowder, Michael. *The Story of Nigeria* (London: Faber and Faber Limited, 1966).

Cruse, Harold. *The Crisis of the Negro Intellectual* (New York: William Morrow, 1967).

Davidson, Basil. *The Growth of African Civilization: A History of West Africa, 1000–1800* (London: Longmans, Green and Co. Ltd., 1965).

————. *The Growth of African Civilization: East and Central Africa to the Late Nineteenth Century* (London: Longmans, Green and Co. Ltd., 1967).

————. *The African Slave Trade* (Boston: Atlantic-Little, Brown, 1961).

Davis, Jackson, Thomas M. Campbell, and Margaret Wrong. *Africa Advancing* (New York: The Friendship Press, 1945).

Dent, Thomas C., Richard Schechner, and Gilbert Moses (editors). *The Free Southern Theatre by The Free Southern Theatre* (New York: Bobbs-Merrill, 1969).

DuBois, W. E. B. *The Suppression of the African Slave-Trade to the United States of America 1638–1870* (New York: Schocken, 1969).

———. *The Autobiography of W. E. B. DuBois* (New York: International Publishers, 1969).

———. *The Souls of Black Folk* (Greenwich, Conn.: Fawcett, 1961).

———. *The World and Africa* (New York: International Publishers, 1965).

English, M. C. *An Outline of Nigerian History* (London: Longmans, Green, and Co. Ltd., 1959).

Ernst, Earle. *The Kabuki Theatre* (New York: Grove Press, 1956).

Essien-Udom, E. U. *Black Nationalism* (New York: Dell, 1964).

Fagg, William. *The Art of Central Africa* (New York: UNESCO, 1967).

——— and Margaret Plass. *African Sculpture* (London: Dutton, 1964).

Feldmann, Susan (editor). *African Myths and Tales* (New York: Dell, 1970).

Forrest, Ronald. *An African Reader* (London: Longmans, Green and Co. Ltd., 1965).

Franklin, John Hope. *From Slavery to Freedom* (New York: Knopf, 1967).

Frazier, E. Franklin. *Race and Culture Contacts in the Modern World* (Boston: Beacon, 1965).

———. *The Negro Church in America* (New York: Schocken, 1964).

Garvey, Amy Jacques. *The Philosophy and Opinions of Marcus Garvey* (London: Frank Cass & Co. Ltd., 1967).

Goodman, Benjamin (editor). *The End of White World Supremacy: Four Speeches by Malcolm X* (New York: Merlin House, 1971).

Gunther, John. *Inside Africa* (New York: Harper and Brothers, 1955).

Hatch, John. *Africa Today—and Tomorrow* (London: Dobson Books Ltd., 1965).

Herskovits, Melville J. *The New World Negro* (Bloomington, Ind.: Indiana University Press, 1969).

Hill, Errol. *The Trinidad Carnival, Mandate for a National Theatre* (The University of Texas Press, 1972).

Howe, Russell Warren. *Black Africa* (London: New African Library, 1966).

Hughes, Langston. *An African Treasury* (New York: Pyramid Books, 1960).

——— and Arna Bontemps. *Book of Negro Folklore* (New York: Dodd, Mead, 1958).

———. *The Langston Hughes Reader* (New York: George Braziller, 1958).

Huma, Albert. *Ancient History* (New York: Barnes and Noble, 1940).

Jahn, Janheinz. *Neo-African Literature: A History of Black Writing* (New York: Grove, 1968).

Johnson, Charles S. *The Negro in American Civilization* (New York: Henry Holt and Company, 1930).

Johnson, James Weldon. *Along This Way* (New York: Viking, 1968).

Jones, Leroi. *Blues People* (New York: William Morrow, 1963).

——— and Larry Neal. *Black Fire* (New York: William Morrow, 1968).

Judd, Peter (editor). *African Independence* (New York: Dell, 1962).

July, Robert W. *A History of the African People* (New York: Charles Scribner's Sons, 1970).

King, Woodie, and Ron Milner. *Black Drama Anthology* (New York: Signet Books, 1972).

Leslau, Charlotte and Wolf. *African Proverbs* (Mount Vernon: Peter Pauper Press, 1968).

Lewis, William H. (editor). *French-Speaking Africa: The Search for Identity* (New York: Walker and Company, 1965).

Locke, Alain. *The Negro and His Music* (New York: Arno Press, 1969).

Logan, Rayford W. *The Negro in American Life and Thought: The Nadir, 1877–1901* (New York: Dial Press, 1954).

Lumumba, Patrice. *Congo My Country* (London: Pall Mall Press, 1962).

Mannix, Daniel P. *A History of the Atlantic Slave Trade* (New York: Viking, 1965).

McCall, Daniel F. *Africa in Time Perspective* (New York: Oxford University Press, 1969).

McKay, Claude. *Harlem: Negro Metropolis* (New York: E. P. Dutton, 1940).

Melady, Thomas Patrick. *The White Man's Future in Black Africa* (New York: MacFadden Books, 1962).

Mellaart, James. *Earliest Civilization of the Near East* (London: Penguin, 1967).

Mitchell, Loften. *Black Drama* (New York: Hawthorn Books, 1967).

Moore, Clark D., and Ann Dunbar (editors). *Africa Yesterday and Today* (New York: Bantam, 1968).

Moore, Gerald. *Seven African Writers* (London: Oxford University Press, 1962).

Mphahlele, Ezekiel. *The African Image* (New York: Praeger, 1962).

——— (editor). *African Writing Today* (London: Penguin, 1967).

Nicol, Davidson. *Africa: A Subjective View* (London: Longmans, Green and Co. Ltd., 1964).

Nketia, J. H. Kwabena. *Ghana—Music, Dance and Drama* (Legon: University of Ghana, 1965).

Nkosi, Lewis. *Home and Exile* (London: Longmans, Green and Co. Ltd., 1965).

Nwoga, Donatus Ibe (editor). *West African Verse* (London: Longmans, Green and Co. Ltd., 1967).

Oliver, Clinton F., and Stephanie Sills. *Contemporary Black Drama* (New York: Charles Scribner's Sons, 1971).

Pankhurst, Richard K. P. *The Ethiopian Royal Chronicles* (London: Oxford University Press, 1967).

Patterson, Lindsay. *Anthology of the American Negro in the Theatre* (New York: International Publishers, 1969).

Pieterse, Cosmo (editor). *Ten One-Act Plays* (London: Heinemann Educational Books Ltd., 1968).

Quarles, Benjamin. *The Negro in the Making of America* (New York: Collier Books, 1964).

Reed, J., and C. Wake (editors). *A Book of African Verse* (London: Heinemann Educational Books Ltd., 1964).

Rive, Richard (editor). *Modern African Prose* (London: Heinemann Educational Books Ltd., 1964).

Roland, Oliver, and Anthony Atmore. *Africa Since 1800* (Cambridge: Cambridge University Press, 1967).

Scott, A. C. *The Kabuki Theatre of Japan* (New York: Collier Books, 1966).

Seligman, C. G. *Races of Africa* (London: Oxford University Press, 1966).

Smalley, Webster (editor). *Five Plays by Langston Hughes* (Bloomington, Ind.: Indiana University Press, 1968).

Smith, Edwin W. (editor). *African Ideas of God* (London: Edinburgh House Press, 1950).

Smith, Robert S. *Kingdoms of the Yoruba* (London: Methuen and Co. Ltd., 1969).

Snowden, Frank. *Blacks in Antiquity* (Cambridge, Mass.: Harvard University Press, 1971).

Stillman, Calvin W. (editor). *Africa in the Modern World* (Chicago: The University of Chicago Press, 1955).

Taiwo, Oladele. *An Introduction to West African Literature* (London: Thomas Nelson and Sons Ltd., 1967).

Wells, Carveth. *Introducing Africa* (New York: G. P. Putnam's Sons, 1954).

Wiedner, Donald L. *A History of Africa South of the Sahara* (New York: MacFadden Books, 1962).

Williams, Eric. *History of the People of Trinidad and Tobago* (Trinidad: PNM Publishing Co., 1962).

Woodson, G. Carter. *Handbook for the Study of the Negro* (Westport, Conn.: Negro Universities Press, 1936).

————. *African Background Outline: Handbook for the Study of the Negro* (New York: New American Library, 1971).

Woodward, C. Vann. *The Strange Career of Jim Crow* (New York: Oxford University Press, 1955).

Wright, Richard. *Black Power* (New York: Harper and Brothers, 1954).

Awiah, Rev. F. J. "Tongo Festivals, Dances and Marriage Customs," Accra, University of Ghana, n.d.

Graham-White, Anthony. "West African Drama: Folk, Popular, and Literary," thesis, Stanford University, 1969; abstract appears in *Afro-Asian Theatre Bulletin*, Vol. 5, No. 1, Fall 1969.

Nketia, J. H. Kwabena. "Multi-Part Organization in the Music of the Gogo of Tanzania," *Tanzania Notes and Records*, No. 68, 1968.

Tenraa, W. F. E. R. "Sandawe Musical and Other Sound Producing Instruments," *Tanganyika Notes and Records*, No. 62, March 1964.

Tracey, Hugh. "The Development of Music in East Africa," *Tanganyika Notes and Records,* No. 63, September 1964.

"Art from the Guinea Coast," Pitt Rivers Museum, University of Oxford, 1965.

"The Language of African Art," Museum of African Art at the Smithsonian Institution, May 24 to September 7, 1970.

"Patterns of Progress: Music, Dance, Drama in Ethiopia," Book IX, Addis Ababa, Ministry of Information, 1968.

Chapter 4

Boateng, E. A. *A Geography of Ghana* (London: Cambridge University Press, 1967).

Braimah, J. A. *The Ashanti and the Gonja at War* (Accra: Ghana Publishing Corporation, 1970).

Busia, K. A. *Purposeful Education for Africa* (The Hague: Mouton, 1968).

Clark, Grahame. *Prehistoric England* (London: B. T. Batsford Ltd., 1940).

Conton, W. F. *West Africa in History* (London: George Allen and Unwin Ltd., 1961).

Cowan, E. A. *Evolution of Trade Unionism in Ghana* (Ghana: Trades Union Congress, n.d.).

Davidson, Basil. *Guide to African History* (London: George Allen and Unwin Ltd., 1963).

Degraft-Johnson, J. C. *African Glory* (New York: Walker and Company, 1954).

Ephson, Issac S. *Ancient Forts and Castles of the Gold Coast* (Accra: Ilen Publications Co. Ltd., 1970).

Fage, J. D. *Ghana: A Historical Interpretation* (Madison: University of Wisconsin Press, 1966).

Foster, Philip. *Education and Social Change in Ghana* (London: Routledge and Kegan Paul Ltd., 1965).

Hatch, John. *The History of Britain in Africa* (London: André Deutsch Ltd., 1969).

Kingsworth, G. W. *Africa South of the Sahara* (London: Cambridge University Press, 1962).

Padmore, George. *The Gold Coast Revolution* (London: Dennis Dobson Ltd., 1953).

Pfann, Helene. *A Short History of the Catholic Church in Ghana* (Cape Coast: Catholic Mission Press, 1965).

McWilliam, H. O. A. *The Development of Education in Ghana* (London: Longmans, Green and Co. Ltd., 1959).

Morell, E. D. *Affairs of West Africa* (London: Frank Cass and Co. Ltd., 1968).

Myatt, Frederick. *The Golden Stool* (London: William Kimber and Co. Ltd., 1966).

Nsarkoh, J. K. *Local Government in Ghana* (Accra: Ghana University Press, 1964).

Oliver, Roland (editor). *The Dawn of African History* (London: Oxford University Press, 1968).

Sampson, Magnus. *Makers of Modern Ghana* (Accra: Anowuo Educational Publications, 1969).

Tufuo, J. W., and C. E. Donkor. *Ashantis of Ghana* (Accra: Anowuo Educational Publications, 1969).

Chapter 5

Agyeman, Nana Yaw Twum Duah. *West Africa on the March* (New York: The William Frederick Press, 1962).

Amissah, M. K. *The Music of Ahanta Kundum* (Legon: University of Ghana, 1965).

Anti, A. A. *Osei Tutu and Okomfo Anokye* (Accra: Ghana Publishing Corp., 1971).

Antubam, Kofi. *Ghana's Heritage of Culture* (Leipzig: Koehler and Amelang, 1963).

Apeadu, Mansa. *Ananse Stories* (London: Longmans, Green and Co. Ltd., 1963).

Barra, G. *100 Kikuyu Proverbs* (London: MacMillan and Co. Ltd., 1960).

Beier, Ulli (editor). *African Poetry* (London: Cambridge University Press, 1966).

Benedict, Ruth. *Patterns of Culture* (New York: Mentor Books, 1946).

Busia, K. A. *The Position of the Chief in the Modern Political System of Ashanti* (London: Frank Cass and Co. Ltd., 1968).

Danquah, J. B. *The Akan Doctrine of God* (London: Frank Cass and Co. Ltd., 1968).

———. *Historic Speeches and Writings on Ghana* (Accra: George Boakie Publishing Company, 1966).

Debrunner, H. *Witchcraft in Ghana* (Accra: Presbyterian Book Depot Ltd., 1959).

Elliott, A. V. P., and P. Gurrey. *Language Teaching in African Schools* (London: Longmans, Green and Co. Ltd., 1963).

Emery, W. B. *Archaic Egypt* (London: Penguin Books, 1967).

Fage, J. D. (editor). *Africa Discovers Her Past* (London: Oxford University Press, 1970).

Flower, F. D. *Language and Education* (London: Longmans, Green and Co. Ltd., 1966).

Fyfe, Christopher, and Eldred Jones. *Freetown: A Symposium* (London: Oxford University Press, 1968).

Gelfand, Michael. *The Sick African* (Cape Town: Juta and Company Ltd., 1957).

Hitti, Philip K. *The Arabs: A Short History* (Chicago: Henry Regnery Co., 1966).

Hodgkin, Thomas. *Nigerian Perspectives: An Historical Anthology* (London: Oxford University Press, 1960).

Huma, Albert. *Ancient History* (New York: Barnes and Noble Inc., 1940).

Johnson, M. (editor). *Salaga Papers*, Volume 1 (Legon: University of Ghana, 19).

Kofi, Vincent Akwete. *Sculpture in Ghana* (Accra: Ghana Information Services, 1964).

Kyerematen, A. A. Y. *Panoply of Ghana* (New York: Praeger, 1964).

————. *Daasebre Osei Tuttu Agyeman Prempeh II Asantehene: A Distinguished Traditional Ruler of Contemporary Ghana* (Kumasi: University Press, 1970).

Mbiti, John S. *African Religions and Philosophies* (New York: Praeger, 1969).

Mead, Margaret. *Sex and Temperament in Three Primitive Societies* (New York: Mentor Books, 1950).

Neal, James H. *Ju-Ju in My Life* (London: George G. Harrap and Co. Ltd., 1966).

Nesbitt, Janice (editor). *Ghana Welcomes You* (Accra: Orientation to Ghana Committee, 1969).

Nketia, J. H. Kwabena. *African Music in Ghana* (Evanston, Ill.: Northwestern University Press, 1963).

————. *Drumming in Akan Communities of Ghana* (London: Thomas Nelson and Sons Ltd., 1963).

————. *Folk Songs of Ghana* (London: Oxford University Press, 1963).

————. *Funeral Dirges of the Akah People* (Achimota: University College of the Gold Coast, 1955).

Opoku, A. A. *Festivals of Ghana* (Accra: Ghana Publishing Corp., 1970).

Ortzen, Len (editor). *North African Writing* (London: Heinemann Educational Books, 1970).

Patten, Margaret D. *Ghanaian Imaginative Writing in English 1950–1969* (University of Ghana: Department of Library Studies, 1971).

Rattray, R. S. *Hausa Folk-lore, Customs, Proverbs* (London: Oxford University Press, 1913).

————. *Religion and Art in Ashanti* (London: Oxford University Press, 1927).

Swithenbank, Michael. *Ashanti Fetish Houses* (Accra: Ghana University Press, 1969).

Van Dantzig, Albert, and Barbara Priddy. *A Short History of the Forts and Castles in Ghana* (Accra: Ghana Museums and Monuments, 1971).

Ward, W. E. *Short History of Ghana* (London: Longmans, 1966).

Yamoah, Felix. *Installation Ceremony of an Ashanti Chief: A Study of Movement* (Legon: University of Ghana, 1971).

Yartey, Francis. *Otufo: A Study of Music and Dance of the Ga-Mashie (Accra) Puberty Rite* (Legon: University of Ghana, 1971).

"From Ghana Folk Art to Kofi Antubam Art," Sponsored by The Ghana

Library Board, The Arts Council of Ghana, and The Ghana Society of Artists, December 1961.

"Ghana Notes and Queries," *The Bulletin of the Historical Society of Ghana,* Volume 9, November 1966, Volume 10, December 1968.

"Music in Ghana," Ghana Music Society, Volume 2, May 1961.

Chapter 6

Beegel, Mary Porter, and Jack Randall Crawford. *Community Drama and Pageantry* (New Haven: Yale University Press, 1916).

Cheney, Sheldon. *The Theatre: Three Thousand Years of Drama, Acting, and Stagecraft* (London: Longmans, Green and Co. Ltd., 1929).

Dubos, Rene. *So Human an Animal* (New York: Charles Scribner's Sons, 1968).

Gassner, John. *World Drama from Aeschylus to Turgenev* (New York: Simon and Schuster, 1951).

———. Modern European Drama from Henrik Ibsen to Jean-Paul Sartre (New York, Simon and Schuster, 1951).

———. *Modern British and American Drama from Oscar Wilde to Arthur Miller* (New York: Simon and Schuster, 1951).

Guthrie, Tyrone. *A Life in the Theatre* (New York: McGraw-Hill, 1959).

Hall, Edward T. *The Silent Language* (Greenwich, Conn.: Fawcett, 1969).

Hatlen, Theodore W. *Orientation to the Theatre* (New York: Appleton-Century-Crofts, 1962).

MacGowan, Kenneth, and William Melnitz. *The Living Stage: A History of the World Theatre* (Englewood Cliffs, N. J.: Prentice-Hall, 1955).

Nicoll, Allardyce. *The Development of the Theatre* (London: George C. Harrap and Co. Ltd., 1966).

Whiting, Frank M. *An Introduction to the Theatre* (New York, Harper and Brothers, 1961).

Chapter 7

Bentley, Eric. *What Is Theatre* (Boston: Beacon Press, 1956).

———. *The Dramatic Event* (Boston: Beacon Press, 1954).

Boulton, Marjorie. *The Anatomy of Drama* (London: Routledge and Kegan Paul Ltd., 1960).

Brooks, Cleanth, and Robert B. Heilman. *Understanding Drama* (New York: Henry Holt and Co., 1945).

Corrigan, Robert U. (editor). *Theatre in the Twentieth Century* (New York: Grove Press, 1963).

Downer, Alan S. (editor). *The American Theatre* (Princeton, N. J.: Voice of America Forum Lectures, 1967).

Hazlett, Uiariam. *Liber Amoris and Dramatic Criticisms* (London: Peter Nevill Ltd., 1948).

Littlewood, S. R. *The Art of Dramatic Criticism* (London: Sir Isaac Pitman and Sons Ltd., 1952).

Richards, I. A. *Principles of Literary Criticism* (London: Routledge and Kegan Paul Ltd., 1967).

Stanislavski, Constantin. *My Life in Art* (New York: Meridian Books, 1956).

Styan, J. L. *The Dramatic Experience* (London: Cambridge University Press, 1965).

Chapter 8

Carroll, J. B. *Language and Thought* (Englewood Cliffs, N. J.: Prentice-Hall, 1964).

Cole, Toby, and Helen Krich Chinoy. *Directors on Directing* (New York: Bobbs-Merrill, 1963).

Doob, Leonard W. *Communication in Africa* (New Haven: Yale University Press, 1961).

Gielgud, John. *Stage Directions* (London: Mercury Books, 1963).

Grotowski, Jerzy. *Towards a Poor Theatre* (New York: Simon and Schuster, 1969).

Heffner, Hubert C., Samuel Selden, and Hunton D. Sellman. *Modern Theatre Practice* (New York: Appleton-Century-Crofts, 1959).

H'Houbler, Margaret N. *Dance: A Creative Art Experience* (Madison: University of Wisconsin Press, 1962).

Hobson, Harold (editor). *International Theatre Annual No. 4* (New York: Grove Press, 1959).

Houghton, Morris. *Moscow Rehersals: The Golden Age of the Soviet Theatre* (New York: Grove Press, 1962).

Kitchen, Helen. *The Educated African: A Country-by-Country Survey of Educational Development in Africa* (New York: Praeger, 1962).

Koestler, Arthur. *The Act of Creation* (New York: Macmillan, 1964).

Laban, Rudolf. *The Mastery of Movement* (London: Macdonald and Evans, 1960).

Liu, Da. *T'Ai Chi Ch'uan and I Ching: A Choreography of Body and Mind* (New York: Harper and Row, 1972).

Mair, L. P. *An African People in the Twentieth Century* (London: Routledge and Kegan Paul Ltd., 1934).

McLuhan, Marshall. *The Medium Is the Massage* (New York: Bantam, 1967).

———. *Understanding Media: The Extensions of Men* (New York: Signet, 1964).

Nicoll, Allardyce. *The Theatre and Dramatic Theory* (London: George G. Harrap and Co. Ltd., 1962).

Polti, Georges. *The Thirty-Six Dramatic Situations* (Boston: The Writer, Inc., 1954).

Spencer, John (editor). *Language in Africa* (London, Cambridge University Press, 1963).

Wright, Edward A. *Understanding Today's Theatre* (Englewood Cliffs, N. J.: Prentice-Hall, 1972).

Acquaye, F. Saka. "The Problem of Language in the Development of the African Theatre," *Ghana Cultural Review*, Vol. 2, No. 1, 19 .

Jones-Quartey, K. A. B. "Tragedy and the African Audience," *Okyeame*, Vol. 3, No. 1, December 1966.

Kennedy, J. Scott. "The Use of Language and the Ghanaian Actor's Technique," Institute of African Studies *Research Review*, Vol. 4, No. 2, 1968.

———. "The Ghanaian Audience Response and Behaviour to a Theatrical Experience of Poetry and Music," Institute of African Studies *Research Review*, Vol. 4, No. 3, 1968.

———. "An Approach to African Theatre," and "University of Ghana Graduates in Drama and Theatre Studies—Direction and Careers," Institute of African Studies *Research Review*, Vol. 5, No. 2, 1969.

Nketia, J. H. Kwabena. "The Language Problem and the African Personality," *African Humanism—Scandinavian Culture: A Dialogue*, Copenhagen, August 13–23, 1967.

Senanu, K. E. "Thoughts on Creating the Popular Theatre," *The Legon Observer* (Accra), Vol. 2, No. 21, October 13–26, 1967.

Chapter 9

Bastide, Roger. *African Civilisation in the New World* (New York: Harper Torchbooks, 1972).

Ben-Jochannan, Yosef. *African Origins of the Major "Western Religions"* (New York: Alkebu-Lan Books, 1970).

———. *Black Man of the Nile* (New York: Alkebu-Lan Books, 1970).

———. *The Black Man's North and East Africa* (New York: Alkebu-Lan Books, 1972).

Breitman, George (editor). *Malcolm X Speaks* (New York: Grove Press, 1966).

Fanon, Frantz. *The Wretched of the Earth* (New York: Grove Press, 1968).

———. *A Dying Colonialism* (New York: Grove Press, 1967).

———. *Toward the African Revolution* (New York: Grove Press, 1969).

Hill, Adelaide Cromwell, and Martin Kilson. *Apropos of Africa* (London: Frank Cass and Co. Ltd., 1969).

The New Africans: Reuters Guide to the Contemporary History of Emergent Africa and Its Leaders (London: Paul Hamlyn, 1967).

Premier Festival Mondial des Arts Nègres (Paris: Editions Delroisse, 1967).

Africa 1968, A Reference Volume on the African Continent prepared by *Jeune Afrique*, 1968.

Algeria: Five Years Later, Ministry of Information, Algiers.

Algiers 1969: News Bulletin, First Pan-African Cultural Festival, OAU, March 1969–June 1969.

INDEX